Divine Power

HARVARD DISSERTATIONS IN RELIGION

Number 19

Divine Power:

*A Study of Karl Barth and
Charles Hartshorne*

Sheila Greeve Davaney

DIVINE POWER:

A Study of Karl Barth and Charles Hartshorne

Sheila Greeve Davaney

Fortress Press   Philadelphia

Library of Congress Cataloging-in-Publication Data

Davaney, Sheila Greeve.
  Divine power.

  (Harvard dissertations in religion; no. 19)
  1. God—History of doctrines—20th century.
2. Power (Christian theology)—History of doctrines—
20th century. 3. Barth, Karl, 1886–1968.
4. Hartshorne, Charles, 1897–   —Contributions in
theology. I. Title. II. Series.
BT98.D29 1986 231 85–45502
ISBN 0–8006–7072–8

1816D86 Printed in the United States of America 1–7072

For my parents Helen Greeve Davaney
and Laurence Francis Davaney
whose support and love
made this work possible

CONTENTS

SHORT TITLES

Information appears here for frequently used works which are cited by short title. A few short titles do not appear in this list, but in each instance full bibliography is given on the page(s) preceding such references.

AD
Charles Hartshorne, *Anselm's Discovery* (LaSalle, Illinois: Open Court, 1965).

An Encyclopedia of Religion
An Encyclopedia of Religion (New York: The Philosophical Library, 1945).

AW
Charles Hartshorne, *Aquinas to Whitehead: Seven Centuries of Metaphysics of Religion* (Milwaukee: Marquette University Publications, 1976).

Barth, *Dogmatics in Outline*
Karl Barth, *Dogmatics in Outline* (New York: Harper & Brothers, 1959).

Berkouwer, *Triumph of Grace*
G. C. Berkouwer, *The Triumph of Grace in the Theology of Karl Barth* (Grand Rapids: Eerdmans, 1956).

BH
Charles Hartshorne, *Beyond Humanism* (Lincoln: University of Nebraska Press, 1937).

CD
Karl Barth, *Church Dogmatics* (Edinburgh: T & T Clark, 1956–74).

CSPM
Charles Hartshorne, *Creative Synthesis and Philosophic Method* (LaSalle, Illinois: Open Court, 1970).

DR
Charles Hartshorne, *The Divine Relativity: A Social Conception of God* (New Haven: Yale University Press, 1948).

Duthie, "Providence"
    Charles Duthie, "Providence in the Theology of Karl Barth," in Maurice Wiles, ed., *Providence* (London: S.P.C.K., 1969).

Ford, "Whitehead's Differences from Hartshorne"
    Lewis S. Ford, "Whitehead's Differences from Hartshorne," in *Two Process Philosophers*

Goodwin, *Ontological Argument*
    George L. Goodwin, *The Ontological Argument of Charles Hartshorne* (Missoula: Scholars, 1978).

Griffin, *God, Power, and Evil*
    David R. Griffin, *God, Power, and Evil: A Process Theodicy* (Philadelphia: Westminster, 1976).

Griffin, "Hartshorne's Differences from Whitehead"
    David R. Griffin, "Hartshorne's Differences from Whitehead," in *Two Process Philosophers.*

Gunton, *Becoming and Being*
    Colin E. Gunton, *Becoming and Being: The Doctrine of God in Charles Hartshorne and Karl Barth* (London: Oxford University Press, 1978).

Hartshorne, "Beyond Enlightened Self-Interest,"
    Charles Hartshorne, "Beyond Enlightened Self-Interest," in Harry James Cargas and Bernard Lee, eds., *Religious Experience and Process Theology* (New York: Paulist, 1976).

Hartshorne, "Development of Process Philosophy"
    Charles Hartshorne, "Development of Process Philosophy," in Ewert H. Cousins, ed., *Process Theology* (New York: Newman, 1971).

Hartshorne, "Divine Absoluteness and Divine Relativity"
    Charles Hartshorne, "Divine Absoluteness and Divine Relativity," in Herbert W. Richardson and Donald Cutler, eds., *Transcendence* (Boston: Beacon, 1969).

Hartshorne, "Divine Relativity and Absoluteness"
    Charles Hartshorne, "Divine Relativity and Absoluteness: A Reply," *Review of Metaphysics* 4 (1950).

Hartshorne, "Interrogation"
    Charles Hartshorne, "Interrogation of Charles Hartshorne," in Sydney and Beatrice Rome, eds., *Philosophical Interrogations* (New York: Rinehart & Winston, 1964).

Hartshorne, "Metaphysics and the Modality of Existential Judgments"
    Charles Hartshorne, "Metaphysics and the Modality of Existential Judgments," in Ivor Leclerc, ed., *The Relevance of Whitehead* (New York: Macmillan, 1961).

Hartshorne, "Modern World and a Modern View of God"
Charles Hartshorne, "The Modern World and a Modern View of God," in Norbert O. Shedler, ed., *Philosophy of Religion: Contemporary Perspectives* (New York: Macmillan, 1974).

Hartshorne, "New Look at the Problem of Evil"
Charles Hartshorne, "A New Look at the Problem of Evil," in Frederick C. Dommeyer, ed., *Current Philosophical Issues: Essays in Honor of Curt John Ducasse* (Springfield, Illinois: Charles Thomas, 1966).

Hartshorne, "Omnipotence"
Charles Hartshorne, "Omnipotence," *An Encyclopedia of Religion.*

Hartshorne, "Omniscience"
Charles Hartshorne, "Omniscience," *An Encyclopedia of Religion.*

Hartshorne, "Process and the Nature of God"
Charles Hartshorne, "Process and the Nature of God," in George F. McLean, ed., *Traces of God in a Secular Culture* (Staten Island, New York: Alba House, 1973).

Hartshorne, "Religion in Process Philosophy"
Charles Hartshorne, "Religion in Process Philosophy," in J. Clayton Feaver and William Horosz, eds., *Religion in Philosophical and Cultural Perspective* (Princeton, New Jersey: Van Nostrand, 1967).

Hartwell, *Theology of Karl Barth*
Herbert Hartwell, *The Theology of Karl Barth* (London: Duckworth, 1964).

Hick, *Evil and the God of Love*
John Hick, *Evil and the God of Love* (Grand Rapids: Eerdmans, 1956).

KD
Karl Barth, *Die Kirchliche Dogmatik* (Zurich: Zollikon, 1932–55).

Keeling, "Feeling as a Metaphysical Category"
Bryant C. Keeling, "Feeling as a Metaphysical Category: Hartshorne from an Analytical View," *Process Studies* 6 (1976).

LP
Charles Hartshorne, *The Logic of Perfection* (LaSalle, Illinois: Open Court, 1962).

Madden and Hare, "Evil and Unlimited Power"
Edward H. Madden and Peter H. Hare, "Evil and Unlimited Power," *Review of Metaphysics* 20 (1966).

Madden and Hare, "Evil and Persuasive Power"
Edward H. Madden and Peter H. Hare, "Evil and Persuasive Power," *Process Studies* 2 (1972).

MVG
> Charles Hartshorne, *Man's Vision of God* (Hamden, Connecticut: Archon Books, 1964).

Neville, *God the Creator*
> Robert Neville, *God the Creator* (Chicago: University of Chicago Press, 1968).

NTOT
> Charles Hartshorne, *A Natural Theology for Our Time* (LaSalle, Illinois: Open Court, 1967).

Parsons, "Religious Naturalism and the Philosophy of Hartshorne"
> Howard L. Parsons, "Religious Naturalism and the Philosophy of Hartshorne," in William L. Reese and Eugene Freeman, eds., *Process and Divinity* (LaSalle, Illinois: Open Court, 1964).

Peters, *Creative Advance*
> Eugene H. Peters, *The Creative Advance* (St. Louis: Bethany, 1966).

Peters, *Hartshorne and Neoclassical Metaphysics*
> Eugene H. Peters, *Hartshorne and Neoclassical Metaphysics* (Lincoln: University of Nebraska Press, 1970).

PSG
> Charles Hartshorne and William E. Reese, eds., *Philosophers Speak of God* (Chicago: University of Chicago Press, 1953).

Reeves, "Whitehead and Hartshorne"
> Gene Reeves, "Whitehead and Hartshorne," *Journal of Religion* 55 (1975).

Robertson, "Conflict of Person"
> John Clifford Robertson, "The Concept of Person in the Thought of Charles Hartshorne and Karl Barth" (PhD. diss., Yale University, 1967).

RSP
> Charles Hartshorne, *Reality as a Social Process* (New York: Hafner, 1971).

Two Process Philosophers
> Lewis S. Ford, ed., *Two Process Philosophers* (Tallahassee: American Academy of Religion, 1973).

Williams, "New Theological Situation"
> Danial Day Williams, "The New Theological Situation," *Theology Today* 24 (1968).

WP
> Charles Hartshorne, *Whitehead's Philosophy* (Lincoln: University of Nebraska Press, 1972).

INTRODUCTION*

The idea of God, its foundations, content, and status have been a source of dispute and uncertainty for much of the modern era and especially for the twentieth century. The development of the physical and social sciences, the rise of critical philosophy and historical consciousness, the growing recognition of pluralism, and the spread of secular worldviews have combined to undermine and seriously call into question the visions of reality and, in particular, the conceptions of God that had characterized Western life for so long. The results of this questioning have been varied. For many the idea of God has simply become unacceptable; although diverse in their reasoning, the final conclusions of such thinkers as Nietzsche, Marx, and Feuerbach have been similar: the idea of God is untenable to modern consciousness.

But for many other thinkers this questioning has meant not that the idea of God must be jettisoned in the present era but rather that it must be subjected to a radical and thoroughgoing reassessment and reconstruction in light of, though not always in agreement with, the insights and assumptions of the twentieth century. That is, while the crisis concerning the status and meaning of the idea of God has resulted for many in the rejection of at least traditional ways of talking about God, it has provided as well the opportunity for others to develop innovative and constructive understandings of God and reality that strive to be coherent and meaningful within, if often critical

*Theology is, at heart, a communal process. While I bear the responsibility for the positions set forth in this book, the book itself would never have been written without the encouragement and support of numerous people. In particular I am grateful to Paula Cooey and Linell Cady, friends, fellow students and feminist cohorts. They have been for years providers of hope and important reality checks in my life. My parents, to whom this book is dedicated, offered both emotional and financial support throughout my graduate school career. Their strong conviction of my worth and their own commitment to intellectual excellence have provided the foundation for my love of scholarship and teaching. And, finally, I am indebted to Professor Gordon D. Kaufman. As advisor and friend, his faith in me has been a profound source of encouragement. For his continued presence in my life, I am grateful.

of, the spirit of the contemporary world. Such attempts at reconceptualization are multiple in number, diverse in approach, and often contradictory in
results. The purpose of this dissertation is to explicate and analyze two such
distinct reinterpretations of the idea of God as they are set forth in the
thought of theologian Karl Barth and philosopher Charles Hartshorne. The
intent is further to focus these respective conceptions of God through a
thoroughgoing examination of Barth's and Hartshorne's understandings of
divine power and the repercussions of that understanding in relation to
human power, freedom, and responsibility.

I have chosen to examine the positions of Barth and Hartshorne and to
focus the study on the subject of divine power for a number of reasons. In
the first place, Barth and Hartshorne represent significantly different and
indeed ultimately contradictory approaches to the question of God. Each
pursues a methodology, assumes guiding principles, and develops material
content that not only offer alternatives to more traditional views about deity
but to each other's position as well. Both in form and content the visions of
Karl Barth and Charles Hartshorne represent if not exhaustive, nonetheless
distinctive twentieth-century choices concerning the idea of God.

In the second place, Barth and Hartshorne are important choices for they
are the leading representatives of two of the most significant modern schools
of theological thought, that is, neo-orthodoxy and process theism. Because
there are other major theological perspectives that cannot be dealt with in
this limited context this thesis does not purport to be a survey of the general
theological scene. Rather, through a systematic comparison of Barth's and
Hartshorne's positions it seeks to provide an introduction to two of the most
noteworthy perspectives that have claimed attention and thoughtful consideration in the twentieth century.

Third, Karl Barth and Charles Hartshorne are significant choices because
although they stand in opposition to each other in fundamental ways, they
also have important concerns and convictions in common. On the one
hand, they both argue, albeit on different premises, for the validity and
meaningfulness of talk about God in response to, or perhaps defiance of, a
modern consciousness that raises serious doubts about such a possibility. In
a century that stands heir not only to the critical thought of Hume and Kant
but also to the claims of logical positivism and historical relativism with
their commonly held doubts concerning the capacities of human reason to
speak in a legitimate manner concerning God, Barth and Hartshorne seek to
establish different and once more secure foundations for that enterprise. On
the other hand, if their respective claims in relation to the form and status of
talk about God seem to challenge certain modern assumptions, the content
of their conceptions of deity embody other very contemporary presuppositions. Increasingly the modern world has come, through the developments
of the sciences and especially historically minded studies, to understand
itself and indeed reality as a whole in dynamic, historical, and social terms,

and the conceptions of God developed by Barth and Hartshorne reflect and cohere with this contemporary tendency to a significant extent. Both Barth and Hartshorne, in contrast to many classical thinkers, argue for an understanding of God as a dynamic, living deity who has a history, a deity whose identity is grounded in relation and whose attributes and characteristics must be understood within such a relational context. And while this commitment to a relational and dynamic interpretation of deity will be seen to produce provocative and contrasting results, especially as it is worked out in terms of divine power, nonetheless it stands as a central and all-important contact between the two thinkers and their perspectives as well as a significant link with the prevailing consciousness of our age.

Thus, the centrality of Barth and Hartshorne to the twentieth-century theological arena and their commonly shared concerns and contrasting conclusions provide the general rationale for examining the work of these two thinkers. However, I have also chosen to focus and give direction to this comparative study through the analysis of Barth's and Hartshorne's specific ideas of divine power, and the reasons for this decision must also be specified. Generally, the focus on power represents an attempt to deal with the vast expanse of these thinkers' work as it pertains to the question of God. Both appear to have an opinion about almost every topic imaginable, and simply to examine the "idea of God" would result, within this limited context, in either insipid generality or overwhelming detail.

However, the idea of divine power has great appeal as a means of giving direction to this inquiry for several more specific reasons. First, divine power has traditionally been a central notion in any conception of God and is so, as well, in the interpretations of deity set forth by Barth and Hartshorne. As such a central idea it is both an important element of any adequate understanding of their particular visions of God and an excellent access to other apsects of these conceptions. This analysis will illustrate in particular the profound connection between the ideas of divine power and conceptions of divine love, freedom, knowledge, and will. Second, the contents of Barth's and Hartshorne's notions of divine power provide very good examples of how guiding presuppositions and methodological approaches lead to or at least influence material claims. Hence, the analysis of the ideas of power will be seen to illustrate the interconnection between form and content and between guiding assumptions and material claims. Third, conceptions of divine power are of central importance because they involve, inevitably, claims concerning worldly powers, freedom and responsibility, and finally interpretations of the meaning and status of evil. As such these notions provide an important point of contact between conceptions of God and understandings of the world; they serve to demonstrate the intrinsic interconnection between theology and anthropology and the profound repercussions of the claims of one for the other. Hence, by focusing on the issue of divine power I hope to examine Hartshorne's and Barth's ideas of God in

a way that illuminates their guiding principles, that uncovers the interconnection of their central ideas, and that finally demonstrates the extent and
importance of theological ideas for subsequent anthropological claims.

Method of Analysis

The intention of this study is therefore to examine the ideas of God
developed by Karl Barth and Charles Hartshorne through the explication
and critical analysis of their respective conceptions of divine power. However, as the above remarks suggest, it is not advisable nor perhaps possible
to understand adequately the ideas of Barth and Hartshorne concerning
divine power in isolation and abstraction from other components of their
reflection which influence or are influenced by these conceptions of power.
On the one hand, the notions of power developed by these thinkers reflect
and follow after the guiding principles and the methodological approaches
that embody such principles. And, on the other hand, the ideas of divine
power have significance and far-reaching implications in relation to their
proponents' understanding of the world and the God-world relationship.
Therefore, in order to take these factors into full consideration the analysis
will proceed in a threefold manner: first, I shall examine Barth's and
Hartshorne's fundamental principles and methodological approaches;
second, I shall give a detailed exposition and critical examination of the
Barthian and Hartshornian conceptions of divine power; and third, I shall
examine the repercussions of these positions in relation to their understandings of the world and especially the ideas of human freedom and responsibility.

In the process of carrying out this threefold approach, I shall not only set
forth, in a comparative manner, these two distinct perspectives but also
further offer a critical evaluation of their respective viability as alternatives
for present-day theological reflection. This critical analysis will be directed
primarily at the question of how internally successful these positions are.
That is, having argued Barth's and Hartshorne's views in the strongest terms
I shall then examine the difficulties and tensions that arise from within the
perspectives themselves. In relation to Barth these conflicts will be seen to
resolve, to a significant extent, around his inability to reconcile his claims of
God's all-determining and independent power with his own alternate assertions of creaturely integrity, freedom, and responsibility. Hartshorne, with a
more socially defined understanding of deity, will be seen to avoid many of
the difficulties posed by Barth's interpretation of power and relationship.
However, his position will be shown to have fundamental and apparently
unresolvable difficulties as well; while Hartshorne avoids many of the
Barthian dilemmas by arguing for a form of receptive power as well as outgoing and agential power, his particular interpretation of such receptivity
will be demonstrated to have both internal contradictions and problematic

implications concerning how the relation of God and world is to be conceived.

On another level, Barth and Hartshorne will be seen as critics of one another, and throughout this study I shall call attention to the ways in which the position of each challenges and calls into question the other. Such opposition will be seen not only in the contrast of their revelational and metaphysical approaches to talk about God but also in their different and often contradictory understandings of power, love, freedom, and knowledge.

On a third level I shall raise critical judgments that challenge these positions externally or on premises other than those articulated and accepted by Barth and Hartshorne. This external form of criticism will be most pointed in a discussion in the concluding chapter concerning Barth and Hartshorne's common failure to take into consideration, in an adequate manner, the claims and challenges of modern historical consciousness. Finally, the concluding chapter will contain as well my overall evaluation and conclusions concerning the possibilities and limitations of these two important perspectives. In that context I shall voice my doubts concerning the viability of these two views while at the same time arguing that they have each made significant contributions to contemporary theological reflection.

Thus, the intention of this dissertation is twofold: (1) the systematic exposition and comparative analysis of the positions developed by Karl Barth and Charles Hartshorne on the power of God, and (2) the critical evaluation of these views as alternatives for contemporary appropriation. Such an analysis will hopefully add to a clearer understanding of these innovative and creative alternatives as well as to a final assessment of their contemporary viability and by so doing contribute in a small manner to present-day theological reflection.

1

BARTH'S GUIDING PRINCIPLES AND
METHODOLOGICAL APPROACH

The central intention of the first half of this dissertation is the explication and exploration of Karl Barth's idea of divine power. Barth, however, speaks of divine power and, indeed, of everything pertaining to God in a very specified and circumscribed manner. According to Barth what can be known and therefore said concerning God is determined in the strictest sense; the sources for knowledge of, and speech about God are severely delimited, completely concretized and localized. Thus, prior to any explication of what divine power signifies for Barth, it is necessary to set forth those determinants which Barth understands to govern what he states about God's power. It is only by examining where his thinking about God commences and how and why this point of departure governs all his theological positions that we will be able to grasp his conception of divine power and his rationale for such an interpretation as well as lay the foundation for the sharp contrast with the Hartshornian position.

The purpose of this chapter, therefore, is to set forth the determining assumptions or guiding principles which establish the foundation for Barth's explicit treatment of the notion of divine power. It also, at least implicitly, points to or indicates that the notion of divine power is already a very important presupposition and component of those principles, that prior to Barth's explicit analysis of the content of divine power such a notion is already operative in a pervasive and fundamental manner. That is, the treatment of Barth's position within this chapter suggests that power is a central element of Barth's guiding assumptions.

Given the constraints of space, it is impossible to analyze in a thorough and critical manner the positions of Barth examined herein. They have been and continue to be today a source of debate and controversy, and any complete analysis would have to enter into the internal Barthian debate in a way that is beyond the scope and purpose of the present discussion. Rather, the intention, at this juncture, is to lay out in a broad and general way the principles and assumptions Barth is working with and the content of these fundamental claims so that we might better understand why and how he

e does. Hence, our analysis must
knowledge and speech about God
is called for, and what assumptions
umanity are entailed in such a pro-

Divine Lordship

d speech about God has its founda-
y one, source: God's revelation of
that God has revealed Godself to
leparture and, indeed, ruling princi-
vhich Barth claims determines —
out God. As such it is imperative
e explicated.
hat Barth begins with what he con-
God's revelation in Jesus Christ.[1]
to demonstrate this claim, momen-
declares it. He takes it to be an
And he does so because he asserts
n the scriptures and proclamation
unters humanity as Lord (CD 1. 1.
meets humanity as Lord means, for
ade known is utterly self-attesting,
expounded, self-grounded. It is its
validation or explanation from any
laim that God encounters humanity
ions as a broad rubric under and
ated. He asserts:

is God in Himself, but because He
wledge of God is always based on
ers in which God exercises in one
and in which He is acknowledged
as God. (CD 2. 1. 23)

miley and T. F. Torrance; Edinburgh: T&T
Where appropriate the German text has been
Zollikon, 1932 – 55), hereafter cited as KD.
mation are God's revelation along with Jesus
a primary and direct sense, the former are so
stresses scripture and proclamation are reve-
parts but because God acts in and through
f God's activity. See CD 1. 1. 131 – 33.

This assertion that in Jesus Christ God reveals Godself as Lord is a far-reaching and multilayered claim for Barth. By saying that God encounters or becomes present to humanity as Lord, Barth wants to characterize, in a radical and fundamental way, both God and humanity and finally the relationship between them. This notion of Lordship is a central key or clue for how Barth thinks God and humanity should be understood.

The Revealed Lord as the Triune God

In relation to God the notion of Lordship expresses the conviction that not only is God revealed in and through revelation but that this is so because God is God's revelation. Revelation, in this view, is not merely the communication of information nor only the transmission of knowledge. Rather, to say that God reveals Godself as Lord means that in revelation God in Godself is present to humanity. It means that revelation is God's own self-interpretation, indeed self-duplication. Barth states:

> The truth of the revelation of God consists first and decisively in the fact that it is His, God's revelation. It is not someone or something else which reveals God, but God reveals Himself. . . . God's revelation is authentic information because in it God is His own witness and teacher. (Ibid., 209 – 10)

In revelation we have to do with none other than God. And for Barth everything depends upon this fact. Only because of this certainty regarding this fundamental matter is there, in the Barthian view, valid and sure knowledge of God (ibid., 209).

But who is this God who is present in revelation? How is this God to be understood? Barth contends that a correct interpretation of this claim that God reveals Godself as Lord, that is, that God is God's self-revelation, leads to an understanding of God as triune or, as traditionally stated, as Father, Son, and Spirit. By this Barth does not mean that the doctrine of the Trinity is directly identical with revelation but rather that the conception of God as triune follows from and is the explication of this fundamental claim that God reveals Godself. The triune interpretation of God is, for Barth, the proper exegesis of the statement that God reveals Godself as Lord. It is important to examine how this primary conviction concerning revelation entails or opens up into this threefold meaning.

This assertion that it is indeed God who reveals Godself means first and foremost that in encountering Jesus Christ humans are not merely coming into contact with another human being (though this too is true) nor are we confronted with Jesus Christ as only a medium or vehicle through which God communicates Godself. Rather, Jesus Christ reveals God because he is, for Barth, to be identified with God.[3] Barth states, "What God reveals in Jesus, and the manner of His revelation of it, namely, in Jesus, are according to the NT not to be separated" (CD 1. 1. 457). To the contrary Barth contends that

> the actual content in the NT texts is at least this, that in Jesus it is God who is found, because in fact Jesus himself cannot be discovered as any one else than God. And it is in Jesus that God is found, because in fact he is not found anywhere else save in Jesus, but in Him He is in fact found. (Ibid., 563)

For Barth, only God can reveal Godself, and, therefore, if Jesus does reveal God this is so because Jesus is God (ibid., 352–53, 465). Thus the claim that God is truly present in God's revelation in Jesus Christ involves an understanding of this presence which affirms the identification of Jesus Christ with God. A particularly helpful approach to Barth's interpretation of this self-revealing God is to examine how Barth understands Jesus Christ to be God's self-revelation. Barth utilizes a variety of biblically based notions to convey what he means by Jesus Christ. Jesus Christ as God's revelation is variously the Word of God, the Son of God, the Act of God, and the Work of God.[4] And in each of these instances Jesus Christ as Word, Son, and Act is God (CD 1. 1. 349; 2. 1. 262–64; 4. 1. 6–7). This twofold assertion that Jesus is God's act and that act is Godself implies several very important factors for how we are to understand God.

This means primarily that, for Barth, God is not to be separated from

---

[3] The status of Jesus Christ within Barth's schema has long been a matter of debate. Barth uses different and even sometimes contradictory language in relation to Jesus Christ. Charles T. Waldrop ("Karl Barth's Alexandrian Christology?" [Th.D. diss., Harvard University, 1976]) gives a lucid account of the several directions of Barth's thought. Waldrop suggests that there is evidence to interpret Barth as claiming that Jesus Christ is the vehicle or medium of revelation but not divine in and of himself but only in virtue of his unique relation with God. That is, what divinity can be ascribed to Jesus is done so by way of association. Waldrop goes on to argue, however, that another and more prominent trend of Barth's thought asserts that Jesus Christ is revelatory, not merely as an indifferent medium, but because Jesus Christ is, by nature and essence, divine. Waldrop strongly supports this second interpretation while recognizing that Barth utilizes the former position as well. It will be clear that I concur with Waldrop's judgment and think that such a claim is central to Barth's overall position. I would further suggest that the medium or vehicle language is often used to stress that the human nature of Jesus Christ has no intrinsic capacity for God as human, and that it functions as the form of revelation because God, in God's eternal primal decision, willed that it do so.

[4] Barth (CD 1. 1. 164) refers to Jesus Christ variously as God's Word, Act, and Son but by so doing he does not intend to indicate some different reality in each instance. Rather they are different ways of pointing to the same reality. For Barth, God's Son = God's Word = God's Act.

what God does. God's being is God's activity. "God is who He is in His works" (CD 2. 1. 260). This means, in the most far-reaching sense, that God is an event, an activity. It means that God not only operates through or behind events or occurrences but that God is this specific event or act (ibid., 262). Barth asserts:

> And in this very event God is who He is. . . . We are dealing with the being of God: but with regard to the being of God, the word "event" or "act" is final, and cannot be surpassed or compromised. To its very deepest depths God's Godhead consists in the fact that it is an event — not any event, not events in general, but the event of His action, in which we have a share in God's revelation. (Ibid., 262 – 63)

Hence, for Barth, God is not to be understood as some static entity or substance whose activity can be distinguished from God's being. Nor is God to be conceived as alien or over against that activity. Instead, God is God's being in act;[5] God is God's decision (CD 1. 1. 178, 181). Thus, what we encounter in revelation is the action of God, and that action is to be understood as God in Godself. God is both subject of God's decision and action and product of such activity. Agent and action are understood as identified in dynamic interrelation and unity.

Barth, however, carries his understanding of God as God's own act or decision much further. Not only is God to be identified with revelation, that is, with Jesus Christ as the decision and act of God, but Barth insists that this understanding of God as God's activity must be extended to and be seen as inclusive of the effect of that activity (ibid., 340). God is also to be identified with God's effect. Barth states that not only must God be identified with revelation but he also declares that God is "not only Himself but also what He creates and achieves in men" (ibid., 343). God is not only the self-creating God and the event of that self-revelation but also "its effect upon men" (ibid.). Barth, therefore, asserts that the God we encounter in revelation must be understood as Revealer, Revelation, and Revealedness or

---

[5] A number of recent commentators on Barth have stressed this identification of God with God's act. See, Eberhard Jüngel, *The Doctrine of the Trinity: God's Being is in Becoming* (Grand Rapids: Eerdmans, 1976); Robert W. Jensen, *God After God: The God of the Past and the God of the Future, Seen in the Work of Karl Barth* (New York: Bobbs-Merrill, 1969); Colin E. Gunton, *Becoming and Being: The Doctrine of God in Charles Hartshorne and Karl Barth* (London: Oxford University Press, 1978).

Another interesting approach to this claim is taken by David H. Kelsey (*The Uses of Scripture in Recent Theology* [Philadelphia: Fortress, 1975] 39 – 50) who sees Jesus' words and acts in Barth's schema as "constituting" his identity by way of enacting and bodying forth his foremost intentions. That is Jesus' identity as ascertained in and through his acts; these acts are not just illustrations of his disposition or identity but rather that identity is truly constituted by his acts. The description of Jesus' acts is therefore the description of his identity.

in traditional language as Father, Son, and Holy Spirit. That is, the God we encounter must be understood as the triune God (ibid., 339–44).

Thus, for Barth, the God with whom we deal in revelation must be conceived of in Trinitarian terms. The God whom we encounter in Jesus Christ is the triune God. This conception of God as triune is not to be understood as some additional notion created by the Church in the early Christian era (though it is that, too) or as an interpretation that follows after and depends upon a previously developed idea of God.[6] Rather, for Barth, the understanding of God as triune, as Father, Son, and Spirit, is demanded by the revelation that encounters humanity.[7]

Stated succinctly, Barth argues that God is present as Lord and that this means primarily that in revelation humanity has to do in fact and finally with God in Godself. He further asserts that the explication of this claim leads to the conclusion that God and God's act of self-revelation are identical and further that the effect of God's act is to be identified with God as well. Therefore, Agent, Act, and Effect, or variously, Revealer, Revelation, and Revealedness are one God. For Barth, to claim that in revelation we truly have to do with God means finally that

> God reveals Himself. He reveals Himself through Himself. He reveals Himself. If we wish really to regard the revelation from the side of the subject, God, then above all we must understand that this subject God, the Revealer, is identical with this act in revelation, identical also with its effect. (CD 1. 1. 340)

Hence, to begin with revelation in Jesus Christ, as for Barth we must, is to begin literally with the Trinity. Barth's departure point is Christological in that he insists that we must begin with Jesus Christ as divine revelation but that means just as surely that we begin with the Trinity. The understanding of God as triune flows directly from his primary and underlying contention that in revelation we have to do primarily with God Godself.

---

[6] Barth (CD 1. 1. 245) is insistent that to begin with revelation means to start with the Trinity or with the encounter with the triune God. Therefore, in his theological treatment of God, he begins with the Trinity and not with the doctrine of God. Barth concedes that this is an unusual procedure in theology and suggests that only Peter Lombard and Bonaventure are to be listed among his forerunners on this account. Nonetheless, Barth is adamant that his interpretation of revelation as God's act demands such a method.

[7] Barth's conception of the Trinity is meant to stress the diversity and unity within the internal life of God without falling into either a monism or a tritheism. By way of avoiding especially the latter, Barth suggests that we understand the threefoldness of God in terms of modes of being rather than in terms of the more traditional but problematic notion of persons. His point is to emphasize the oneness of God while giving that oneness a dynamic and vital character.

Finally, the statement "God reveals Himself as the Lord" is the "root of the doctrine of the Trinity" (ibid., 353).

This notion of God as triune in turn functions to undergird and solidify Barth's claim that in Jesus Christ we have to do with true and valid knowledge of God and hence that everything we can and must say about God comes forth from this source and, indeed, must be judged against this revelation. If Jesus Christ is God and if the effect is revelation, the Holy Spirit, then in revelation we have certain and guaranteed knowledge of God. In no other way for Barth can we make any claims about God that are anything more than human speculation about the world and humanity.

Divine Lordship as Ontic Independence

Barth's assertion that we begin with the encounter of God as the Lord, that is, that all thinking and speaking about God commences with the fact, the reality of God's self-revelation has several further implications which must be brought to the foreground. As will be clear, these implications follow from and are part and parcel of what has gone before. They are, for the most part, developments or entailments of what has been stated above. But it is necessary to unpack them in order to grasp more clearly the far-reaching ramifications of Barth's claim while keeping in mind that it is the triune God to which they refer.

Barth's assertion that we encounter God as Lord, that in revelation we are confronted with Godself, means first that this event must be understood as grounded entirely in itself (ibid., 134–35). This revelation has no ground outside of or beyond God's own activity. To encounter God as Lord is to encounter the God who is Lord and Subject of God's own activity. Barth states:

> According to Scripture God's revelation is a ground which has no sort of higher or deeper ground above or behind it, but is simply a ground in itself, and therefore as regards man an authority from which no appeal to a higher authority is possible. Its reality and likewise its truth do not rest upon a superior reality and truth, are under no need of an initial actualization or legitimation as a reality from any other such point, and are also not measured by reality from any other such point, and are also not measured by reality and truth such as might be found at such another point. . . . On the contrary, God's revelation has its reality and truth wholly and in every respect—i.e., ontically and noetically—within itself. . . . Revelation is not real and true from the standpoint of anything else, either in itself or for us. It is so in itself, and for us through itself. . . . And that we sum up in the statement, God reveals Himself as the Lord. (Ibid., 350–51)

Divine Lordship, therefore, indicates that God's revelation is not only God's act but also that that activity has its source wholly and completely in itself. It is not a reaction to or a result of any other act or condition. Human events and worldly occurrences come about in reaction to or as out-growths of previous happenings within the world. As will be seen, such a conception of activity as responsive in nature is central to Hartshorne both in relation to the world and God. But, for Barth, while this reactive charac-ter is true of creaturely action it is not true in terms of God's decision and act. No situation or occurrence within the worldly sphere is to be under-stood as in any way the source, foundation, or prior condition for this unique event of God's act. It is grounded upon and flows out of itself. It is ontically independent (ibid., 350).

Viewed negatively, this ontic independence or self-grounding is to be understood to mean that God's revelation of Godself, though it takes place in and to the world, can never be reduced to a function of or a factor in the world (CD 1. 2. 135). The reality which is God's revelation is not in any way a possibility of humanity or the world. "God is the constant Subject of revelation" (ibid., 1). As such God never "becomes the predicate or object of our existence or action. He becomes and He is manifest to us. But this very becoming and being is and remains a determination of His existence. It is His Act, His Work" (ibid., 1. 134). To be ontically independent means, for Barth, that God's revelation of Godself, that God for and present to us, is a sovereign divine act, an act of divine lordship.

But, perhaps even more importantly, Barth wants to view this self-grounding, this ontic independence, in positive terms, in terms of what it says about God in Godself. Thus, revelation means that God is present to and for humanity. This reality or fact of "God for us" is that with which we must always begin. But, for Barth to say that God's revelation or God for us is grounded in Godself means that God in Godself is not different from or alien to the God humanity encounters in revelation. To the contrary, God in Godself is the prior ground and possibility of God for us and as such God in Godself is not unlike the revealed God but is also act, decision, relation-ship, that is, Trinity.[8] God's external revelation is grounded in and reflective of God's antecedent internal reality (CD 1. 2. 476; 2. 1. 48 – 49).

This intimate connection between God in revelation and God in Godself means for him, as well, that in no way can we assume that there is a hidden, unknown God behind the God of revelation. There is no God beyond or above the God we encounter in Jesus Christ. Speaking of this encounter, Barth asserts:

> The inner truth of the lordship of God as the one supreme and true lordship revealed and operative in His proclamation and action—the inner truth and therefore also the inner strength of His self-demonstration as the Lord, consists in the fact that He is Himself from

[8] Barth, *Dogmatics in Outline* (New York: Harper & Brothers, 1959) 28.

eternity to eternity the triune God, God the Father, the Son and the Spirit. (CD 1. 1. 474; 2. 1. 47)

Thus, the possibility for revelation and, following upon that, the truth and validity of this "God for us" is grounded in the prior fact that God is not different in Godself. There is no "Deus absconditus" at the back of revelation (CD 2. 1. 210). Barth's original claim that in revelation we have to do with God and not someone or something else is, for him, substantiated by this fact that God's revelation to and for us is grounded in and reflective of God's own internal life.

But Barth is insistent that this fact that God for us is the true and real expression of Godself must be understood in the light of another fundamental claim: the self-grounding and self-revelation of God is utterly free. Divine freedom means two central claims in this connection and each is of equal significance.[9] The first sense in which God is free is that it is within God's possibility to become other than Godself. That is, the reality of God's self-revelation in Jesus Christ and its grounding in God's own internal reality indicate that God is such that God can make Godself known and can communicate Godself to others and do that not only in the eternal reality of God's own internal life but can, without diminution of God's divinity, do so as well in and to the world (CD 1. 1. 2, 263, 267–68, 372; 2. 1. 11). Barth insists that God's essential freedom means that "it was not to Him an inalienable necessity to exist only in the form of God, only to be God . . . only to be the eternal word and not flesh. He was not committed to any such 'only' . . . He had this other possibility: the possibility of divine self-giving the being and fate of man" (CD 4. 1. 180). In this sense, God's freedom means that God can reveal Godself, that it is within God's power and capacity to be for us and not only in Godself (ibid., 179–80). So, God's Lordship means that "it becomes possible in His freedom that He should be our God" (CD 1. 2. 31).

However, for Barth, divine freedom signifies another equally significant fact. God's freedom does indeed mean freedom to be "God for us" but it also means that God is not for us because of any necessity either on God's side or humanity's. Barth insists upon this adamantly. God's revelation is grounded in God in Godself but this grounding does not in any way indicate a necessity for that revelation (CD 1. 1. 195–98; 2. 1. 57). The fact that

---

[9] Barth also posits another sense in which God is free, i.e., free in relation to Godself; God is free in God's own internal life. But freedom in this sense does not mean the same thing for Barth that it means in relation to God's activity toward humanity. In the latter case Barth takes freedom to mean freedom of choice, a capacity to do one thing or another. But in the former case freedom does not imply choice but rather the capacity to be oneself. That is, in relation to God's own internal freedom Barth wants to say that God is free to be Godself but God is not free to be other than Godself.

God in Godself is the source and, hence, the guarantor of that revelation does not imply that that revelation had to occur.

So it does not rest upon any necessity in the divine nature or upon the relation between Father, Son and Spirit that God becomes man. . . . That is, in His Word becoming flesh, God acts with inward freedom, and not in fulfillment of a law to which He is supposedly subject. His Word is still His word apart from this becoming, just as Father, Son and Holy Spirit would be none the less eternal God, if no world had been created. (CD 1. 2. 135)

Thus freedom for humanity and the world is counterbalanced by freedom from any compulsion or need to be so related to the world. Divine Lordship consists both in freedom to be for humanity and the world and in freedom from any necessity in relation to that world. This Barthian notion of divine freedom, especially in its latter expression of freedom from necessity of any world, will be seen to clash significantly with the Hartshornian conception of divine freedom. Hartshorne, in contrast to Barth, argues that while God is indeed free, such freedom does not entail that God could exist apart from a world but rather that some world, some nondivine reality, is necessary.

For Barth, however, it is precisely this twofold freedom for and from humanity and the world that permits God's relationship with the world to be understood as a loving relationship. In Barthian terms, "Love is free or it is not love" (CD 3. 3. 110). For a relationship to be loving it cannot be coerced or take place by necessity. Both the fact of the relationship and the character of the relationship must be free if it is to be gracious and loving.

Thus, divine freedom becomes a primary basis for his claim that God is truly a gracious God. On the one hand, God need not love the world or humanity because God already in God's own inner trinitarian life exists in fellowship and love. God "does not need a fellow in order to be love, or a companion in order to be complete" (CD 4. 1. 39). Hence, in contrast to what Hartshorne will be seen to claim, no necessity can be said to be the basis for the God-world encounter. On the other hand, the very fact that God loves in Godself means that God is able to love and that it is not alien or foreign to God's nature. It is not a capricious or unnatural act to love. Rather, divine fellowship with humanity is grounded in and corresponds to God's own trinitarian life of love (CD 2. 1. 275, 441, 463).

For Barth, therefore, this freedom from both necessity and caprice, reflective of God's loving relatedness *a se*, becomes the ground for understanding God's relationship with the world as a gracious one. In Jesus Christ, God's revelation of God's true self, humanity encounters a God who without needing to, has freely chosen to create fellowship between God and nondivine reality. God in Godself is self-completed and self-satisfied love but nonetheless in an overflow of love God enters into relation with the world. Barth sums up his conviction in this way:

In Jesus Christ, God has manifested himself, as a God who while being perfectly free and self-sufficient yet does not wish to be alone. He does not wish to act, exist, love, labor, work, strive, vanquish, reign, triumph without man. He does not wish, therefore, for his cause to be his alone. He wishes it to be also the cause of man. ... Even if there are men without God, there is, from the Christian viewpoint, no God without men.[10]

Hence, love and freedom are inextricably interwined. In revelation humanity encounters the God who is Lord and that Lordship entails God's fundamental freedom from the world. But this freedom also points to the capacity and possibility of relationship which is grounded in God's own self-relatedness. God's love *a se* is seen as the basis of God's love *ad extra* and God's freedom is the guarantee that this relationship is truly loving in character.

Barth, however, in order to undergird and emphasize this totally free character of God's revelation insists that a distinction must be maintained between God for us and God in Godself. God for us or divine revelation is, indeed, grounded in God's own internal identity and hence is truly God. But Barth wants to assert that these two cannot be collapsed into one another. God in God's revelation is none other than God, but God must not be reduced to God's revelation (CD 1. 1. 37; 2. 1. 75, 260). In order to maintain God's Lordship Barth insists these two are distinct. We begin with God's communication to us but that very communication indicates God's freedom.[11] Barth does not mean to undercut his primary assertion of the essential connection between the two. Instead, it is precisely by making such a distinction that Barth seeks to reaffirm God's Lordship and freedom and, hence, the validity and reality of revelation:

All we can know of God according to Scripture testimony is His acts. All we can assert of God, all attributes we can assign to God relate to these acts of His. ... Although the operation of God is the essence of God, it is necessary and important to distinguish His essence as such from His operation in order to remember that this operation is a grace, a free decision, also to remember that we can only know about God, because, and so far as He gives Himself to our knowledge. ... God gives Himself to man entirely in revelation, but not in such a way as to give Himself a prisoner to man. He remains free, in operating, in giving Himself. (CD 1. 1. 426)

Thus, God is true in God's acts but never in such a way that God is no

[10] Barth, *Prayer According to the Catechisms of the Reformation* (Philadelphia: Westminster, 1953) 38.

[11] John Dillenberger (*God Hidden and Revealed* [Philadelphia: Muhlenberg, 1953] 132) stresses this distinction and its ramifications for Barth's position.

longer Lord and Subject of that act. Yet, although Barth wants to distinguish between God in Godself and God for us, he is insistent as well that God for us is no arbitrary or capricious act (CD 2. 2. 25). If revelation is not grounded in some worldly basis neither is its source the belated whim of an impulsive God. Instead, God for us, God's decision to reveal Godself to humanity is an eternal act, an eternal decision. God was never not God for us—even in eternity, even prior to the advent of the world (ibid., 8–9, 25–26, 101). Indeed Barth is so insistent upon this claim that he understands God's decision to reveal Godself to humanity in Jesus Christ, to elect humanity into fellowship with Godself, as the basis and reason for the creation of the world at all. Election of God's primal decision to be for and with humanity becomes, in this schema, the foundation for God's creative activity. (The other side of this claim is that Jesus Christ is God's decision from all eternity to be for humanity and not just a response to a fallen humanity. Jesus Christ is not to be understood as purely a stopgap measure or panacea for a creation that went awry.) And further, the recognition of this basis for creation is taken to be the only perspective from which an adequate understanding of the world's relation to God is to be obtained. Hence, Barth asserts that the distinction between God for us and God in Godself—and therefore divine freedom—can be maintained while at the same time God's revelation need not be viewed as an arbitrary or nonself-grounded act.

Barth, therefore, derives from the conviction that God's self-grounding involves both the capacity for relationship with that which is other than God and the freedom from any necessity for such a relationship. And he further holds these two freedoms together through the notion of the free and gracious primal decision of God to be for humanity and by so doing supports and undergirds the continuity of God's self-revelation in Jesus Christ and God's own internal life. Thus, it is finally in God's free and loving decision to be for humanity, grounded in God's eternal life, that humanity encounters God as Lord, and it is only in such an encounter, with all of these implications, that humanity finds certain and valid knowledge of God.

Divine Lordship as Noetic Independence

We have been examining the content and implications in relation to God of Barth's claim that God reveals Godself in Jesus Christ and that in that encounter God is present to us as the Lord. The intention now is to explore what such a claim entails for humanity. In order to lay a foundation for such an examination, it is necessary briefly to draw some conclusions concerning the parameters of human knowledge of God that flow out of Barth's position as articulated thus far.

Two of Barth's claims and their implications for human knowledge of God must be reemphasized. They are, as has been suggested above, interrelated assertions, and each involves the same ramifications for human knowledge of God. The first is the general claim that in revelation we have to do with God's act that is Godself. This means several things in terms of human knowledge of this act. It means, in a primary way, that God is to be encountered here in Jesus Christ and nowhere else (CD 1. 2. 243; 2. 1. 318–19; 4. 1. 45). Jesus Christ is God's act and because God and God's act are identified in a fundamental way, only Jesus Christ as that act can be the source of human knowledge of God. Barth states that in encountering God in Christ, we discover that God is not to be met elsewhere:

> So far as it is attested for us in Holy Scripture as the reality of God's revelation, the reality of Jesus Christ has also a strictly critical significance. When we are told in it that God is free for us here, we are also told restrictively that He is not free for us elsewhere. It limits the freedom of God for us to itself. It tells us that only here, in this manness of God, in the God-ness of this man, is God free for us. (CD 1. 1. 28, 34)

To know God is to know God only in and through Jesus Christ and that which attests to him. It is only in this exclusive, historical, concrete place that we have a true and valid source for knowledge of God.

Barth's emphasis upon the identity of God with God's act and hence upon the "event" character of divine revelation also supports, undergrids, and indeed radicalizes this localization or specification of locus of God's revelation to humanity. The event character of revelation involves the further fact that this act or event can never become a mere datum of knowledge, a piece of information to be manipulated or controlled. Knowledge of God brings with it the recognition that the object of that knowledge can never become an object like other objects. It always maintains its primary character of free and sovereign event. Thus God must not only be understood as free Lord in relation to Godself but also as Lord in relation to human knowledge of God.

The second general claim that has such far-reaching ramifications for human knowledge of God is the assertion that this act or event which is God is ontically independent. This means that knowledge of God cannot be grounded in any dimension or facet of human life or worldly reality. (Revelation takes place through Jesus Christ and hence through a worldly reality. But Barth emphasizes that this is so because of God's ruling activity not because Jesus as a human being possessed any capacity to reveal God.) Knowledge of God cannot be, so to speak, read off the world. This is another way of reiterating that it is only in and through Jesus Christ that any valid knowledge of God is to be discovered.

The fact of God's act and this act's ontic independence points to and demands a very particular epistemology in relation to the knowledge which has God as both its source and object. It demands that this knowledge follow after God's revelation. Barth rejects, in a way that will be seen to contrast sharply with Hartshorne's claim for metaphysical and public knowledge of God, any notion of a priori knowledge concerning God (CD 2. 1. 4 – 5). Only knowledge that is gained retrospectively, after and following upon God's activity, is real and valid knowledge. The exclusive locus of God's revelation, the event character of that revelation, and the independent self-grounding of that event all demand that the path we must follow in any knowledge of God be a completely a posteriori path (ibid.). God acts; God is this act. Any knowledge or speech concerning God must flow from this source.

This claim is followed by the recognition that although human concepts and ideas must be used to think and speak of God, this ontic independence points as well to utter inadequacy and incapacity of those ideas to express the truth which they encounter. If words and ideas do convey some knowledge of God it cannot be because they in themselves are reflective of that reality. It can only be because God is Lord, too, of this dimension of reality.

Thus, Barth draws radical conclusions from his conviction that knowledge of God follows from rather than precedes the act of God. He concludes that not only is God Lord in terms of Godself but that when this claim is explicated as it has been above we must conclude that God is Lord as well of humanity and, in particular, of humanity's knowledge of God. Put differently, Barth asserts that God, though object of human knowledge, is nonetheless Lord and Subject and Ruler of that knowledge and indeed of the knowing process itself. Barth proposes that in relation to God we must assert a completely realistic epistemology in which the object of knowledge controls the knowledge itself. And he makes the further and even more far-reaching claim that God determines the how of that knowledge, the very process of knowing itself. For Barth all of this is the self-evident outcome of the assertion that humanity encounters God as Lord. At this juncture it is necessary to explicate and elaborate just what this claim of Lordship entails for human knowledge and the human process of knowing.

1.2 Noetic Independence and Human Knowing

The previous concern has been with what Barth's assertion of divine Lordship entailed for his understanding of God. Now the corresponding affirmation of divine Lordship in relation to humanity must be examined. It will be clear that, for Barth, the assertions set forth in this section follow from and depend upon the above examination and indeed are only separated for the purpose of analysis. And as Barth's, conception of the former expression of Lordship might be summed up in the notion of ontic independence, so divine Lordship in this second sense might be character-ized as noetic independence or noetic Lordship. It is necessary, at this point, to analyze what this noetic lordship might possibly involve for Barth.

For Karl Barth God is truly known to humanity in Jesus Christ. This means, for him, that God becomes an object of human apprehension, an object of human cognitive processes (ibid., 13–14, 181). Knowledge of God to be knowledge does and must entail this "objectivity" of God. Barth states: "If God becomes the object of man's knowledge, this necessarily means that He becomes the object of his consideration and conception" (ibid., 14, 205). God is thus to be understood as an object of human cognition and as such Barth means primarily that God is encountered as over against and distinct from the knower and as that which is capable of being apprehended by the human knower.[12] However, Barth qualifies and characterizes God as object in a very stringent manner. For, though God is an object to be known, apprehended and conceived by the human knower, this divine object is so in a manner unlike all other objects of human knowledge (CD 1. 1. 149; 1. 2. 172; 2. 1. 21; 4. 2. 119–20). To understand what Barth means in this connection it is first necessary to examine briefly how he understands human knowing generally.

Barth's epistemology or theory of knowledge concerning elements or objects that are not ontically independent, that is, not God but rather are worldly objects of knowledge, is somewhat idealistic.[13] That is, he believes that in the normal human cognitive process, the knower controls and, indeed, determines the object of knowledge. In the sphere of worldly knowledge, the knower governs the known. In Barth's words, "We are masters of what we can apprehend. Viewing and conceiving means encompassing, and we are superior to and spiritually masters of, what we can encompass" (CD 2. 1. 188).

However, God never becomes an object in this manner. God, as object of human knowledge, is never controlled or governed by the knower. God's noetic independence means that

> God does not belong to the objects which we can always subjugate to the process of our viewing, conceiving, and expressing and therefore our spiritual oversight and control. In contrast to that of all other objects, His nature is not one which in this sense lies in the sphere of our power. (Ibid., 187)

Thus, in relation to God, Barth posits a radically realistic epistemology in

---

[12] James Brown (*Subject and Object in Modern Theology* [London: SCM, 1955]) examines the difficulties of Barth's insistence upon maintaining that God is object and subject at the same time and in relation to the same activity.

[13] Brown (*Subject and Object*, 149) suggests that "it is possible to suspect a vestigial survival of Barth's Kantianism" in his analysis of human cognition. He goes on to say that perhaps Barth is more Kantian than Kant in this matter. He states: "But even Kant knew that this did not mean that man made either himself or his world (ibid.)."

which the object of knowledge effects and controls the knowledge of it. Barth appears to reject any notion that any object other than God possesses any significant integrity or independence over against its knower. Instead, he stresses that all objects of human knowledge other than God are constituted in a significant way by the knower. On the contrary, God always remains Subject and Lord even as object (CD 1. 2. 172; 4. 2. 146–47).

Barth, while recognizing the difficulty in grasping how this can be so, nonetheless maintains that in the human encounter with God in revelation true and valid knowledge takes place. This knowledge must, however, be considered an utterly unique form of knowledge, that is, it must be considered faith-knowledge.

Faith, for Barth, is the process by and through which humans encounter God in Jesus Christ and in the scriptures and proclamation that attest to him (CD 2. 1. 12). It is the activity in which knowledge of God comes about. But as such, Barth insists, it is an occurrence in which God remains Subject and Lord. Barth not only wants to assert that the divine object of faith-knowledge refuses to be controlled or domesticated, he also wants to claim that God remains the Lord and Subject of the knowing process as well. God is Lord of the faith process not only by being an object that evokes an affirmative and believing response from the knower, that is, as the objective basis of knowledge. God is also Lord by determining the subjective response from the knower. That is, God is Lord as God's own effect upon humanity, as the Holy Spirit. Barth expresses this claim in the following manner:

> The Spirit of God is God in His freedom to be present to the creature, and so create this relation, and thereby to be the life of the creature. And God's Spirit, the Holy Spirit, particularly in revelation, is God Himself, so far as He can not only come to man, but be man and so open up man for Himself, make him ready and capable, and so achieve His revelation in him. Man needs revelation, as surely as he is lost without it. He thus requires that revelation should become manifest to him, i.e., that he should become open to revelation. But that is not a thing within the power of man. It can only be God's own reality if it does happen, and it is therefore a thing only in God's power, that it can happen. It is God's reality, by God being subjectively present to men not only from without, not only from above, but also from within, from beneath. It is reality, therefore, by God not only coming to man, but meeting Himself from man's end. (CD 1. 1. 516)

Thus, faith is the work of the Holy Spirit. Recognizing the profound difficulty with this notion, Barth carefully qualifies his claim in two directions. The first way he qualifies the activity of the Spirit in human believing is to assert that the Spirit and the believer are very separate realities. The Spirit cannot be identified with humanity or its capacities in any form or manner. "In the outpouring of the Holy Spirit, God remains God. The statements about the operations of the Holy Spirit are statements the Subject of which God is not man, and under no circumstances could they be transformed into statements about men" (ibid., 528). Human beings can never be identified with this Spirit and hence God remains the Lord "even and precisely when He Himself enters our hearts as His own gift, even and precisely when He 'fills' us" (ibid., 532). Barth will entertain no notion of mystical union here.

Barth also puts forth another and equally important qualification concerning the Spirit as the Lord and Subject of the knowing process called faith: although God initiates, determines and, in effect, completes this process, nonetheless this act of faith-knowledge is wholly and truly an act of the human knower. The Spirit determines human beings for God but that, insists Barth, does not detract or deny the self-determination of those believers (ibid., 230). Barth does not want to undercut or subvert human knowledge, freedom, or self-determination. He does not want to posit some super entity working in but unconnected with the human knower. Nor does he want to suggest some mysterious transformation of humanity takes place (CD 1. 1. 272; 1. 2. 242–43; 2. 1. 213). Hence, this activity of the Spirit by and through which humans encounter God "has nothing whatever to do with a magical inversion of the interrelated totality of our physico-psychical human life by supernatural factors and forces" (CD 1. 2. 266). Instead, our human self-determination is still active, but we are so only in such a manner that those acts of human knowledge and self-determination are enclosed in and presuppose the previous determination and activity of God (CD 1. 1. 137–38, 281, 529). Human beings determine themselves but that self-determination is "imposed upon us" (CD 1. 2. 273). Barth fully recognizes the grave difficulties entailed in maintaining divine Lordship in such terms as these. However, to begin with that initial claim of lordship entails affirming both God's control and human freedom and self-determination. And his final word in the face of these difficulties is that in faith we know that this is so, though how it can be remains a mystery (ibid., 233).

Thus, Barth's original assertion that in Jesus Christ we encounter God as Lord can be seen to entail many important claims for how humans know God and in what that knowledge consists. He has insisted that, on the one hand, God never can become an object of human disposal or control. God even as the object of knowledge remains Lord and "indissolubly Subject" (CD 1. 1. 438). On the other hand, the human process of knowing and apprehending God is also directed and determined by God as Lord. God not only elicits response but also in some mysterious manner also initiates, establishes, and directs that response from the side of the knower. God is noetically independent both insofar as God rules that which is known and the process of knowing itself. God remains Lord both objectively and subjectively in the faith process (CD 2. 1. 204).

As has been seen, God is Lord on both sides or ends of the knowing process. But Barth wants to be very explicit that this fact is only known in and through this process itself. That is, humans only know God as Lord, and hence for Barth as the true God, in this faith activity.[14] No other form of knowledge leads to this understanding. Hence the only knowledge of God that is valid and real is faith-knowledge. Faith and knowledge are not antithetical.[15] Rather, it is only through faith that knowledge takes place (CD 1. 1. 261). But this means as well that in faith-knowledge all other ways to God are denied as impossible accesses to God. As God's ontic independence localized and concretized the locus of God's revelation, God's noetic lordship reiterates and reasserts the exclusive nature of God's revelation of Godself. To say that God encounters humanity as Lord means finally that humanity must look only here and only in this way. No objects in the world, including humanity, can point to or reveal God in themselves. Knowledge of God cannot be seen as an aspect of or an outgrowth from knowledge of the world. Instead, it is God's revelation in Jesus Christ that reveals and makes clear the meaning and the content of the world and of humanity. Moreover, this Lordship clearly entails, the further claim that humanity has no capacity in itself to encounter and know God. This claim of cognitive incapacity will be seen to conflict fundamentally with Hartshorne's assertion that humans possess the innate rational capacity to know God. But for Barth, the God humans encounter in faith is a God who makes Godself known as utterly unknowable in relation to any innate

---

[14] Barth argues that it is not only through revelation that human beings come to knowledge of God but also that it is in this faith process that humans come to recognize that God is such that humans cannot come to God on their own, i.e., that God is unknowable to human beings. Philosophical agnosticism or claims of ignorance or the mind's inability are not the kind of claims Barth is trying to make in this context. For him, this kind of ignorance and our recognition of it are human possibilities. They flow out of the mind's capacity to recognize its own limits and they do not have God as their object, even though it may be unknowable. It is only within the faith process that humans come to realize the radical unknowability of God and human incapacity for this God. Thus for Barth valid knowledge of human ignorance and lack of capacity are enclosed as well within God's activity. Because of this Gustav Wingren (*Theology in Conflict: Nygren, Barth, Bultmann* [Philadelphia: Muhlenberg, 1958] 108–9) offers a basically incorrect interpretation when he suggests that Barth really begins with an anthropological presupposition, even though it be negative, of human incapacity for God. Barth, in the end, encloses this assertion of incapacity within the lordship of God and it in no way functions except in relation to revelation and as it is circumscribed by revelation.

[15] This central claim that faith is not irrational runs through Barth's work. The relation of faith to rational knowledge is a special concern in his work, *Anselm: Fides Quaerens Intellectum* (London: SCM Press Ltd., 1960). In this work he expresses the conviction that true knowledge and faith are not antithetical but rather that knowledge can only follow upon and presuppose faith. Knowledge is a function of faith. Faith is not, therefore, a repudiation of rational knowledge.

human capacity.[16] Anything and anyone that humans can know, and hence control, is not this God.

> What man can know by his own power according to the measure of his natural powers, his understanding, his feeling, will be at most something like a supreme being, an absolute nature, the idea of an utterly free power, of a being towering over everything. This absolute and supreme being, the ultimate and most profound, this "thing in itself" has nothing to do with God. It is part of the intuitions and marginal possibilities of man's thinking, man's contrivance. Man is able to think this being, but he has not thereby thought God. God is thought and known when in His freedom God makes Himself apprehensible. . . . God is always the One who has made Himself known to man in His own revelation, and not the one man thinks out for himself and describes as God. There is a perfectly clear division there already, epistemologically, between the true God and the false gods.[17]

Thus Barth, grounding his position in the ontic and noetic lordship of God in God's revelation, rejects both the possibility of the world's revealing God apart from Jesus Christ and the possibility of human beings' being capable of any revelation apart from the ruling activity of this Lord. There is no natural knowledge of God and hence no natural, nonrevelation-based theology.[18] There is only the encounter with God in Jesus Christ in and through which God reveals Godself as Lord.

1.3 Summary Remarks

The intention of this chapter has been to set forth and unpack in broad terms, the foundations of Karl Barth's talk about God and the implications

---

[16] CD 1. 2. 257–58; 2. 1. 40, 44, 188; *Dogmatics in Outline,* 17–24.

[17] *Dogmatics in Outline,* 23–24.

[18] Barth's conclusion (CD 1. 1. 1, 3, 45; 2. 1. 173) in relation to all this is that theology or talk about God cannot take place except within the context of faith and only with the presuppositions of faith being its basis and critical principle. Thus, as part and parcel of his very guiding assumptions goes the radical rejection of any "natural" knowledge of God. "Natural," within this interpretation, means apart from Jesus Christ and this means apart from any true access to knowledge. Knowledge not determined by God's ruling power in the context of faith is really illusion and falsehood. This is the rationale which forms the basis for Barth's rejection of natural theology in all its forms, whether pietism or the *analogia entis* of the scholastics and the Catholic tradition. Any position that does not commence with Jesus Christ and which is not guided and criticized from this perspective alone is rejected by Barth. There is an inherent and insurmountable contradiction, for Barth, between revelation-based theology and natural theology. For further discussion of the issue of natural theology, see Henri Bouillard, *The Knowledge of God* (New York: Herder & Herder, 1968) 24–31; Regin Prenter, "Das Problem der natürlichen Theologie bei Karl Barth," *ThLZ* 10 (1952) 607–12.

of such determining assumptions. These foundations were explored through the examination of Barth's central and all-controlling claim that God has revealed Godself in Jesus Christ as Lord and through the explication of the assumptions underlying such a claim and the repercussions that flow from this assertion. The conclusions from this examination can be seen to be several.

First, Barth has sharply delimited the arena where knowledge about God is possible. All knowledge about God is limited to that sphere circumscribed by Jesus Christ and the scriptures and proclamation which attest to him. Knowledge beginning in or being controlled by the criteria and principles of another sphere will not be valid. Hence, history, anthropology, and science, as well as all other areas of strictly human knowledge, including Hartshornian-type rational philosophy, are unilaterally rejected by Barth. Knowledge of God is knowledge under the constraint of the ruling Lordship of Jesus Christ (CD 2. 1. 6–9). In contrast to these claims for localized and not general knowledge of God, Hartshorne will be seen to assert that such knowledge is a public and universal possibility open to all rational beings who reflect deeply enough. As such it will be a function not only of God's activity but of the innate human capacity to reason.

Second, Barth has insisted that within the limited sphere of revelation true and valid knowledge of God and the real nature and purpose of humanity and the world are possible. Thus Barth does not conclude that speech about, and knowledge of, God are to be ruled out but only that they are to be controlled by this prior fact. God's revelation is the presupposition, basis, content, and criterion for all talk of God. By making such a claim for valid knowledge of God Barth is calling for a form of knowledge not governed by the rules or criteria of ordinary knowledge. He is asserting a validity based not upon human norms of certitude but a divine guarantee of truth and validity. The concluding chapter of this dissertation will return to this Barthian assertion and will raise questions concerning the acceptability of such circumvention of all human criteria from the perspective that maintains that no knowledge escapes its human foundations, not even knowledge of God.

Third, the explication of Barth's understanding of divine Lordship has indicated not only his interpretation of the source of knowledge of God but also something of his conception of the identity and nature of this God. Thus, it was seen that the God who is revealed as Lord is the triune God who lovingly and freely enters into relation with the world. But while this Lordship points to the divine capacity to be "for us" such power depends upon the prior ontic independence and self-sufficiency of the triune God. Divine Lordship means, finally, that God can be and is truly in relation with the world, but that apart from that relation God is, in Godself, self-completed and fulfilled. Thus, ontic independence and self-sufficiency lie at the heart of the Barthian understanding of God. The treatment of divine power in the following chapter will further elucidate this claim for divine independence while the second half of this dissertation will analyze the profound contrast of this Barthian independence with what will be seen to be Hartshorne's claim that God and the world ontologically imply one another and cannot be understood apart from one another.

Given these guiding principles and their implications it will now be possible to state in a much more explicit and detailed manner, Barth's conception of divine power. On the one level, it will be seen how Barth understands Jesus Christ to be the reflection and embodiment of divine power and our only guide to what power means in relation to God. From this perspective it will become clear that Barth offers a specific and radical interpretation of divine power determined by his Christological center of analysis. On another level, it will also be necessary to make explicit the notion of power which is underlying all that Barth says, that is at the very heart of his procedure as a whole. Hence at this juncture, we must proceed to the delineation and explication of the idea of divine power as set forth by Karl Barth.

2

DIVINE POWER
ACCORDING TO BARTH

It is now possible and necessary to examine Barth's conception and treatment of God's power both in terms of his explicit and formal analysis of divine power and in relation to his more concrete illustration and application of his conception of such power. His position will be examined on several levels and from several different directions, all of which are interconnected and reinforce one another. First, the investigation will set forth what might be termed Barth's formal definition of divine power as a perfection of the divine being. Within this context, it will be possible to delimit, on the one hand, those understandings of power which Barth rejects in relation to divine power and, on the other hand, to examine Barth's positive interpretation of divine power in terms of God's knowledge and will. Second, I will put forth and analyze Barth's concrete interpretation of divine power as paradigmatically manifested in and revealed through the life, death, and resurrection of Jesus Christ. Through this twofold approach it will be seen that Barth does not separate these two levels but rather understands them in continuity with one another, the one being the attempt to set forth the parameters for his interpretation of power and the categories through which this power can be conceived, and the other being the paradigmatic manifestation or exemplification of those categories.

Throughout this inquiry it will be important not only to be aware of Barth's explicit treatment of the notion of divine power but also to be alert to how that notion was already implicitly operative in Barth's methodological assumptions as set forth in the preceding analysis. That is, it is important not only to determine the conclusions Barth draws concerning divine power but also to recognize the extent to which his convictions concerning this power already function as an intrinsic and determining presupposition underlying his explicit position.

2.1 Power as a Perfection of the Divine Being

Barth commentator G. C. Berkouwer has stated, concerning Barth's position, "*In and through Christ* we must learn *who God is* and *what the really divine is and can do.*"[1] And Barth's conclusion was that in and through Jesus Christ humanity encounters and comes to know God as the one who loves in freedom. First and last this must be said of God and any further statements concerning God must be grounded in and reflective of this basic assertion. Anything else attributed to God must not contradict or oppose this claim but rather be a development of it.

Barth, although insistent that this basic definition be the center from which all else flows and to which all returns, nonetheless asserts that it is possible and proper to elaborate the assertion that God is the one who loves in freedom. That is, to say that God freely loves allows humans to say other things as well concerning God. And he develops and analyzes what these further assertions might be under the rubric of divine perfections.

For Barth, the divine perfections are ways of bringing out or explicating the fundamental claim that God is the one who freely loves. And as such they do not add anything new, extra, or foreign to that being (CD 2. 1. 331). Rather, in setting forth the divine perfections, Barth insists, "We are only naming Him again and yet again as the One who loves in freedom" (ibid.). To speak of God's perfections is not to say anything other or different than that God freely loves. It gives depth, concrete meaning, and definite contour to that claim. And it is within the context of Barth's analysis of these perfections that he sets forth his definition of divine power.

Several further important observations are necessary for an adequate understanding of Barth's position. First, he deliberately chooses to speak of God's perfections rather than the often-used notion of attributes. For Barth, the term attributes implies or indicates a quality, characteristic, or capacity which is held in common with others (ibid., 332). In relation to God Barth rejects any such suggestion. God does not share God's attributes in common with any other being. Rather, they are God's alone; indeed God is God's perfections. God's perfections are identical with God's being and as such "every individual perfection in God is nothing but God Himself" (ibid., 333). Hence, the divine perfections are God's essentially and properly in a singular and unique fashion. This means further that if these attributes can be applied to other realities besides God they can be so only in a derived and relative fashion. Only God can be understood to possess or be these perfections inherently. All other realities can only be understood to have them, not be them, and indeed to have them in a derived and improper way (ibid., 442–43, 542–43). Hartshorne, in contrast to this Barthian claim, speaks of much of what Barth terms perfections as attributes and sees all actuality as possessing them inherently and sees God as possessing them in a preeminent fashion. They are characteristics shared commonly by all

[1] G. C. Berkouwer, *The Triumph of Grace in the Theology of Karl Barth* (Grand Rapids: Eerdmans, 1956) 126.

reality and therefore the language of proper versus improper and inherent versus derived is not appropriate in Hartshorne's schema but is replaced by the terminology of preeminent versus nonpreeminent. This will be seen to be especially true of power.

However, Barth is concerned through his understanding of perfections to protect, on the one hand, the unity of divine being and, on the other hand, to insist that this unity of God's being and perfections implies a superiority to and independence from all other realities. But, Barth also has another and, for him, equally important concern which underlies his treatment of divine perfections. This concern takes the form of the claim that although the perfections of God must be understood as identified with God's being and hence as indicating a fundamental unity in God, they must equally be understood to be real and literal descriptions of that being. What Barth is rejecting here is the claim that divine attributes or perfections are merely human ways of talking about God and that in reality God exists apart from or behind these perfections in supreme and utter simplicity (ibid., 329). Instead, Barth asserts that to begin with God as the one who loves in freedom, instead of a notion of pure and simple being, and to understand the divine perfections as the concrete embodiment of this reality means that it is proper and indeed necessary to apply these perfections to God in a literal and thoroughly realistic manner. To speak of God's power or grace or patience is to describe God's being in a literal, nonmetaphorical manner. And furthermore, Barth insists that to speak in such an exact and concrete way does not call into question God's unity, for all these perfections are the perfections of the one loving and free God, and each is grounded in and reflective of that essential unity. God is fully present in, and as, each perfection.

Hence, Barth claims that by beginning with the God who loves freely and by understanding the divine perfections as descriptions of that being, it is possible to conceive of both simplicity and multiplicity, unity and diversity as proper and essential to God and that these in no way contradict one another but can be shown to correspond to each other (ibid., 332).

It is under this rubric of divine perfections, understood as inherent in God and literally descriptive of God, that Barth explicitly and formally examines the notion of divine power. With these underlying claims in mind, we must now consider Barth's formal and explicit analysis of divine power.[2]

---

[2] Barth uses a variety of terms that are translated in the English edition of CD as "power." They include *die Macht, die Kraft, die Gewalt, das Vermögen,* and *die Potenz.* The term most frequently used by Barth, and almost exclusively so in his formal analysis, is *die Macht* which carries not only the sense of strength or force but also authority. Barth's term for omnipotence is almost always *die Allmacht.* When he is referring to nondivine power he fluctuates between *die Macht* and *die Kraft* for the most part, while utilizing the other terms on occasion.

Delimitation of Divine Power

Barth treats the divine perfections as a means of analyzing and elaborat-
ing upon his fundamental assertion that God is the one who loves in freedom. And for the purposes of analysis he considers these perfections as
either perfections of love or freedom. However, he also is insistent that this
division is a heuristic device and that just as love and freedom mutually
imply each other in relation to God, each of the perfections must continually
be understood in light of all the others.[3] It is within this schema that Barth
examines divine power as a perfection of God's freedom.

Barth's consideration of power as a divine perfection represents his formal
and explicit definition of God's power and as such it can be divided into two
interconnected but distinct segments. The first is comprised of what might
be termed Barth's delimitation of divine power (CD 2. 1. 543). That is, he
seeks to determine what kinds of power are ruled out in relation to God and
thereby indicate what might be properly understood as divine power. The
second focus for Barth consists of his more strictly positive defining of what
is involved in speaking of God's power, that is, the analysis of divine power
in terms of God's knowing and willing (ibid.).

Barth asserts that to begin with the conviction that God reveals Godself
in and as Jesus Christ, and thus as the God who freely loves, involves a
number of very important, far-reaching, and ultimately determinative implications for any conception of divine power. It means first and fundamentally that we can look only here and nowhere else for an understanding of
divine power. However, it must be stated at the outset that although Barth
is adamant that Jesus Christ is the determining criterion for all that follows,
exactly how Barth derives these assertions exclusively from Jesus Christ is
not made clear. Indeed, at times, despite his initial claim, Barth states his
position concerning divine power with little or no explicit reference to Jesus
Christ at all. This is especially true in relation to Barth's treatment of power
in terms of God's all-determining knowledge and will. The result is that
Barth's treatment of God's power under the rubric of the divine perfections
and his later emphasis upon the cross as the manifestation of power sometimes appear to be in tension. The question of whether this tension is real

---

[3] CD 2. 1. 344–50. Much of what Barth says concerning power is very much like his position on freedom. On the one hand, he explicitly labels power as a perfection of divine freedom and in that sense power sounds like a subset of freedom. On the other hand, there are
times when Barth appears to almost equate the two or even make freedom sound like a subset
of power, i.e., a kind of power. At various points he makes the following statements: "Thus
God's power might also be described as God's freedom" (*Dogmatics in Outline*, 46–47); "Freedom means ability, possibility, power—power in its illimitability or its equality over against
other powers" (CD 1. 2. 674). Barth's underlying concern is, I would suggest, that freedom is
never understood in relation to God as empty but always as efficacious, as able to effect its
will, and power is never understood as simply force but as freely informed decision.

or can be resolved will be raised later in the analysis but at this juncture let it suffice to state that Barth claims a determining relation between Jesus Christ and the following assertions though what that casual connection is appears at times obscure.

Whether or not Barth always follows his own principles consistently in this matter, nonetheless he claims that this strict localization of the knowledge of God's power means that we cannot begin with any general or universal idea of power and then apply it to God in some super- or preeminent manner. No abstract notion of power can be attributed to God. Divine power is always this God's power and as such it is distinct, unique, and specific; it is the power that can be known only from what God has done, does, and will do in God's act, that is, in Jesus Christ.

This primary and overarching claim involves several other elements that can be explicated. On the one hand, it entails the rejection of any attempt to define God in terms of power itself.[4] To speak of divine power does not and must not mean that power is divine. Power is divine only insofar as it is this God's power. This claim involves no deification of power in and of itself. The subject, God, must always define the content and meaning of the predicate, power. No reversal can be permitted. Indeed "power itself" refers to that which is opposite of the power revealed in the one who loves in freedom. It points rather to tyranny, chaos, and freedom from all restraint. He points out that

> God is not "power in itself." The essence of all power, namely ability, possibility, freedom as a neutral existence, absolute freedom, abstract ability, power in itself, is an intoxicating thought. . . . But it is not "the Almighty" who is God; we cannot understand from the standpoint of a supreme concept of power who God is. . . . The power of God, real power is opposed to "power in itself."[5]

Hence, God defines power, not power God. But, on the other hand, Barth also stresses that the God who is revealed in Jesus Christ is the omnipotent and almighty God. Barth, by asserting that power is not God, is not calling into question God's omnipotence. Rather, he is insisting that how we understand power and omnipotence must be circumscribed and determined for us by the God who is and has this power rather than God's being determined by preconceived ideas of what power means. It is from Jesus Christ that we will learn the meaning and scope of operation of true omnipotence.

These preliminary claims lay the foundation for further specification and delimitation of the idea of divine power. One such important specification

---

[4] Ibid., 524, 565; *Dogmatics in Outline,* 47–48.
[5] Barth, *Dogmatics in Outline,* preceding note.

which Barth sees following from his initial assertions involves the rejection
of a conception of divine power as simply or preliminarily might, force, or
physical possibility. What this rejection entails can best be understood in
terms of Barth's distinction between *potentia* and *potestas.* *Potentia* refers to
physical possibility, potency, or might. But *potestas* involves not only the
notion of power and ability but also the added dimension of authority, of
legitimate power. And in relation to divine power these two can never be
separated; God's power is not only mighty, it is also always righteous, moral,
and legal. It is not only force, it is authority as well. Barth states:

> To let this subject give content and definition to the concept of power
> means concretely that the power of God is never to be understood as
> simply a physical possibility, a *potentia.* It must be understood at the
> same time as a moral and legal possibility, a *potestas.* God's might never
> at any place precedes power, but is always and everywhere associated
> with it. . . . It is power which is the origin of legality and is always exer-
> cised in the fullness of this legality. . . . What God is able to do *de facto,*
> He is also able to do *de jure,* and He can do nothing *de facto* that He can-
> not also do *de jure.* . . . God's moral and legal possibility is also His
> physical. His *potestas* is complete *potentia.* (CD 2. 1. 526; 4. 2. 97)

Further, God's power is not moral, righteous, and legitimate because it
corresponds to or is determined by some higher authority or universal law.
"God does not stand under any alien law, any general truth and possibility
and presupposition embracing and conditioning and limiting both Himself
and the world and man" (CD 4. 1. 529). Rather, God is the source and origin of all legality and righteousness and authority and God is this not only
in relation to Godself and divine power but in relation to humanity and the
world as well. God is the true and primary law-giver "not *ex lex* but Himself
lex and therefore the source and norm and limit of all *leges*" (ibid.). God's
power is legitimate power because it is grounded in God's own internal self-
ordering, and God's internal relations and relations with the world do not
contradict that self-ordering and self-imposed harmony but are the expression of it.

Another delimitation or clarification of the idea of divine power, profoundly significant for Barth, consists in the fact that God's power must not
be understood solely in terms of God's activity within the world (CD 2. 1.
526 – 28). That is, God's power must not be reduced to God's omnicausality. It is important to elaborate what is entailed in this assertion, and it will
be clear that Barth's position in terms of power closely follows the distinctions set forth in the preceding chapter concerning "God for us" and "God
in Godself."

Barth insists, as always, that God's power is exercised in a true form in
God's relation with and activity in the world. In what God has done, does,
and will do we truly encounter divine power. There is no other different

kind of power that stands behind God's activity in the world. Affirming this, Barth states:

> Of course it is God and God alone, who is active in His work, and He has revealed Himself within it. His omnipotence, then, is naturally the power manifest in His activity, the power in the activity of the One who has fulfilled and does and will fulfill this work, and who reveals Himself as the One He is within this work. We have neither to fear nor hope nor in any sense to expect that He will be utterly different, and not the Shepherd of Israel and Lord of the Church, in other works not known to us or in His divine essence. (Ibid., 527)

However, for Barth, God's power cannot simply be reduced to or equated with this power expressed in the worldly sphere. God is omnicausal but not only omnicausal. God's work takes place by virtue of divine power but divine power is not exhausted in this activity and relation. That is, divine power is not simply a relation between God and a reality totally distinct from God. "It is not the case that God is God and omnipotence omnipotence only as He actually does what He does" (ibid.). Barth insists upon this distinction for several reasons. On the one hand, without such a distinction Barth fears God would simply be identified with the powers and forces in the world. There would be no way to distinguish God from the workings of the universe. And Barth wants to maintain that God works omnipotently within the world while he asserts at the same time that divine power and worldly power are not the same but that each has its own integrity and sphere of activity. It will be seen also that Hartshorne, while not reducing God's action to the workings of the universe, nonetheless understands there to be a much closer connection between the two. He maintains, as well, in contrast to Barth, that God's action and power is always in some manner responsive to creaturely reality.

On the other hand, Barth argues that to understand divine power solely in terms of omnicausality would bind God to the world and hence call into question Barth's most basic assertion of God's fundamental independence of the world. That is, lacking this distinction, God would be understood as powerful only in relation to a reality distinct from and over against the divine being and not in terms of God's own existence. God would be, in this case, omnipotent only in relation to that which is not God, and therefore the perfection of omnipotence would have as its correlate the necessary existence of a world. Barth adamantly rules out such necessary existence on a nondivine level. While power is in ordinary usage a relational term signifying the reality of more than one entity, Barth, in order to safeguard the independent status of God, understands divine power in nonsocial terms. Thus, Barth rejects the identification of divine power and omnicausality because it could lead either to the denial of the distinction between God and the world or it could make such a distinct reality necessary to God. Either implication is unacceptable within the Barthian schema though both resurface within Hartshorne's vision.

Thus, Barth rejects any simple collapse of God's power into God's causal activity, of "God in Godself" into "God for us" (ibid., 528). But in order to do that he must forsake a relational, other-oriented conception of power and interpret divine power as first and foremost the power of self-grounding, self-positing, and self-conditioning. God's power consists primarily in the capacity to be Godself as Father, Son, and Spirit and to live of and by Godself. Divine power is first triune self-sufficiency and only secondarily the power to be in relation with ontologically distinct realities. Such an insistence upon a self-referential conception of power rather than on a more socially defined understanding of power will be seen to be not only in conflict with Hartshorne's interpretation of power along relational lines but will also be shown to cause problems in understanding the status of creaturely power and integrity.

This conception of God's omnipotence as primarily God's power to be Godself points to what Barth considers a further specification of divine power. This power is no neutral, indifferent, or blind power (ibid., 532 – 34). Rather, it is power to be the trinitarian God and as such capacity it is "a specific capacity, i.e., a power which is not empty but has real content, not neutral but wholly and utterly concrete" (ibid., 532). This particularizing and indeed circumscribing of divine power involves several important dimensions which must now be examined.

Every other capacity that God has flows from, follows after, and indeed is a manifestation of this power to be Godself (ibid.). But this does not mean that God therefore has the capacity, the power to do anything. Barth emphatically asserts that "God cannot do everything without distinction" (ibid., 533). To say that God is omnipotent means for Barth that God has the capacity to do, not everything, but all that which confirms and manifests God's being (ibid., 522 – 23). God cannot contradict or deny God's own being; such contradiction and denial are not possibilities of God's omnipotence. Hence, God's power is not power in general but the specific power to be Godself, to be this God.

Far more is, however, entailed in this deliniation of divine power. First and primarily, Barth asserts, it is God and only God who determines what is possible for God, what confirms and what denies God's being (ibid., 535 – 36). Neither other realities nor some sort of metaphysical categories determine divine possibilities and hence the scope of divine power. God can do anything that God determines is possible for God. Thus, God is the standard and the basic measure of what is possible in relation to Godself.[6] This does not imply limitation for Barth but rather self-limitation and hence true

---

[6] Barth, *Dogmatics in Outline*, above n. 4.

omnipotence. What is ruled out is not true power but wanton license. Barth states: "We cannot accept the idea of an absolutely possible or impossible by which even God's omnipotence is to be measured. On the contrary, we have to recognize that God's omnipotence is the substance of what is possible" (CD 2. 1. 534). Thus, God defines the limits and conditions of God's own power and thereby claims God's power as God's own.

Barth comes to further conclusions in this area. He declares that not only does God determine the limits of the possible in terms of Godself but that God is the standard and ground of what is possible outside of and apart from God as well. There is no basis for reality apart from God and God's powerful decisions. "We have, indeed, to keep an inflexible grip on the truth that God is omnipotent in the fact that He and He alone and finally (because He is who He is) controls and decides what is possible and impossible for Himself and therefore for all" (ibid., 535). This delimitation of creaturely reality and possibility extends to and includes what might be termed logical and metaphysical necessity. God determines metaphysical categories, not vice versa. For Hartshorne, once more, this will be shown not to be the case; metaphysical principles are not the product of divine decision in the way they are for Barth but are finally the "way things are" both for God and the world. Barth rejects this kind of thinking and declares instead:

> Up to and including the statement that two and two make four, these do not have their value and truth and validity in themselves or in a permanent metaphysical or logical or mathematical system which is "absolute" in itself, i.e., independently of God's freedom and will and decision. They have their value and truth and validity by the freedom and will and decision of God as the Creator of all creaturely powers. As such God is also the basis and origin and limit of all that is creaturely possible. (Ibid.)

Thus, to state in a summary fashion, Barth posits that divine omnipotence is not without limits in relation to itself and to humanity and the world. However, this power is not circumscribed by any power outside God, by any creaturely power or by something intrinsic to the nature of power itself. Rather, what is possible for God in and for Godself and therefore for the world is determined by God alone. In sum, Barth asserts, in terms of divine omnipotence the "limit of the possible is not, therefore, self-contradiction, but the contradiction of God" (ibid., 536).

This contention that God cannot do everything indiscriminately but rather sets the limits of God's own possibility leads Barth to make a final specification concerning divine omnipotence: although God's power is circumscribed by God's own self-determination it is nonetheless power over and superiority to every other power (ibid., 538–40). This claim involves several elements. First, Barth's assertion that God is omnipotent over everything does not mean that there are no other powers. There are indeed powers other than God but they are grounded in God and are real and legitimate only insofar as God is their basis and limit (ibid., 522–23). Only God has, or is, power in Godself. Only God is self-sufficient power. All other realities are given power by God; their power is derived, not intrinsic power. God, in God's omnipotence, "permits them to exist as powers apart from and besides His power" (ibid., 538). Although there are a plurality of powers in the universe, this does not, as it does for Hartshorne, point to a social theory of power in which all realities possess inherent power. Rather, God as the source and ground for all powers remains superior to and independent of all other powers, limiting, controlling, and determining them. In no way can these derived powers be understood to control and determine God. In terms of power the relationship between God and all other realities is not one of mutual conditioning or social reciprocity. It is not a symmetrical relation but an asymmetrical one. Barth contends:

> God is superior to all other powers. . . . God is not in the series of these worldly powers, perhaps as the highest of them; but He is superior to all other powers, neither limited nor conditioned by them, but He is the Lord of all lords, the King of all kings. So that all these powers, which as such are indeed powers, are *a priori* laid at the feet of the power of God. In relation to Him they are not powers in rivalry with him.[7]

Thus, a multiplicity of powers exist but they do so not in competition with God but rather under God's own controlling power and in the service of that power. A more explicit examination of Barth's understanding of this coexistence of divine and worldly powers will be undertaken in the following chapter. It is sufficient to say at this juncture that Barth insists upon both the reality and legitimacy of worldly powers and, at the same time, the complete determination of those powers by God.

He also contends that God's power over everything embraces not only what he considers real and legitimate powers grounded in God but also what he terms the "powers of opposition" (CD 2. 1. 538). God's omnipotence governs and determines not only what God positively wills and affirms but also ultimately controls that which God does not will but which runs counter to the very being of God. God is, in this schema, the source and controller or Lord of all possibility. But God is also the Lord of the impossible. That is, God's power is finally superior to evil as well as the source of all good. Divine power is, thus, power which can never be defeated. It can appear to be called into question or assailed in our world but from the perspective of God it can never be completely or really challenged. In sum, Barth's claim is that the omnipotence of God must be affirmed in terms of

---

7 Barth, *Dogmatics in Outline*, above n. 4.

both legitimate and illegitimate powers, real and unreal powers. Divine power, though specific and determinate, nonetheless is power over and indeed through all things, and no other power, either good or evil, falls outside the sphere of God's omnipotence.

Thus, Barth asserts that by localizing the sphere wherein knowledge of divine power may be obtained certain implications follow that delimit and circumscribe what might be said concerning God's power. By centering on the claim that God is encountered in revelation as the one who loves in freedom, Barth posits that a number of things must be rejected or ruled out in relation to divine power. This power cannot be conceived of as power in itself, nor simply as might, nor as only omnicausality, nor as neutral or blind force, nor as conditioned or controlled by external powers. Rather, such a centering point leads to the assertions that God defines the meaning and content of power, that this power is not only might but legitimate authority; that God is not only powerful in and through the world but first and primarily in Godself; that this power in Godself consists in the very capacity to be Godself, and as such is the basis for all other possibility; and finally, that as such divine power rules and determines all other powers, both legitimate and illegitimate. And further, through this delimitation process, Barth has defined power in at least two ways: the first, being God's power in relation to Godself, involves the capacity to be and maintain Godself, and the second, being God's power in relation to the world, consists in the capacity to affect and completely determine all reality distinct and separate from Godself. And finally, he has asserted that divine power, understood in such terms, does not negate the existence of other powers but, in fact, acts as their source and ultimate guarantee. Our subsequent analysis will have to determine how Barth further defines and delimits divine power and whether such an understanding can in fact support his insistence upon the reality of other powers.

This process of delimiting or distinguishing divine power from other powers has provided a sound basis for understanding Barth's conception of divine power. But for him this process has been basically negative in character and it is now necessary to turn to what Barth considers the analysis of divine power in positive terms, that is, divine power conceived in terms of God's knowing and willing (ibid., 543). For Barth, as well as for Hartshorne, to speak of divine omnipotence is in fact to speak of God's knowledge and will.

Divine Omnipotence as the Power of God's Knowledge and Will

Barth declares that to allow God's revelation in Jesus Christ, rather than a general concept of power, to determine the understanding of divine omnipotence ultimately means that God's power must be interpreted as the power of God's knowledge and will (ibid.). In Jesus Christ God is encountered not as a blind or indiscriminate force, an anonymous might, but as a conscious and purposive I. And it is only in terms of that consciousness and will that God's power is to be interpreted at all.

Following more classical arguments and his own insistence upon the priority of God's self-grounding, the first claim Barth sets forth is that God's knowledge and will are identical with God's essence. Reflecting the position that God's being and God's act are one, Barth contends that God's knowledge and will cannot be separated from God's being but rather "God's knowledge is God Himself and again God's will is God Himself" (ibid., 549). There is, as Barth has repeatedly asserted, an essential unity between the divine being and activity. Barth's concern, expressed in this position, is that God's activity of knowing and willing not be swallowed up or disappear into the idea of God's being. It is as God knows and wills Godself and only as such, that God is God. And further, it is this primary self-knowing and self-willing that constitute the basis for any divine knowledge or willing in relation to humanity and the world. God first knows and wills Godself and only then and as such does God know and will the world.

Corresponding to this initial assertion, Barth also states that God's knowledge and God's will are to be identified as well. "God's knowledge is His will and God's will is His knowledge" (ibid., 551). But such a statement is made with great care by Barth. He posits it because he is concerned to insure the unity of God's essence and activity. He does not, however, want such an assertion to result in the denial of either knowledge or will in God. His concern is that the equation of knowledge and will will result in the expungement of both from the divine essence as mere anthropomorphisms, that one may be reduced to the other, or that primacy will be ascribed to one while the other will be referred to only figuratively (ibid.). For Barth all of these possible interpretations are unacceptable and must be consistently rejected. Rather, both knowing and willing must be understood as intrinsic to divine being and neither God nor divine power must be understood apart from them. For Barth this is essential if it is to be maintained that God is a person and further that God, as a personal being, loves humanity and the world (ibid., 548). Thus, in order to maintain both the identity with God's being but also the distinct and literal characteristics of knowing and willing, he suggests that the two are most adequately conceived as coextensive, that is, what God knows God wills and what God wills God knows (ibid., 551). Nothing falls outside the realm of the other. In contrast, Hartshorne denies the coextensiveness of divine knowing and willing; while God knows all there is to know much that takes place is not in accordance with God's will nor does that divine will possess the capacity to bring about all that it would wish to have occur.

In order to understand more clearly Barth's association of power with knowledge and will, it is necessary to explore in detail Barth's conception of the scope of divine knowing and willing and their relation to their objects.

This can best be accomplished by the explication of Barth's claim that God's knowledge and will are superior in relation to all that is distinct from God, keeping in mind that Barth claims he derives this conception of superiority from Jesus Christ though he does not tell us how. This claim of superiority is made and grounded in the preliminary assertion that God first and primarily knows and wills Godself and by so doing posits and maintains God's own being. This divine self-consciousness and self-willing is of a somewhat different nature than God's knowing and willing of realities distinct from Godself.[8] In this first instance God's knowing and willing coincide and are identical with God's being and with each other. As such they occur simultaneously with their object. And although Barth understands the two types of activity to be in continuity with one another, with the divine self-consciousness and self-willing forming the basis for both the fact and the superiority of God's knowledge and purposive activity in relation to the world, it is important nonetheless that the distinctive nature of these forms of activity be kept in mind.

Barth develops the assertion that God's knowledge is superior to its objects in two distinct but interconnected ways; the first concerns God's omniscience and the second deals with God's foreknowledge. God's

---

[8] Barth offers an interesting variety of theories about the knowing process. On the one hand, he examines the human side of cognition and offers at least two theories concerning that. First (CD 2. 1. 188–89), he offers a somewhat idealistic interpretation of human knowledge of the world speaking of knowledge as controlling the object in some way and declaring that we are the masters of what we know. (At other times he sounds much more realistic in his interpretation with human knowledge following its object.) Second (1. 1. 102–3, 148–49, 152, 178, 217), Barth makes a definite and radical shift in his epistemological claims when he is speaking about human knowledge of God. He claims that this knowledge is totally a posteriori knowledge. It follows after its object and is utterly shaped by the object, not the object by the knower. In this sense it is a realistic epistemology. But Barth offers an interesting twist. Humans never "possess" this knowledge; it is never universally present or fixable. Rather it is always an event and as such is not permanent. Instead both its initial fact and its continued presence depends upon the object, God. It does not become datum or static fact. In relation to God's cognitive activity Barth introduces another set of epistemological interpretations. God's knowledge of the world can be understood in radically idealistic terms. God's knowing of its objects precedes the existence of those objects and indeed is the source and ground for their existence. In this sense, God as knower of the world is radically superior to and independent of that world. The knower, in this case, conditions and indeed constitutes the object known and not the reverse. And finally, in relation to God's knowledge of Godself, Barth asserts that since God's knowledge or act is identical with God's being, there is no split between that knowledge and its object; they occur simultaneously and God's knowledge (along with God's will) constitutes God, i.e., it is by virtue of God's self-knowing and self-willing that God is. God does not exist apart from this knowledge or will. Thus Barth offers a variety of epistemologies that not only point to differences in degree or perfection of knowledge but essentially refer to different kinds of knowledge, and when examined this variety raises the question whether the notion of knowledge to cover all of them is not misleading.

knowledge is omniscient knowledge because it is complete and all-embracing. Nothing exists outside the scope of divine knowledge and further, within that range, God knows everything as it is, "in exactly the sense proper to it" (CD 2. 1. 553). Contrary to the classical conception of divine knowledge in which God knew all reality as actual, Barth insists God knows reality distinct from Godself as differing and contrasting kinds of reality and therefore real and literal distinctions occur in God's knowledge. He makes a primary distinction between what God knows and evaluates positively and what God knows and evaluates negatively. In the former instance, God knows both what is actual and what is merely possible and knows them as that which God affirms (ibid., 552–53). In the latter instance, divine knowledge is understood to extend to include knowledge also of that which is not affirmed but rejected, that is, knowledge of evil or in Barth's terms, the "impossible." Even though Barth denies the validity and hence, as we will presently see, the actuality or real being of this rejected reality, it does not thereby escape divine knowledge. "In the form of His turning away from it, it is no less the object of the divine knowledge than that which is before Him" (ibid., 554). Barth claims that that which is not known at all by God, either positively or negatively, is "*ipso facto* null and void" (ibid., 553). And he also declares, "That which is not knowable and known by Him does not exist, either as actuality or possibility, as being or nonbeing, good or bad, in bliss or perdition, life or death."[9]

Another way Barth expresses the omniscient quality of divine knowledge is to characterize it as penetrating (CD 2. 1. 558). By this Barth means that not only is the range of God's knowledge all-embracing in that God knows all things singularly and externally but also internally and interconnectedly. God's knowledge has depth. Divine knowledge is thus characterized by intension as well as extension. Therefore, divine omniscience is a "knowledge which is absolutely clear, plain, definite, and intensive in exhaustiveness. Everything which is in any way knowable is known by Him" (ibid., 555).

Barth, in stressing the comprehensiveness and penetrating character of divine knowledge, wants to indicate not only the scope and depth of God's knowledge but also the particularity and definiteness of God's consciousness. Divine cognition is not knowledge in general but knowledge with specific and concrete content and as such forms the foundation and limit of

---

[9] CD 2. 1. 552–53. Barth is intent to distinguish between total lack of being or no-being and what will be examined in the next chapter as *das Nichtige* or nonbeing or negative being. The former is simply nothing, empty or blank nothing and refers to that which simply does not exist in any form, positive or negative. The latter refers to that which, though lacking positive actuality, nonetheless has a strange sort of negative being and exists as a potent, though utterly negative, force in the world.

all reality.[10] In Barth's view, "It is the knowledge of God—with it His will—which defines the limits of being. For this reason God's knowledge, as it embraces all things—all that is—is a knowledge which is definite, not limited from without but by itself. There is no limit set to it" (CD 2. 1. 553). Just what Barth means by this statement that God sets the limits of being can be more fully understood through the explication of his second claim that God's knowledge is superior to its objects in that it is foreknowledge.

Foreknowledge (*das Vorherwissens*) or *praescientia* has several dimensions for Barth. First, it does indeed consist in knowing all things that are distinct from God prior to their actual existence (ibid., 558). But Barth, while acknowledging that foreknowledge refers to prior knowledge, prefers to focus his attention in this regard upon what he terms the independence of divine knowledge from all its objects. Temporal priority is an aspect of this independence but not its sum total. By this independence Barth means that not only does divine knowledge follow after and correspond to its objects but, far more importantly, God's knowledge is the eternal presupposition of all that exists in possibility or actuality, as being or nonbeing, in general and in detail (ibid.). Foreknowledge means the absolute priority, ontologically and thereby temporally, of God's knowledge in relation to everything that is distinct from God.

Several very important implications are entailed in such an epistemology. First, there are conclusions to be drawn in relation to the realities outside of God. This conception of divine knowledge entails the assertion that all things distinct from God are first the content of God's knowledge and then and only as such do they exist in distinction and separation from God. In this schema, God's knowledge of the objects, not generally or in relation to indeterminate possibility but in detail and as completely determinate, precedes the existence of the object, and indeed this knowledge is the prior condition and finally the cause for that existence. Barth states, "Everything that exists outside Him does so because it exists first and eternally in Him, in His knowledge" (ibid., 559; KD,2. 1. 629). And again he claims, "It is not that God knows everything because it is but that it is because He knows it" (CD 2. 1. 559; KD 2. 1. 629). Thus, the object known is dependent upon and determined and circumscribed by the knower. The divine knower is independent of that which is the object of knowledge.

This epistemology involves significant implications in relation to God as well. It means that as knower God is not passive but entirely active. Stated one way, God, as knower, is not conditioned or determined in any sense by that which is known. The process of divine knowing is indeed a process

---

[10] Ibid., 553, 556. For Barth, God also sets the limits of human knowing and willing. That is, humans can only know and will either what God knows and wills in an affirmative sense or what God rejects. Humans cannot know or make a choice not first delineated by God's knowing and willing.

which conditions and limits God but it is always a matter of self-conditioning and self-limitation, not worldly determination. Thus, passivity, dependence, and receptivity in relation to the world are not elements intrinsic to God's cognitive activity. Stated in a more positive manner, divine knowing can be understood in terms of God's sole and preeminent agency, that is, God's knowledge can be understood in the active and causative terms of a divine decision. And the content of God's knowledge can be understood as the product of that free decision, not as a response to any external reality. Thus, the "created corresponds to the foreknowledge and it is only for this reason that the divine foreknowledge corresponds to the created" (CD 2. 1. 560; KD 2. 1. 630). This prospective and fully active character of divine knowing, as well as willing, represents a sharp contrast to the Hartshornian perspective. For Hartshorne, divine knowledge is creative and conditioning but not prospectively determining in the Barthian sense, and while divine knowing is active in character it will be seen to contain a retrospective and responsive element as well.

Barth develops an understanding of divine willing which corresponds to what he has maintained concerning divine knowing. God's will is understood, as is divine knowledge, to be superior to all realities distinct from it. In a parallel manner to his analysis of divine knowledge, and in contrast to what Hartshorne will be seen to claim, Barth asserts that divine will is superior to all its objects, in the first instance, in that it is a complete and exhaustive will (CD 2. 1. 555–57). Everything distinct from God is within the scope and control of the divine will. This is the case in relation to both possibility and impossibility, both being and nonbeing. On the one hand, everything that exists does so by virtue of God's will and, moreover, it exists in precisely the manner in which it does under the rule and determination of that will. On the other hand, even that which is impossible, that which exists only in the strange form of negative being does so not outside the control of God's decision and will or in real challenge to that will but finally because of its permission and under its auspices and determination (ibid., 556). God's rejection of negative being and impossibility is a powerful and all-encompassing rejection. That which is denied and judged as evil does not therefore escape God's will but in its own particular form affirms the all-powerful nature of that will. Thus, in this Barthian schema, God's omnipotent will, but as it affirms and as it denies, is definitive, embracing and determining all of reality. Barth asserts:

> Only what can be and is willed by Him is. It is by God's affirming and
> accepting will that the actual is and also the possible which has not yet
> received actuality from God's will or may receive it. But it is by God's
> refusing and rejecting will that the impossible and non-existent before
> Him is, since it is only by God's rejecting will, His aversion, that it can
> have its particular form of actuality and possbility. . . . There is no out-
> side this sphere. The sphere of His will is the sphere of spheres. (Ibid.)

And finally, it must be stated that, as with divine knowledge, God's all-embracing will is a specific concrete will. It is not will in general, not a non-particularized volition. Rather, the divine will is active in a particular, determinate way and hence, although its sphere includes all reality, it is nonetheless fixed and definite. God's will is exhaustive in scope but, precisely for this reason, it is specific in character and as such it corresponds to and is coextensive and in harmony with God's knowledge. God wills only what God also knows (ibid., 555). God's decisions are always fully aware and God's purpose is always a conscious one.

Barth asserts, as well, that God's will is superior to its objects in that it is completely independent of these objects (ibid., 560–62). This means, in general terms, that everything exists because of and in accordance with God's will, that God's will precedes and has priority over all other realities. God's decision in this view is the basis for and cause of all else. This independence signifies, more significantly, that God's will is not conditioned or determined by any other reality or will distinct from Godself. God's will is free from other realities in that it is not limited or defined by them:

> God is not dependent on anything that is not Himself, on anything outside Himself. He is not limited by anything outside Himself and is not subject to any necessity distinct from Himself. On the contrary, everything that exists is dependent on His will. It is conditioned by Him and happens necessarily in accordance with His will. And His will is pure will, determined exclusively by Himself, to act or not act, or to act in a particular way. (Ibid., 560; KD 2. 1. 631)

Thus, in the Barthian schema, this independence rules out any notion of a "relation of mutual limitation and necessity" between God and the world (CD 2. 1. 560). The world is conditioned by God, not God by the world. God and the world do not exist in a relationship of reciprocal determination. The relationship is asymmetrical in nature. And as with divine knowledge, Hartshorne, in his turn, rejects this independent and all-determining character of divine willing and argues instead that God's actions are responsive and hence, at least in part, dependent in nature upon the world.

Barth wants to make several other claims in relation to this independence. On the one hand, he contends that although God is not determined by any external will or reality, God is nonetheless self-determined. And this means that in an important, if not altogether clear way, God is conditioned in relation to the world. By freely choosing to know and will a reality distinct from Godself, God also decides to determine Godself in a particular way (CD 2. 2. 169). God defines Godself, not necessarily, but freely choosing to define, that is, know and will the world. God need not have so determined Godself, but in the free decision of knowing and willing the world God has in fact made such a determination. Barth asserts:

God's will in relation to His creation is conditioned, yet not by the
creature but by His own will as Creator, by the conditions to which He
has Himself subjected and continually subjects His creature. It is not
conditioned from outside itself, by another. In no sense is it a powerless
will, an empty wish, mere volition. On the contrary, whatever God wills
also comes about. . . . Always and everywhere His will is operative and
it is only conditioned and limited by itself and in this sovereignty it is
the determination and delimitation of all things and occurrence. (CD 2.
1. 596; KD 2. 1. 673)

Thus, God is conditioned, affected in relation to the world in the sense
that if God had never known nor willed the world, God could and would
have been different, though no less God. God is this specific God because
God freely chose to know and will this distinct reality. It is God's act of
self-determination, not an external worldly determination, which conditions
God. And further, it is this divine self-determination that forms the foundation for worldly reality as well.

On the other hand, Barth also wants to assert that although God's
knowledge and will precede all reality and, in fact, determine reality distinct
from God, this external reality nonetheless also possesses freedom, integrity,
and the power of self-determination. God's determining knowledge and will
do not cancel worldly self-determination but rather establish it. This is so
because God knows and wills God's creatures as free and self-determining
realities (CD 2. 1. 560, 585–86, 596, 598). What such a claim entails is the
subject of the next chapter, but let it be noted at this juncture that Barth
maintains both that all-pervasiveness of God's power as knowledge and will
and the self-determination and freedom of those who exist within that
sphere and further that the two claims do not contradict each other but ultimately imply each other (ibid., 586).

There is one final claim that Barth reiterates pertaining to God's knowing
and willing, and it both underscores all that he has claimed in relation to
omnipotent knowledge and will and indicates, as well, some of the
difficulties which emerge with such a conception. This claim is that divine
knowing and willing must under all circumstances be understood as real
knowing and willing (ibid., 563–65; KD 2. 1. 634). It is knowing and willing in a literal, not figurative or allegorical sense. Barth's concern, as in a
parallel manner in relation to God's being, is that divine consciousness and
decision not be absorbed in or compromised by its identification with power.
It is as knowing and willing, and only as such, that God is omnipotent.
Divine power has no other form or manifestation except that of knowledge
and will, and therefore omnipotence must never be separated from God's
consciousness and purpose.

Barth, however, recognizes that when omnipotence is associated with
knowledge and will in the manner he suggests, certain questions concerning
the literal character of that will and consciousness emerge. Indeed, Barth

states the question himself:

> The question is raised at once at our starting-point by the fact that God's knowledge is the knowledge of divine omnipotence and is therefore omnipotent knowledge. But if this is the case, how can it be knowing, i.e., consciousness and conscious representation of itself and other objects? If God knows Himself and all things in one unique act, to what extent does He really know? (CD 2. 1. 564)

> How can an omnipotent will really be a will, a purpose, the setting of a goal, a resolve? (Ibid., 587)

Although Barth raises these questions his attempt at resolving them is not altogether satisfactory. He essentially replies to his own questions by suggesting that the literal character of divine will and knowledge will be safeguarded if his starting-point in revelation is always the controlling principle of analysis and interpretation. If revelation, God's encounter with humanity, is focused upon them, God's activity can never be understood as anything but a personal, purposive, and fully conscious act, and as such an act it will always entail those distinctions that are intrinsic to literal knowing and willing: the differentiation between the real, the possible, and the imposssible; the distinction between being and nonbeing; and the difference between divine self-determination and world-determination (ibid., 589).

However, although Barth asserts that by keeping to revelation this conscious and purposive character of divine power is protected, it is not at all clear that this response truly resolves his concerns delineated earlier; it is not at all certain that Barth has overcome the difficulty through argumentation rather than mere pronouncement. How can knowing and willing which take place "in one unique act" also consist in these differentiations which entail distinctions in terms of time, character, and kind? Barth's understanding of God's eternity, though lacking in clarity, might be seen to mitigate, if not completely cancel, some of the difficulty surrounding these issues (ibid., 608–10). God knows and wills eternally and so, this has meant traditionally, in one act. However, Barth for his part suggests that eternity not be understood primarily in opposition to or as a negation of time—and as such lacking in any distinction between past, present, and future; beginning, middle, and end; or purpose, realization, and goal. Rather, Barth conceives of God's eternity as involving these distinctions but involving them in a manner unique to divine reality and contrasting to all human experience of such differentiations. Humans experience the past, present, and future asymmetrically, one-directionally, and as characterized by a certain discontinuity. For God, however, this is not so. Barth contends:

> What distinguishes eternity from time is the fact that there is in Him no opposition or competition or conflict, but peace between origin, movement and goal, between present, past and future, between 'not yet,'

'now' and 'no more,' between rest and movement, potentiality and actuality, whither and whence, here and there, this and that. In Him all
these are *simul*, held together by the omnipotence of His knowing and
willing, a totality without gap or rift, free from the threat of death under
which time, our time, stands. (Ibid., 612)

Thus, Barth would have us believe, according to his interpretation of
eternity, that true differentiation and distinction occur in the divine
knowledge and will but that they do so without any of the temporal
qualification or distinction in nature that characterize creaturely experience.
These qualifications result not so much from the "nature" of past, present,
and future but from humanity's creaturely and imperfect experience of
them.[11] Thus past, present, and future, though somehow distinct, nonetheless occur simultaneously in God but are nonsimultaneous, imperfect,
divided, and even opposed for creaturely reality (CD 2. 1. 608, 611).
Hartshorne, in contrast to these Barthian claims, understands the discontinuity between past and present and future to be intrinsic to all time and
not just to human imperfect experience of that temporal progression. God,
although experiencing the temporal flow of reality more perfectly than
humans do, will nonetheless not experience the past, present, and future
simul but will still experience them as intrinsically different from one
another. Therefore, the type of solution proposed by Barth for conceiving of
the relation between God and time will be, from the Hartshornian perspective, an unacceptable one that empties temporal existence of its very meaning and significance.

Given Barth's position concerning these matters it is possible to draw
some conclusions as to how he envisions the relation of creaturely temporal
existence (including its asymmetrically defined distinctions between past,
present, and future) and the divine knowing and willing of that experience.
First, as can be concluded from the foregoing discussion, Barth insists that
God's knowing and willing of reality distinct from Godself takes place apart
from and prior to the actual and temporal existence, in the creaturely sense,
of those realities. In this sense God's knowledge and will are pretemporal
and as such are complete and determinate, not probable or uncertain, apart
from their objects; and they are thereby above and uncircumscribed by all
human distinction of past, present, and future (Ibid., 558–59; KD 2. 1.
629).

Second, following upon the claim of divine independence, Barth also
asserts that although God's knowledge and will are complete eternally (in
this instance eternal means apart from and prior to creaturely time) this does

---

[11] Barth (CD 2. 1. 624) asserts that he can make such claims because God is understood, in
his schema, as the Lord of time and as such God is not subjugated to time but time is a servant of God.

not mean that these realities exist or are actual in any way eternally. They are known and willed prior to temporal existence but are themselves not eternal. Barth points out that

> it is true that God knows and wills temporal things eternally, that He can know them and will them and really does know and will them, in their temporal existence because he is eternal, and that He co-exists with them as the One who is eternal. But this does not permit us to reverse the matter and say that they for their part eternally co-exist with Him and His eternity. . . . God knows them and wills them. In this way they are certainly present in Him from eternity, enclosed in the Now of eternity before their existence and without it. But they have their existence and also their co-existence with God only in the positive act of divine creation. (CD 2. 1. 614)

Hence, Barth wants to claim that God's knowing and willing are complete and determinate independently of and prior to the actual existence of creaturely reality, *and* that there is a contrast between the divine eternal knowing and willing of creaturely reality and the actual existence of that reality. Both of these claims are made to the same purpose: to safeguard the unconditioned, independent, and causative character of divine activity. However, problems arise once more. On the one hand, it must be asked if the latter contrast between divine knowing and willing and the actual existence of creaturely reality does not raise questions concerning the former claim of completeness. If there is a distinction between divine knowing and the actual existence of creatures, does this not suggest that the coming into actuality of creaturely reality would have as its correlate an alteration in the content of divine knowledge that would register the change? And would not such an alteration call into question the complete priority and independence of God's knowledge? On the other hand, if both this distinction and the complete and independent character of divine knowing are maintained, does this not in turn raise questions concerning the significance and meaning of actual creaturely existence for God?

Barth's analysis is not clear or adequate concerning how these questions are to be resolved. However, once again his concept of eternity provides a clue, if a far from satisfactory solution, to the difficulty. Although God is pretemporal, God also accompanies, encloses, and indeed follows after creaturely time. "Time itself is in eternity. Its whole extension from beginning to end, each single part of it, every epoch, every lifetime, every new and closing year, every passing hour: they are all in eternity like a child in the arms of its mother."[12] By this poetic statement Barth appears to be

---

[12] Ibid., 623. Barth has received much criticism about his treatment of time and eternity even from those who consider themselves Barthians in some fashion or other. For a selection of comments on this topic see Gunton, *Becoming and Being* 177–81; Jensen, *God After God:*

saying that while creaturely existence is not coextensive with divine reality, divine existence is coextensive with creaturely reality. That is, Barth is asserting, in a manner very difficult to comprehend, that while God's eternal knowing and willing do not entail the simultaneous actual existence of their creaturely objects, the temporal, historical occurrence of these creaturely objects always has as its simultaneous counterpart divine knowledge of these happenings. With this claim, coupled with his notion of the simultaneity of God's pretemporal, cotemporal, and post-temporal existence, Barth is maintaining, on the one hand, the internal harmony of the pretemporal divine knowing and willing of creaturely existence with the divine accompaniment of that reality, and, on the other hand, he is insisting that the significance of the latter is not negated by the former. Thus, Barth wants to maintain the sovereignty and independence of the divine knowing and willing in relation to all objects distinct from God while at the same time asserting that these realities are not superfluous or insignificant to God.

All this is extremely difficult to make sense of and comprehend. But despite the unclarity, Barth's central conviction is clear: divine knowing and willing (i.e., divine power) are to be interpreted as essentially independent, unconditioned, and causative in nature. They are never to be understood as even partly responsive to or dependent upon their objects. The repercussions of this conception of power are far-reaching and involve the rejection of any idea of an open or indeterminate future (at least from the divine perspective), as well as a very particular notion of creaturely freedom and self-determination.

It is important to develop a bit more fully what Barth wants to maintain concerning his conception of divine power and the power of a person, the omnipotence of a conscious, purposive I and to develop how such a claim can be understood to qualify and clarify further Barth's understanding of divine power.

2.2 Divine Power as the Power of the Cross

Barth asserts from the outset that God's power must be understood from the perspective of Jesus Christ. Centering upon this conviction, he has sought, first through the differentiation of divine power from other types of power and second through the positive association of that power with God's knowing and willing, to conceive of divine power as God's power and as such personal, conscious, and purposive power. In all this he has consistently distinguished divine omnipotence from all forms of neutral force, pure

The God of the Past and the God of the Future, Seen in the Work of Karl Barth (New York: Bobbs-Merrill, 1969) 67, 152; and Danial Day Williams, "The New Theological Situation," *Theology Today* 24 (1968) 453.

causality, or arbitrary and capricious might. And this process of differentiation and association allows Barth to conclude, in a sense, where he began—with the revelation of God in Jesus Christ as the one who loves in freedom.

For Barth, power understood apart from or in disjunction from divine knowing and willing can only be understood in opposition to and as negation of love. As Barth earlier contended that love must be free and not coerced, he now asserts that it must also be conscious and purposive. And omnipotence (conceived as the power of a personal, conscious, purposeful I) does not stand in opposition to this love but rather in the closest, most fundamental connection. "A mere blind force can possess power and efficacy, but it cannot love. . . . There is love only where there is knowing and willing" (CD 2. 1. 599). And it is in Jesus Christ that we encounter the God who consciously and purposefully loves humanity, and hence we meet the omnipotence which is not opposed to love but which is only expressed in, and as, divine care and benevolence. In revelation, humanity discovers God's love, and "because it meets us there as omnipotence, we must now say as the final thing about God's omnipotence that we must recognize the omnipotence of the divine knowing and willing, the only real omnipotence, as the omnipotence of love" (ibid.). *why not also this am power?*

Thus, the fundamental word must be that power and love are bound together inextricably in Jesus Christ. What this means and how Barth fills and gives further content to the idea of divine power may be ascertained by examining Barth's treatment of Jesus Christ as the crucified one.

Divine Lowliness and the Nature of God

It is only in Jesus Christ that God's power is definitively revealed. This is so, in Barth's view, because in Jesus Christ God has become flesh, has become human. Barth's central Christological definition is that in, and as, Jesus Christ God truly and literally condescended to become a man (CD 4. 1. 432). Thus, God's omnipotence is identified with Jesus Christ and anything that is said concerning power in terms of Godself or in relation to its operations in the world must be anchored in this fundamental fact of divine condescension into the sphere of sinful humanity. The task at hand is to explore what this condescension implies for Barth's conception of divine power, that is, how God's omnipotence and God's lowliness in Jesus Christ correspond to one another.

The preceding chapter stressed Barth's fundamental conviction that in Jesus Christ we truly have to do with God for Jesus Christ *is* God. This primary claim leads Barth to conclude that in Jesus Christ God truly condescends to become other than Godself, to go "into the far country" and in so doing to take on not only the constraints and limitations of creaturely existence but to take upon Godself as well the burden of human sin and guilt. If God truly exists in Jesus Christ, the question must be asked what this self-abasement and indeed, for Barth, humiliation tell us about God and God's power.

The overarching claim that Barth puts forth is that this humiliation and lowliness do not deny, contradict, or mask God's deity and omnipotence but rather reveal, affirm, and reflect that divine stature and power (CD 2. 1. 517; 4. 1. 134, 158–59, 184–87, 417, 419, 533; 4. 2. 84). For God truly to enter the worldly sphere does not in any way compromise, challenge, or stand in conflict with who God is in Godself but rather is the ultimate manifestation of that God. Barth maintains: *[handwritten: this is not what I meant ... he rejects a god who changes]*

> God is always God even in His humiliation. . . . The divine being does
> not suffer any change, any diminution, any transformation into some-
> thing else, any admixture with something else let alone any cessation.
> The deity of Christ is the one unaltered because unalterable deity of
> God. He humbles Himself, but He did not do it by ceasing to be who
> He is. He went into a strange land, but even there and especially there,
> He never became a stranger to Himself. (CD 4. 1. 179–80)

Barth elaborates upon this claim that God's condescension reveals rather than obscures God's deity by emphasizing two further assertions. The first is Barth's conviction that in Jesus Christ what is revealed is God's free and powerful capacity to enter into relationship with humanity in such a manner. The condescension of God in Jesus Christ is grounded in God's capacity to be Godself but also to be with another and indeed to become another. Whatever else may or must be said concerning God, it must be stated that God is the one who is capable of becoming other than Godself. Barth stresses, as always, that this capacity implies no necessity, either to be alone or to be with and as another (ibid.). Rather, the capacity for conde-scension is the reflection of God's free and all-powerful will. It is the capac-ity to be self-determining in the most far-reaching sense. As the previous section underscored, who God might be is determined not by external stan-dards of possibility but by God in Godself. God alone determines the scope of God's possibilities. Barth asserts that this deity is truly expressed "in the fact that it has such power over itself and its creature that it can become one with it without detriment to itself" (CD 2. 1. 616).

Barth also suggests that the fact that God humiliates and abases Godself by entering the human sphere entails as well another, much more controver-sial, assertion concerning God in Godself. Barth posits that the very fact that God truly condescends in Jesus Christ signifies that condescension and humility are not alien to God in Godself but are also proper to God apart from God's relation to humanity and the world. Barth argues this important point as follows. The Son of God became human as Jesus Christ and the occurrence was an act of free obedience on the part of the Son to his Father. It was not an accidental or arbitrary act but a specific act of conscious and willed self-determination. And this self-determination, this obedience took the form of abasement and humiliation in the world. But this act cannot be conceived as contradicting the internal trinitarian relationship but rather the condescension and obedience of Jesus Christ in becoming human must be understood as grounded in and reflective of the eternal obedience of the Son to the Father. God is capable of obedience and humility in relation to the world because this is first and primarily a mode of relationship within the intertrinitarian life; it is a mode of God's own conscious and willed determination of Godself. Barth states:

> We have not only not to deny but actually to affirm and understand as essential to the being of God the offensive fact that there is in God Himself an above and a below, a *prius* and a *posterius*, a superiority and a subordination. And our present concern is with what is apparently the most offensive fact of all, that there is a below, a *posterius*, a subordination, that it belongs too in the inner life of God that there should take place within it obedience. . . . His divine unity consists in the fact that in Himself He is both One who is obeyed and Another who obeys.[13]

Barth is aware that it is difficult to grasp how one God can be characterized in both fashions, as one who is obeyed and at the same time one who obeys, one who is exalted but also lowly. But for Barth this claim is at the heart of a trinitarian understanding of God and he is adamant that neither be relinquished. If Jesus Christ is the revelation of God, then this dynamic must be upheld. Barth asserts concerning Jesus Christ:

> His witness is that although the two are different in God they do not confront one another in neutrality, let alone exclusiveness or hostility, but in the peace of the one free divine love, so that there is no contradiction, no gaping chasm between them. He attests that the height and depth are both united, not merely in the love in which God wills to take man to Himself, and does take him, but first in the eternal love in which the Father loves the Son and the Son the Father. He attests that their one eternal basis is in this eternal love. He attests a divine height and superiority and ruling authority which are not self-will or pride or severity, which do not cramp God, but in which He is free to stoop to the lowest depth in His whole sovereignty. And He attests a depth and subordination and willing obedience in God in which there is nothing of cringing servility and therefore of suppressed ill-will or potential revolt, but which are achieved in freedom and therefore in honour rather than need or shame or disgrace, in which God is not in any sense smaller but all the greater. (CD 4. 2. 352)

---

[13] CD 4. 1. 200–201. Berkouwer (*Triumph of Grace*, 312–14) recognizes and discusses the difficulties of this double claim on Barth's part by stating that it eventually leads to the asking of the question, "How can *God* be foresaken by *God*?"

Barth, thus, while insisting upon the reality of divine obedience and subordination, is equally adamant that this condescension and abasement does not represent a discontinuity or conflict of God with Godself. The incarnation, the life, and the death of Jesus Christ cannot be understood as God against God. Rather, these are expressly the manifestation of the divine power of self-determination. Understood as being grounded in and reflective of God's primary power of self-determination, humiliation, and lowliness are not therefore forms of weakness or powerlessness. Rather, they are the product and expression of divine omnipotence.

Further, this condescension and subordination represent, for Barth, not only this primary exercise of divine power as self-determination but are also the locus for the secondary form of divine power, the power of world-determination. It is in and through the lowliness of Jesus Christ that God most powerfully and fully conditions and determines creaturely existence. Thus, Jesus Christ is not only the manifestation of God's power to be God-self but also the supreme form of divine power in relation to humanity and the world. And, in the Barthian schema, the crucifixion of Jesus Christ is the fulfillment of God's condescension into the creaturely realm, of God's way "into the far country," and as such is the ultimate revelation of this twofold divine power.

Divine Omnipotence as Manifested in the Crucifixion

The crucifixion, for Barth, is the act whereby God reconciles Godself to the world and through which the covenant fellowship between God and humanity is restored. As such it is the culmination of God's way "into the far country," the fulfillment of God's power in lowliness. This suffering and death become, therefore, the paradigm for understanding the exercise and thereby the character of divine omnipotence both in relation to Godself and the world. As Barthian commentator G. C. Berkouwer suggests, the cross becomes, for Barth, the epistemological principle for understanding divine power.[14]

There are several convictions that underly these claims set forth by Barth which, although implicit in the above, must be explicitly stated here. The first is that the life and death (and resurrection) of Jesus Christ are a whole. By focusing upon the crucifixion Barth does not mean to suggest any discontinuity between the life and death but rather wants to stress that the cross is the ultimate expression of that free obedience and humility which character-ized the life of Jesus Christ. Second, Barth assumes always and fundamen-tally that it is God Godself who is humiliated, suffers and dies on the cross. Barth accepts no suggestion that on the cross it is only the human Jesus who

---

[14] Berkouwer, *Triumph of Grace*, 312.

suffers and somehow the Son of God remains unscathed in secret majesty behind the cross on Golgotha (CD 2. 1. 517). Rather, it is not only, but first and primarily, the Son of God who suffers and dies here.

Barth takes his claim even further. He insists that not only does Jesus Christ, and hence God the Son, suffer on the cross but so does the Father. Barth does not want to collapse these two divine modes of being but does want to assert that by sending the Son, the Father chooses to sympathetically align Godself with suffering and sinful humanity and hence does not stand aloof or unaffected by this occurrence. Going counter to those who have denied the suffering of the Father, Barth maintains the literal participation of both the Father and Son in the suffering and crucifixion of Jesus Christ. Arguing this, he states, "There is a *particula veri* in the teaching of the early Patripassians. This is that primarily it is God the Father who suffers in the offering and sending of His Son, in His abasement."[15]

It can thus be stated that, according to Barth, what occurs in the crucifixion is that Jesus Christ, in an act of incomparable obedience and self-giving, takes upon himself the guilt of sinful humanity and the accompanying rejection and wrath of God and by so doing reconciles the world to God. But Barth does not only wish to stress that God is truly in reconciliation but also that it is because of—and only because of—this divine presence that such a reconciliation could be accomplished. Barth expressed the centrality of the divine presence in this reconciliation process by claiming that Jesus Christ can accomplish this feat because of the twofold fact that as God he has (1) the capacity to submit himself to the judgment of God, that is, the power to determine himself in this manner, and (2) the power to be equal to that judgment and wrath (CD 4. 1. 12–13, 129–30). Because it is God acting, the reconciliation can be affected. For Barth, the all-important claim is that

> because He was God Himself, He could subject Himself to the severity of God. And because He was God Himself He did not have to succumb to the severity of God. . . . That double proof of omnipotence in which God did not abate the demands of His righteousness but showed Himself equal to His own wrath; on the one hand by submitting to it and on the other by not being consumed by it. (CD 2. 1. 400; KD 2. 1. 450)

Reconciliation is true and efficacious not because humanity has made amends or assuaged the righteous wrath of God by virtue of its own activity.

---

[15] CD 4. 2. 357. Berkouwer (*Triumph of Grace,* 307) has difficulty with the notion of God's suffering. He states that "once foot is set on this road there is no logical place at which to stop. The process of drawing conclusions must then be pursued to the end. It then becomes necessary to speak of what can and does happen *in* God in the way of curse, suffering and *death.* In this connection it is eminently noteworthy that Barth frequently speaks about the 'passion of God' but not so unqualifiedly of the 'death of God.' "

Rather, it is efficacious because God, in the humiliation and suffering and death of Jesus Christ, has taken the human burden of sin and guilt as God's own and only in this work has restored fellowship. The power of God and hence the efficaciousness of the act are made doubly manifest in God's capacity to surrender and yet not be destroyed nor annihilated by such an action.

It is now time to examine explicitly the content of Barth's claim that it is in the cross that we have the truest exemplification of divine power and the point from which all other manifestations of God's omnipotence must be interpreted. To state Barth's position succinctly, in the crucifixion and death of Jesus Christ the Son of God surrendered Godself to both the wrath of God and the sinful rejection of humanity and precisely in this abasement, subjugation, and impotence was triumphant and all-powerful. It is at this point of utter weakness and impotence that God is fully omnipotent. But what does Barth mean by this? Is he suggesting a new definition of power in relation to God that that which the world understands as weakness is really powerful? Is he positing that suffering and with it passivity are proper notions to apply to God? Is Barth contending that God, in Jesus Christ, is truly conditioned and determined by human action—even unto death on the cross? And if this is so how can it possibly be reconciled with the claims of omnipotence as independent knowing and willing and of the unconditioned character of divine power? By way of answering these questions we must look more closely at what is entailed in Barth's claim.

First, although Barth affirms that both the Father and Son participate in this suffering, he offers as well a very particular and sharply delimited understanding of this divine suffering. It is essentially active in character. God, in both the modes of Father and Son, remains the subject and Lord of this occurrence. The Father is predictably subject in that it is as Father that God freely sends the Son. But the active passion of the Son is more interesting and as such more difficult to grasp. Barth asserts that the suffering and death of Jesus Christ, although acts of subjugation and obedience, are completely active in character because they are freely chosen by Jesus and take place only on the initiative of such divine choice; that is, they occur first and foremost as events of divine self-determination, not as determination by the world. God, in Jesus Christ, becomes a victim, an object in humanity's temporal history but this fact has its origin in and is completely controlled by the eternal free decision of God. In relation to the suffering and death of Jesus Christ Barth contends:

> We must first emphasise generally that . . . in it as a passion we have to do with an action. That in it the subject of the Gospel story became an object does not alter this fact. For this took place in freedom of this subject. . . . But it is with free self-offering of this kind and therefore with an act and not a fate that we have to do in this passion. (CD 4. 1. 244–45)

There is another sense in which God is always the subject of this passion, and that in relation to it, as with all other occurrences, God does not relinquish control, God does not become other than the all-powerful and all-determining Lord. Ultimately, although God in Jesus Christ submits Godself to both the forces of evil and the wrath of God, because Jesus Christ is God he can survive this subjugation. Because he is God, Jesus Christ, even on the cross and in death, cannot be truly challenged or threatened but is acting in omnipotence. Thus God, both as initiator and as controller of the passion itself, remains subject of this occurrence. God remains subject, even as victim, because the passion of Jesus Christ is primarily and fundamentally an act of self-determination, and as such it is also an act in and through which God ultimately determines the other forces and powers involved—not they God. Barth states:

> God *could* do it because in His omnipotence He is capable of this
> handing-over, because in His self-abasement—far from committing any
> breach against His own nature—He causes His omnipotence to con-
> quer, and because the concealment and darkness and mire to which He
> gave Himself are quite unable to diminish His divinity. (CD 2. 2. 493)

We must inquire what this insistence upon God as active subject of this passion says about this suffering and about the cross. First, we must ask if there is true passivity or receptivity in this suffering and humiliation. Barth certainly wants to maintain that God is object here, literally suffers and is affected. That is, he is concerned to assert that this action is passion (CD 4. 1. 238). And the fact of the crucifixion certainly involves the action upon Jesus Christ by other forces and powers. Nonetheless, Barth always encloses this receptive or passive side of the cross within the primary action of God. The cross is first and foremost a product of divine self-determination and other-determination. It is not the result of determination of God by the world. Thus finally, God's passivity in the crucifixion appears to be a form of divine activity. And any understanding of divine receptivity or passivity that emerges from reflection upon the cross must interpret such passion from the perspective of God's primary action, not vice versa. Thus, if God is conditioned by the world (a claim Barth often sounds like he is making), this conditioning can only be understood as secondary, dependent upon, and finally as an expression of God's primary self-determination.

This leads to the all-important question of what is meant by the claim that in this passion God's power is clearly revealed. Given Barth's emphasis upon the active and ultimately controlling character of that suffering, it is necessary to conclude that although God is powerful in impotence and weakness, God's power must not be simply identified with or defined as impotence or weakness. That is, Barth is not offering a new definition of power as powerlessness. He is not suggesting a new divinization of weakness and passivity. Just as "power in itself" was rejected as inappropriate in relation to God so, too, is abstract or general powerlessness. "There is no lowliness which is divine in itself and as such. There is therefore no general principle of the cross in which we have to do with God (in principle)" (ibid., 191–92).

Thus, Barth can be interpreted to mean that although divine power is revealed through powerlessness and passion, this is not the same as identifying God's power with this impotence and passivity. Rather, it is precisely because God is omnipotent, both self-determining and hence world-determining, that God's power can take this form. God's self-offering and subjugation reveal that God's power is so unique and so great and superior that it transcends and encompasses what for humanity are so often the oppositions of activity and passivity, power and powerlessness. "His omnipotence is that of a divine plenitude of power in the fact that (as opposed to any abstract omnipotence) it can assume the form of weakness and impotence and do so as omnipotence, triumphing in this form" (ibid., 187). Thus it can be seen that the tension between the passivity of the cross and the all-determining nature of divine knowing and willing are apparently resolved by Barth through the interpretation of that passivity as a form of divine decision and self-determination, not as a product of creaturely conditioning. Here, too, God's action remains independent, autonomous, and causative rather than reactive or responsive in nature.

Thus, divine power is active in powerlessness but is not to be merely equated with weakness and impotence. But while this claim may resolve the tension between God's power as active and unconditioned and the seeming passivity of the cross, does not this interpretation, on another level, call into question Barth's initial claim that Jesus Christ is our only way of understanding divine power? If divine power is not identified with this passion but only works through it, does there not remain the suspicion that lurking behind the cross there is another form of power that could just as well exercise itself in other forms or through other mediums, including coercion or tyranny? [16] This sense of uneasiness is supported when it is remembered that behind the cross there stands the Father who, as Father, suffers but certainly does not die and who remains as the one who resurrects Jesus Christ from the dead. When this is kept in mind it appears to erode Barth's claim that the power of God is definitively revealed in Jesus Christ. [17] Despite Barth's claim to the contrary, there remains the suspicion that although lowliness is not improper to God, the real power is behind the cross and Jesus is merely an occasion for the illustration of that power.

---

[16] There remains in Barth, despite his efforts, the ever-present fear or danger that when "God-for-us" and "God-in-Godself" are identified but not collapsed, that somehow God in Godself is different. Barth wants at all cost to avoid this but nonetheless it remains always at the back of his position.

[17] Berkouwer, *Triumph of Grace*, 312.

Barth attempts to avoid this difficulty by affirming that although God cannot be reduced to God's acts in the world, including the act of the crucifixion, neither can God be divorced from them. That is, his position is grounded in the conviction that although divine power cannot be said to be only operative here and in this way, it must be said to be truly exercised here and wherever else we may encounter it; it will always have, though not the same form, the same character and purpose as it does in Jesus Christ. Thus, in whatever form God's power takes it will always be exercised as loving and free and in the service of God's decision to be with and for humanity. And when this conviction is combined with the above stated interpretation of the cross as active, not passive in character, Barth is convinced that any tension between God's power and God's action in the cross or any tendency to separate the two will be understood as a misunderstanding. Rather, God's power is always active and determining, on the cross and elsewhere, and it always has as its purpose in that action the gracious and loving desire of God to be with and for humanity.

Thus, Barth concludes that because God's power is revealed in Jesus Christ in the service of reconciliation, of God's gracious activity toward the world, then we can—and indeed we must—always understand love and power in conjunction and not in separation. God's power is the active power of self-determination and world-determination, but what Jesus Christ reveals is that such determination is always loving and benevolent in nature. There is finally no disparity between God's independent knowing and willing and God's abasement on the cross nor between the power behind the cross and the love expressed on the cross. God's power is always active in nature, but the purpose of that activity is always to love the world and its creatures.

This intimate association of love and power revealed in God's act of reconciliation points to a final claim that might be drawn out of Barth's position. That is, although God's power is not exhaustively exercised here, it is paradigmatically expressed, that is, it is appropriately and properly manifest here and in this manner. What is meant by this is that although Barth does not identify divine power with weakness and suffering as such, the connection of power with love in the self-offering of Jesus Christ indicates or delineates those forms of power which might be said either to correspond to or contradict God's revelation of Godself as loving. That is, although Barth might reject any assertion that as omnipotent God can only act in one particular way, he might, however, agree that we can say that there are certain forms this power can never take, for example, oppression, tyranny, or cruelty. The cross, then, might be understood as a principle which does not tell us precisely the form in which God will always exercise God's power, but does delineate the character that power will always manifest.

There is one final dimension of Barth's notion of divine power determined by Jesus Christ that must be mentioned. The crucifixion is not the final word, though it may be the definitive one. The resurrection, too, is an expression and exercise of divine power. But what must most importantly be said here is that the divine omnipotence revealed in the resurrection in no way contradicts or stands separate from the divine omnipotence of Jesus' self-offering on Golgotha. It is not the case that the resurrection represents either the real divine omnipotence or a different kind of omnipotence. Rather, the resurrection is the perspective from which the triumph of the cross, the reality of reconciliation, is made known (CD 4. 2. 133). And in so revealing, it is an exercise of divine power, of the power whose character, Barth states, must be from this perspective understood as light, liberation, knowledge, and peace (ibid., 310 – 16). The resurrection is, finally,

> the revelation that the love of God for the world estranged from Himself attained its end in this action and passion, that He, the humble servant of God, is our righteousness, i.e., that our own wrong has been set aside in and with the judgment accomplished and suffered by Him, and our own new right has been established by Him. (Ibid., 4)

2.3 *Summary Remarks*

The intent of this chapter has been to examine Barth's understanding of divine power. As a means of accomplishing this task Barth's position has been considered in terms of his analysis of divine power as a perfection of God's being and in terms of his conception of the crucifixion of Jesus Christ as the primary manifestation of that power. Out of this analysis several broad concluding statements can be set forth, but with them several questions must be raised as well.

Stated in the most fundamental terms, Barth declares that divine power must always be understood as the power of the triune God, of the Father, Son, and Spirit. And as such, Barth defines this power in two ways: as the power or capacity to determine and maintain Godself and as the capacity to determine, in and through God's act of self-determination, all realities distinct from God. This self- and other-determination, further, must be understood exclusively in terms of divine knowing and willing and thus as conscious and purposeful acts—as the acts of a personal I.

This basic definition of power as divine self-determination and the subsequent understanding of omnipotence as world-determination allow Barth to conclude that no other powers condition or challenge God's power because all are grounded in and controlled by God's primary act of knowing and willing Godself. Rather, God, in this act of self-knowing and willing, defines the realm of God's own possibility and hence the world's. Given these qualifications of what divine power entails, the life and especially the death of Jesus Christ can be understood not as a contradiction to be explained away but instead as the greatest and most significant manifestation of divine power.[18] They can be seen as such a manifestation in several important ways.

On the one hand, because God always remains the subject of this event and as such the initiating and ultimately controlling factor, powerlessness — not generally but in this instance — emphasizes the intrinsic independence of and control over external realities by God rather than divine dependence upon and conditioning by these realities. The cross rather than indicating any powerlessness or weakness on God's part, underscores the divine superiority and independence of all creaturely reality. God acts with equal omnipotence in all circumstances, in apparent impotence as well as strength, as object as well as subject, and as servant as well as Lord. On the other hand, because God truly becomes flesh and suffers and dies, Barth again contends it can be maintained that in God's self-determining, God also chooses to be conditioned and determined by the world. For Barth, this worldly conditioning and determination are secondary and are always circumscribed and enclosed within God's self-determination, but they are not therefore not real. God is different because of the world. It is not self-evident, however, that Barth can maintain both these claims. What does it finally mean to say that God determines both Godself and all things — down to the details — but that in this determination God allows Godself to be conditioned and determined by creaturely reality? Is God truly determined by the world or only by God's determination of it? Does the extent or compass of divine power not call into question the claim that God is in any way truly conditioned as the crucified Jesus Christ?

It is not only the all-determining scope of divine power which raises this question but also Barth's conception of that power in terms of knowing and willing. Barth contends that divine power is not just a greater power than other powers, a power among kindred powers, but is different in kind. And when he speaks of it as superior and omnipotent knowing and willing, it is understood to precede all other realities and to be prior to them. This led us to ask whether Barth's God is truly affected or conditioned in any way by the world or humanity, or whether in fact — as a function of divine self-determination — God is only conditioned by God's independent and prior knowledge and willing of the world and not the world itself. That is, if Barth's solution, suggested above, of divine eternity does not offset his adamant claim of divine power as independent and ultimately nonsocial power, then we are left with the question of whether creation, history, and humanity have literal significance. In an all important sense, is that divine self-determination not already accomplished prior to the world's existence, and at best can the world only be understood as the arena where that self-

---

[18] Barth states: "God cannot be greater than He is in Jesus Christ" (*Prayer According to the Catechisms of the Reformation* [Philadelphia: Westminster, 1953] 23).

determination is "exhibited" or played out? If Barth, given his fundamental insistence upon God's all-controlling determination and his understanding of that determination as self-completed knowing and willing, remains unconvincing concerning the equal importance of the actual existence of that creaturely reality, then even the cross comes in danger of being regarded as at best a dramatization of what is already settled or at worst a charade in which God is never really challenged, not truly powerless, and never really victim.

Thus, because Barth insists upon God's self-determination and determination of the world in the terms in which he does, any attempt to claim that the world and humanity also condition and affect and contribute to the divine life must be called into question. And with this the question arises concerning the character of that power as loving, or rather divine power as the power of love. On the one hand, this association of love and power is supported by Barth's insistence that this power is conscious and purposive, that is, that capacity of a person who can acknowledge and enter into relationship with another. Going along with this is also Barth's ever-present insistence that divine power and love as God's power and love are always free, never necessary or coerced. Thus, they maintain the character of spontaneous self-giving. However, on the other hand, it must be asked if this interpretation of the determination of God as self-determination not world-determination does not also include a weakening of Barth's connection of power and love. In ordinary usage, the notion of love includes some social element; it refers to a kind of interaction that involves at least a small degree of reciprocity and mutual conditioning. Even self-sacrificial love has a responsive and receptive element. But Barth does not interpret divine love along such social lines; while he stresses the claim that divine love involves freedom from necessity, he appears to reject the idea that it also entails reciprocal conditioning, even in relation to the cross and Jesus' love for humanity. Therefore, insofar as one argues for a more socially defined conception of love, either on the basis that love intrinsically involves interaction, not just action, or perhaps on the basis that divine love as revealed in Jesus Christ entails reciprocity between God and the world, then Barth's claim will be open to question; in such a case love and power, as Barth defines it, will be difficult or impossible to identify with one another. However, if one accepts the Barthian conception of divine power as active and determining power, then a notion of love that does not entail mutual interaction will follow. What cannot be maintained is an identification of a social notion of love as interaction and mutual conditioning with a nonsocial notion of power as one-directional and all-determining action.

We have been looking at Barth's conception of power and what that says about God's self-determination and the possibility of God's being determined in some way by the world. What has emerged from this analysis is the conviction that Barth understands divine power as essentially independent, unconditioned, and causative in nature and that such an understanding either denies the conditioning of God by the world or so radically encloses the significance of that determination of God by the world within God's own self-determination that its meaning is no longer clear. It is now time to examine how this conception of divine omnipotence is explicitly worked out in terms of God's determining of the world and realities apart from God. And by way of focusing this discussion God's power will be investigated in light of the question of evil, and of human determination, freedom, and responsibility.

3

DIVINE POWER AND WORLDLY REALITY
ACCORDING TO BARTH

The discussion of the preceding chapter revolved around Barth's understanding of divine power, its nature, character, and exercise. Stated in summary form that examination concluded that, from Barth's perspective, divine power must be understood solely as this God's power and therefore as distinguished from all other forces or powers. This delineation of divine power was seen to lay the foundation for Barth to conceive of God's power in terms of personal knowing and willing. Divine power interpreted as such conscious and purposeful action lead Barth, on the one hand, to conceive of it as all-determining and omnipervasive and, on the other hand, to understand divine power as intimately connected with divine loving. Thus, love and omnipotence come to entail one another in this schema, and the cross becomes the moment of ultimate manifestation of both, of a love which is always and completely efficacious and of an omnipotence which is ever gracious.

We have reached the juncture where it is necessary to examine how this gracious power is active in relation to the world. The structure of and the principles which govern this relation between divine and human activity have been set forth in the preceding chapter, but in order to fully understand their implications it is important to explore how that structure and principles are manifested in relation to particular questions and situations. As is evident from Barth's analysis of divine power as the power of God's superior and independent knowledge and will, the notion of omnipotence is important to every aspect of Barth's schema. For Barth there is no arena in which this power is not operative and all-pervasive. It is therefore impossible, within the limited scope of this study, to examine every power where this notion is relevant. Instead, in this chapter I propose to analyze those points both where the extent and character of divine power are most clearly exhibited and where the questions and difficulties arising from such a conception of divine power are most vividly in evidence. By way of doing this, I will examine Barth's understanding of evil and sin, his conception of divine providence and finally, coming back to our original point of departure in Chapter 1, his notion of faith. Through this analysis it will become evident that I do not believe that Barth can maintain all his claims in a consistent manner and that such difficulty raises serious questions about the coherency and viability of his position. At every juncture of our analysis the relation between God's power, understood as all-determining, independent and causative, and creaturely action and integrity will be seen to be problematic. Hence, the following analysis will attempt both to set forth Barth's position and to explore the problems that I have come to understand as intrinsic to that position.

3.1 The Problem of Evil and Sin

In order to understand adequately the scope and meaning of Barth's conception of evil and sin, it is necessary first to set forth Barth's view of the intrinsic goodness and perfection of creation. It is only against such a background that both Barth's notion of radical evil and his conception of the all-pervasive divine power can demonstrate their full impact and importance.

For Barth, the true meaning of creation, as of everything else, can only be ascertained from the perspective of faith. That is, creation can only be truly understood from that perspective shaped and determined by knowledge of Jesus Christ. The content and significance of creation cannot be independently determined but rather they are, so to speak, read back into creation from the point of revelation.

What is revealed in Jesus Christ is not only the knowledge of creation tied to Jesus Christ, but the fact that first and primarily Jesus Christ is the ontological foundation for creation itself (CD 3. 1. 29). That is, in revelation the eternal divine decision in Jesus Christ is understood as the ontological ground for any and all reality distinct from God. Jesus Christ is God's eternal decision not to be God alone but to enter into fellowship and become a covenant-partner with a reality distinct from Godself. Creation, understood from this point of view, becomes the arena in which God actualizes that eternal self-determination and in the context of which God establishes, maintains and fulfills, in Jesus Christ, God's covenant with humanity. Barth claims that revelation informs us that the "secret, the meaning and the goal of creation is that it reveals, or that there is revealed in it, the covenant and communion between God and man" (ibid., 377).

This intimate connection between God's decision for covenant and creation leads Barth to make a number of important and in this context highly relevant claims concerning the nature of that creation. First, this means that creation, as the product of God's decision, is not hostile or even neutral to God. As the effect of God's all-powerful knowledge and will it is the actualization of those, and only those, possibilities which affirm God; as God's creation it is inherently and completely good. Barth under no circumstances will allow the suggestion that God could or would create a reality which in any manner contradicts, denies, or opposes God.

Given this fundamental claim, Barth also, however, asserts that this goodness of creation has a twofold form: a positive and a negative aspect. And it is in this double distinction of creation's goodness that we first begin to encounter Barth's delineation of what is to be understood as evil. For although Barth contends that creation has a negative side, he also is adamant that this aspect does not contradict his primary claim of creation's intrinsic goodness but rather is a manifestation of it and hence must be very carefully distinguished from real evil.

The Shadowside of Existence

In the Barthian schema creation is good but that goodness takes the form of a dialectic and is characterized by contrast and marked by antithesis. In one form it is positive and in another—and in our context this is what is of interest—it is negative. This latter dimension of creation's goodness Barth labels creation's "shadowside" (*die Schattenseite*), and under this designation he refers to such aspects of creaturely reality as obscurity, limitation, decay, loss, failure, age, and death (CD 3. 3. 297). What is all-important here is that the reality of this negative dimension does not involve the rejection or denial of the goodness of creation. It is not to be identified with evil but rather acknowledged as the product of God's knowing and willing, and as such it is good.

> It is irrefutable that creation and creature are good even in the fact that all that is exists in this contrast and antithesis. In all this, far from being null, it praises its creator and Lord even on its shadowy side, even in the negative aspect in which it is so near to nothingness. (Ibid.)

It is only in Jesus Christ that this ultimate harmony and unity of creation is made known. Outside of revelation it is impossible for humans to reconcile the two aspects (CD 3. 1. 378; 3. 3. 295–96). They are always experienced as contradiction. But in Jesus Christ God took upon Godself both aspects, and the contradiction of creation was made God's own and as such was revealed to be the result of God's will and causative knowledge and hence good.[1]

---

[1] CD 3. 3. 301. Barth (CD 3. 1. 388–414) recognizes that many aspects of his idea of creation as inherently and totally good resemble the optimistic evaluation of such thinkers as Leibniz and his conception of the best of all possible worlds. However, Barth asserts that his own position has a fundamentally different grounding; his evaluation of the world as good lies only in his prior faith in the knowledge of God as Creator and Savior of the world. The affirmation of the goodness of creation is based "unequivocally on the judgement of the Creator God" (ibid., 411). Only from this perspective, Barth argues, can the true goodness and

Why this twofold form of creation should be good—indeed be better than only a positive creation—is not made absolutely clear by Barth. In one sense, God's wisdom might simply be said to transcend ours and that therefore this assertion of creation's goodness in this double form is not open to analysis but only acknowledgement in response to Jesus Christ (CD 3. 3. 297). But in another way Barth offers a more explicit reason. The negative aspect of creation points to the creatures' complete and utter need of their Creator. The shadowside of creation indicates that creaturely reality is "something, yet it is something on the edge of nothing, bordering it and menaced by it and having no power of itself to overcome the danger" (CD 3. 1. 376). The shadowside of existence, understood as part of the good creation, emphasizes that God wills to be humanity's Helper, Lord, and Savior and reveals that neediness and dependence are not evil but the proper stance of God's creature (ibid., 375–76). It becomes as such the mark of creaturely perfection and that dimension in respect to which God most fully reveals God's gracious will and power (CD 3. 3. 295–96). Barth states:

> For all we can tell, may not His Creatures praise Him more mightily in humility than in exaltation, in need than in plenty, in fear than in joy, on the frontier of nothingness than when wholly oriented on God? For all we can tell, may not we ourselves praise Him more purely on the bad days than on good, more surely in sorrow than in rejoicing, more truly in adversity than in progress? (Ibid., 297)

Thus, creation in its negative aspect is not contrary to God. Rather it is a legitimate aspect of God's creation and as such must never be confused with real evil. There is "no common ground between it and nothingness, the power inimical to the will of the Creator and therefore to the nature of His good creation, the threat to world-occurrence and its corruption" (ibid., 296). Yet, this negative aspect of creation exists in a unique relation to real evil. Barth uses spatial imagery to express this relationship; he asserts that the shadowside of creation, though not the same as evil, sits at the edge of creation, near to nothingness or that which God has not affirmed but rejected (ibid., 350). And as contiguous to nothingness the shadowside is a manifestation of the creatures' need of their Creator.

However, it must be said that Barth, although imaging the shadowside of existence as contiguous with real evil or as he will label it, *das Nichtige*,[2] does

---

also the reality of evil be taken seriously.

[2] Barth's term *das Nichtige* has been translated in a variety of ways. The translators of the English edition of CD have rendered it "nothingness." Geraint Vaughan Jones ("God and Negation" *SJT* 7 [1954]) labeled it the "inimical principle of Negation." Arthur C. Cochrane (translator's note to Otto Weber, *Karl Barth's Church Dogmatics* [London: Lutterworth, 1953] 187) states that there is no precise English equivalent and that Barth has formed the term

not understand that proximity to indicate any positive possibility or propensity within God's good creation for that evil. God's creation, as a product of God's will and knowledge has as its inherent capacity only those possibilities which affirm God. As such "there is no capacity for nothingness in human nature and therefore in God's creation, nor is there any freedom in this direction as willed, ordained and instituted by God" (CD 3. 3. 356).

Thus, creation as the product of God's decision for covenant, is wholly and utterly good. As such its negative aspect must be conceived as part of creaturely reality indicating especially the proper dependent stance of the creature. It is not to be conceived of as evil nor as the foundation or basis for sin and evil, that is, as the weak link in creation. Now we must turn to the examination of this evil with which the shadowside of existence is not to be identified and attempt to understand how it crosses the frontier and enters God's good creation for which it is not true possibility.

The Reality of Radical Evil

With the background provided by Barth's assertion of the goodness of creation and his understanding of the shadowside of existence as part of God's decision for humanity and hence as a God-affirming and thereby creature-affirming possibility, it is now possible to turn full attention to Barth's particular conception of evil or, as he most often terms it, *das Nichtige.* And it is in relation to such an analysis of real and radical evil that the full magnitude and implication of Barth's notion of divine power are exhibited and, along with this, the difficulties and questions which such an idea of power entail.

It must be stated at the outset that the question of evil is, for Barth, not only important but also highly problematic. This is so for several reasons. First, the very knowledge of evil presents a difficulty. On the one hand, evil in this schema is absolutely rejected as a part of God's good creation. In no way can it be regarded as a product of God's self-determination or world-determination. Hence, evil and creaturely existence have no common ground, and thereby any "natural" knowledge of evil is ruled out (ibid., 331–32, 350). What humans can know of their creaturely reality, within

---

from the German adjective *nichtige.* Cochrane, hoping to capture the negative sense of evil and destruction, translates the term as the "Nihil." Herbert Hartwell (*The Theology of Karl Barth* [London: Duckworth, 1964] 117–18), speaks as well of the "Nihil" but he states that he has chosen this rendering as a means of conveying not only the negative aspect but also God's rejection and defeat of this factor. Berkouwer (*Triumph of Grace* [Thetford, Norfolk: Fontana Library, 1974]) often refers to it as chaos. And John Hick (*Evil and the God of Love* [Grand Rapids: Eerdmans, 1956] 133), recognizing the difficulties of an adequate English translation, prefers to simply repeat Barth's own term, *das Nichtige.* I have followed the translators in quotes and followed Hick's method of repetition in my own analysis.

this context, is only, at most, the negative limit of our own consciousness and experience, that is, the shadowside of existence and not genuine evil (ibid., 350). Therefore, the creature encounters and indeed is a victim of this radical evil but "of itself, the creature cannot recognize this encounter and what it encounters. It experiences and endures it. But it also misinterprets it" (ibid.).

On the other hand, knowledge of evil is further complicated by the fact that although the good creation has nothing in common with *das Nichtige,* nonetheless this reality has entered into creation, threatened and corrupted it. Thus, the "existence, presence and operation of nothingness . . . are also objectively the break in the relationship between Creator and creature" (ibid., 294). That is, when we deal with the question of evil we are not examining a reality external to us but rather a reality which, though having nothing in common with the good creation, is nonetheless intimately connected with creaturely existence. And because of this reality true knowledge of God, creation, and evil is distorted and made impossible.

Barth, however, asserts that although humanity's sinful condition and creaturely status rule out any "natural" knowledge of *das Nichtige,* a true understanding of this reality is possible through Jesus Christ. In Jesus Christ, God not only affirms the goodness of creation and God's love of and faithfulness to humanity and the world but does so by clearly differentiating Godself from that which is evil, confronting it, naming it for what it is, and ultimately defeating it. For Barth, genuine knowledge of evil is possible, for in Jesus Christ

> there is revealed not only the goodness of God's creation in its twofold form, but also the true nothingness which is utterly distinct from both Creator and creation, the adversary with whom no compromise is possible, the negative which is more than the mere complement of an antithetical positive, the left which is not counterpoised by any right, the antithesis which is not merely within creation and therefore dialectical but which is primarily and supremely to God Himself and therefore to the totality of the created world. (Ibid., 302)

Therefore, in Jesus Christ, as God became flesh, existence of genuine evil is made known as that which both opposes God and assaults and threatens God's creation as well. In the cross of Christ is revealed that which is antithetical, alien, and adverse to God's self-determination and loving determination of the world. And further, the death of Jesus Christ points to the gravity and seriousness of this opposing reality (ibid., 304). *Das Nichtige* is no mere apparent evil but rather the radical and mighty opponent of God.

But Jesus Christ reveals not only the existence of this opposing power and the seriousness of its assault but also, and most importantly for Barth, the divine triumph over this challenger. The cross of Jesus is that point at which God's power is most fully manifested. God is opposed by *das Nichtige,*

but in the cross of Jesus "God Himself comprehends, envisages and controls.
. . . For God is Master of this antithesis. He overcomes it and has already
overcome it" (ibid., 302).

Thus, in Jesus Christ both the gravity and ultimate relativity of *das
Nichtige* are made known. Yet, finally, this revelation does not remove all
the difficulties concerning knowledge of evil. For what is revealed in Jesus
Christ is the utter incomprehensibility, unintelligibility, and inconceivability
of evil. Our knowledge of evil is confused and lacks coherence not only
because of our own human status and the fact that we look in the wrong
direction but also because in and of itself *das Nichtige* is that which lacks all
reason and basis; it is the impossible possibility. Thus, given creaturely and
sinful conditions of humanity and the fundamental incomprehensibility of
das Nichtige, Barth from the outset warns that all that we say concerning evil
will reflect these basic difficulties and that indeed, in relation to nothingness,
we have a clear exemplification of the "necessary brokenness of all theological thought and utterance" (ibid., 293). Yet despite these difficulties Barth
asserts that much can and must in fact be said concerning the nature and
operation of *das Nichtige* and its relation to God's activity.[3]

Seeking to understand the nature and operation of that which opposes
God and God's creation, he concludes that *das Nichtige* is most adequately
understood as that which God did not will, as that which God in God's
creative work rejected and denied. It is that possibility which God in God's
creative and positive decision to be with and for humanity ruled out as
either hostile or neutral to that determination:

> Nothingness is that from which God separates Himself and in face of
> which He asserts Himself and exerts His positive will. . . . God elects
> and therefore rejects what He does not elect. God wills and therefore
> opposes what He does not will. (CD 3. 3. 351)

This understanding of nothingness as that which God did not will but

---

[3] A number of Barth commentators think that what Barth does indeed go on to say concerning *das Nichtige* is highly speculative and somewhat contrary to his own injunction against
philosophical or mythological speculation and that it cannot be developed from those sources
Barth claims to be all-important, i.e., Jesus Christ, scriptures, and tradition. Rather than *das
Nichtige* being an idea flowing out of the biblical witness, it is instead in most commentators'
views (including Berkouwer, Hick and Duthie) a highly speculative idea. Hick (*Evil and the
God of Love*, 149) calls it a "product of Barth's own fertile and fascinating mind." Charles
Duthie ("Providence in the Theology of Karl Barth," in Maurice Wiles, ed., *Providence* [Lon-
don: S.P.C.K., 1969] 65) agrees with this assessment of Barth's position as mythological speculation and asks "is his whole conception anything other than a piece of unconvincing mythol-
ogy?" And Berkouwer (*Triumph of Grace*, 222–23) asks if Barth has not overstepped his own
limit of the incomprehensibility of evil and if this idea of *das Nichtige* is not "under the control
of speculative ideas."

rejected entails a number of important and far-reaching claims and corresponding implications. First, as such a rejected and denied possibility *das Nichtige* cannot be understood to exist either as God exists or as do creatures. On the one hand, God exists and has actuality as the one self-determining and self-affirming reality and, on the other hand, creatures exist as posited by and grounded in God's positive willing and creation. Reflecting his previously stated claim, Barth asserts that God, as the one self-positing and self-determining reality, is the only standard and basis of what is truly possible and that therefore only that which corresponds to this self-determination and affirms it has a ground for positive being. Hence, only God in a primary sense and creation secondarily can be said to exist. For Barth "only God and His creature really and properly are" (ibid., 349). *Das Nichtige* as that which opposes and is hostile to God has no such divine grounding and therefore cannot be comprehended in terms either of God or God's good creation. In this sense, the fact that it exists and the manner of that existence "can be explained neither from the side of the Creator nor from that of the creature, neither as the action of the Creator nor as the life-act of the creature" (ibid., 292). Rather, *das Nichtige* must be understood as a third and distinct factor whose reality is not grounded in God's positive will and whose existence is an entirely different and indeed contradictory mode from that of God or creation.

Rejected as a product of God's positive willing and hence as a real possibility, *das Nichtige* nonetheless has a certain reality and exists in a way peculiar to itself. It exists as the object of God's nonwilling and it has reality as God's *opus alienum*. What Barth means by these corollary ideas of divine nonwilling and *opus alienum* are of great import and interest in this context. For Barth, God wills positively Godself and creation in fellowship with Godself. By so willing God rejects those possibilities which would run counter to this covenant relationship. But just as God's positive affirming will bears fruit in creation, so too does God's rejecting will bear, as it were, the negative fruit of *das Nichtige*. Barth argues that God's nonwilling does not have as its object simply blank or empty being but rather this negative reality; the corresponding object of God's negative will is not "no-thing" but a highly potent force opposing and menacing all of God's *opus proprium*, all of God's creation. Barth contends:

> But nothingness is neither God nor His creature. Thus it can have nothing in common with God and His creatures. But it would be foolhardy to rush to the conclusion that it is therefore nothing, i.e., that it does not exist. God takes it into account. He is concerned with it. He strives against it, resists and overcomes it. If God's reality and revelation are known in His presence and action in Jesus Christ, He is also known as the God who is confronted by nothingness, for whom it constitutes a problem, who takes it seriously, who does not deal with it incidentally but in the fullness of the glory of His deity, who is not

engaged indirectly or mediately but with His whole being, involving
Himself to the utmost. If we accept this, we cannot argue that because
it has nothing in common with God and His creature nothingness is
nothing, i.e. it does not exist. That which confronts God in this way
and is seriously treated by Him, is surely not nothing or non-existent.
In light of God's relationship to it we must accept the fact that in a
third way of its own nothingness it 'is.' All conceptions or doctrines
which would deny or diminish or minimise this 'is' are untenable from
the Christian standpoint. Nothingness is not nothing. . . . But it 'is'
nothingness. (Ibid., 349; KD 3. 3. 402)

Barth, thus, on the one hand, denies any commonality of *das Nichtige* with
God's positive will and its product, creation, and by so doing hopes to maintain both God's lack of direct responsibility for the existence of evil and the
intrinsic goodness of God's creative work. On the other hand, Barth establishes the reality and thereby the seriousness of evil by understanding it as
the outcome of God's nonwilling. In this manner Barth hopes to maintain
both that creation is good and that evil is real. An examination of what
other claims and implications are entailed in such a position will make it
clear that, despite his hopes to the contrary, Barth has grave difficulty
balancing these various assertions.

One all-important claim that follows the above is Barth's insistence that
although *das Nichtige* is real, it must not be understood in any sense whatsoever as an autonomous reality existing independently of God. This rejection
of any independent status in relation to *das Nichtige* can be stated in several
ways. First and foremost it involves an unequivocal denial of any dualism.
As was indicated in the preceding chapter, for Barth, God's power is all-
pervasive and encompasses not only creation as the product of God's positive knowing and willing but also *das Nichtige* as the product of divine
nonwilling. Barth maintains that *das Nichtige* exists but that it does not do
so outside of and over against God's all-determining power. *Das Nichtige,*
though utterly opposed to God, cannot be understood as a principle whose
reality can be explained or understood in separation from God. Barth
states, "Without God, in this case without His wrath and rejection and
judgement—even nothing could not be present or of any power or consequence" (CD 3. 3. 77).

Das Nichtige is further qualified by Barth's claim that it would not exist at
all except for God's positive and creative activity. That is, without God's
eternal decision and that decision's actualization in creation *das Nichtige*
would not be in any sense. It is brought into being because of God's decision to create a good world. As such it only exists as a strange by-product of
God's knowing and willing (CD 3. 1. 123). What Barth wants to maintain
here is the priority of God's positive knowing and willing over divine rejection and denial; God denies, but that denial has no independent validity
and takes place only in relation to and for the sake of God's positive and

creative decision. Thus, Barth asserts *das Nichtige* is qualified both by the fact that it is a product of divine nonwilling and by the fact that such divine rejection follows after, depends upon, and ultimately serves God's positive and creative activity.

Barth also makes another—an indeed ultimate—qualification of *das Nichtige*. Not only must it be recognized that this menacing opponent has no independent status, it must also, and perhaps most importantly, be understood that even this subordinate and dependent existence of *das Nichtige* is only transient and has no perpetuity (CD 3. 1. 123). Indeed, this enemy of God and creation has already been defeated and overcome in Jesus Christ and has thereby ceased to exist even in its peculiar negative form. There are several latent dimensions involved in this claim.

First, corresponding to the assertions that God's nonwilling is not commensurate with God's willing and that therefore God's *opus alienum* must not be understood as equal in stature to God's *opus proprium* but rather only as subsidiary and subordinate to God's creative activity, Barth insists that as such it must be understood not as an eternal, permanent opponent of God and creation but rather as a temporary, passing one (ibid., 360–61). It must not be conceived as a constant factor balancing God's positive activity. Rather, *das Nichtige*, as the *opus alienum Dei*, becomes superfluous as God brings to completion God's true creative purpose. Barth states:

> As God fulfils His true and positive work, His negative work becomes pointless and redundant and can be terminated and ended. It is of major importance at this point that we should not become involved in the logical dialectic that if God loves, elects and affirms eternally He must also hate and therefore reject and negate eternally. There is nothing to make God's activity on the left hand as necessary and perpetual as His activity on the right. . . . God is indeed eternally holy, pure, distinct and separated from the evil which is nothingness. But this does not mean that He must always strive with this adversary. (Ibid., 361)

And it is in Jesus Christ that the positive will of God actualizes itself fully, and therefore from the perspective of Jesus Christ *das Nichtige* must be understood as completely and finally overcome. If the menace and gravity of *das Nichtige* is revealed in Jesus Christ, so is God's victory over it. In Jesus Christ it is made known that not only is *das Nichtige* subordinate to God but that because of the cross of Jesus it can no longer be said to exist in any mode at all, not even a negative one. *Das Nichtige* is no more:

> From the act of atonement which has taken place in Jesus Christ it is clear that in evil we do not have to do with a reality and power which have escaped the will and work of God, let alone with something that is sovereign and superior in relation to it. Whatever evil is, God is its Lord. We must not push our attempt to take evil seriously to the point of ever coming to think of it as an original and indeed creative counter-

deity which posits autonomous and independent facts, competing seriously with the one living God and striving with Him for mastery. Evil is a form of that nothingness which as such is absolutely subject to God. We cannot legitimately deduce this from a mere contrasting of the idea of evil with the idea of good. But we can say it in the light of fact that in Jesus Christ, in His death . . . we see evil overcome and indeed shattered and destroyed by the omnipotence of the love and wrath of God. (CD 4. 1. 408, 409; 3. 3. 362–63)

Hence, from Jesus Christ, we learn of God's ultimate control over *das Nichtige*. All adequate interpretations of *das Nichtige* must understand it fundamentally as that which was but is no longer. However, Barth also admits that although this defeat is objectively true, humanity still experiences *das Nichtige* as though it were real and potent. It is, in truth (i.e., in Jesus Christ) already rendered innocuous, yet a semblance or shadow of it still remains masquerading as reality (CD 3. 3. 366–67). Barth, asserting that God does indeed ultimately control and rule *das Nichtige*, must answer how even this semblance can remain to menace creation. He responds by insisting that God's power is indeed all-encompassing and that therefore even this semblance or echo of *das Nichtige* can be understood to remain only under the decree of God and therefore in the service of God's knowledge and will. "In this already innocuous form, as this echo and shadow, it is an instrument of His will and action. He thinks it good that we should exist 'as if' He had not yet mastered it for us" (ibid., 367).

Barth concludes, after having begun with the assertion of the absolute negativity of *das Nichtige*, that because God's rule encompasses even this, *das Nichtige* must be understood finally to serve God and to be an instrument of divine purpose. *Das Nichtige* as that which utterly opposes and is hostile to God and God's creation nonetheless comes to be seen as the servant of the very reality it seeks to destroy. Thus, Barth claims:

Finally, because in this form still left to it nothingness exists and functions under the control of God, we must say that even though it does not will to do so it is forced to serve Him, to serve His Word and work, the honour of His Son, the proclamation of the Gospel, the faith of the community, and therefore the way which He Himself wills to go within and with His creation until its day is done. (Ibid.)

From the above analysis Barth can be seen to offer a broad and ambitious understanding of evil. Indeed he might be interpreted as wanting it all ways at once. First, he is insistent that evil is genuine and radical and must be taken with the utmost seriousness. Yet he also is adamant that it does not escape the reach of divine power and that God controls and rules *das Nichtige*—not just in God's ultimate victory over it but even in its very origin. And this rule is so complete that *das Nichtige* comes to serve that which it opposes; it is finally an instrument of God's good purpose. But finally,

Barth also wants to avoid the stumbling block of all conceptions of God as omnipotent; he wants to deny that God must be understood as responsible for the existence of evil. He claims to circumvent this difficulty by asserting that *das Nichtige* results not because God wills it but as an effect of divine rejection. Can Barth indeed have it all these ways? Or, does his position ultimately entail either the denial of divine omnipotence, at least in its Barthian formulation, or the reinterpretation of *das Nichtige* in ultimately positive terms?

To answer these questions, we must first ask, granting that *das Nichtige* is genuine and real evil, can it be said to exist in any necessary fashion? That is, we must inquire if that evil exists because God could not prevent it, that it comes into being as a necessary correlation to creation. [4] We shall see that for Hartshorne, evil, or at least the possibility of evil, is just such a necessary and intrinsic correlation to creation, but Barth's response, given what we discovered in the preceding chapters, must be assumed to be an emphatic "No." This assumption must be made for several reasons.

First, any claim that God could not prevent evil implies that God is somehow subordinate to a necessity independent of Godself. Such an assertion runs counter to Barth's fundamental claim that it is God and God alone who determines what can be understood as necessary or possible—including logical or metaphysical necessity. Thus, any independent necessity to which God, too, might be understood to be subjected is definitely ruled out and with it any hint of dualism or the existence of independent or competing powers.

This notion of necessity is also called into question on two other, slightly different grounds. On the one hand, any such notion would seem to contradict the fact that God indeed conquers and destroys evil, contradictory to the highest degree if God could not help creating evil but could ultimately do away with it. [5] In this case, God's omnipotence, in the all-encompassing form Barth suggests, would be seriously qualified and called into question. Instead of God's being, as Barth insists, the one real power from which and in subordination to which all other powers—positive and negative alike—exist, God would be one, though perhaps the greatest, power among competing powers. Such a reciprocal and social understanding of divine power

---

[4] Hick (*Evil and the God of Love,* 143) agrees that the question of necessity must be raised. He asks, "Is there . . . a necessary connection between good and evil such that good inevitably drew evil in its wake, whether God wished this or not?" David R. Griffin (*God, Power and Evil: A Process Theodicy* [Philadelphia: Westminster, 1976] 166) also raises questions concerning this necessity and concludes that if God could not create good actuality without also creating *das Nichtige* as well, then this is a strange form of power. He states: "The idea that God's power, since it is different from ours in being omnipotent, also differs from ours in that it necessarily gives some sort of actuality to that which is not willed, is quite paradoxical. It seems more a form of impotence than desirable power."

[5] Hick (*Evil and the God of Love,* 144–45) also raises this question.

is adamantly denied by Barth and with it any suggestion that God can be determined by external factors.

And finally, any hint that an independent necessity mandates that creation has as its corollary some negative reality appears called into question by the fact that God also exists and is actual, and yet, in Barth's schema, there is no eternal antithesis to this divine reality.[6] If *das Nichtige* is to be conceived as the necessary corresponding negative reality to positive actuality, it would suggest that some form of eternal opposition must be conceived in relation to God. But, although in Barth's view *das Nichtige* opposes God, it only comes into existence with creation and hence in no way can be understood as the eternal opposite to God. Although God's willing of creation seems to entail the existence, albeit negative, of *das Nichtige*, God's eternal willing and positing of Godself involves no such corresponding reality.[7] Hence once more, the idea of a necessity to which God is bound appears ruled out.

Thus, our first and fundamental response must be that the existence of *das Nichtige* does not indicate any external necessity to which God can be understood to be subordinate. We cannot conclude therefore that God could not prevent evil. Now we must ask if evil is genuine, and not merely apparent, and if God's power is all-encompassing, embracing even logical and metaphysical necessity, must we conclude therefore that God is indeed responsible for evil—that God freely chose *das Nichtige*?

---

[6] There is, as Berkouwer (*Triumph of Grace*, 220) points out, a sense in which what God rejects has eternal status; God eternally constitutes Godself, determines Godself and thereby exists in self-distinction from that which God is not. That is, God eternally knows what God rejects for what it is—opposition to God. But Barth does not give this rejected possibility the status of eternally existing (either in relation to God's self-determination or God's eternal knowledge and willing of creaturely reality). *Das Nichtige* as that which opposes God and the world does not come into its own peculiar existence until creation is brought into being. It does not exist eternally in opposition to God, though God's rejection of it is eternal. God's eternal self-constitution, although it involves a distinction between what God is and is not, does not appear to involve the eternal actuality, even negatively, of that rejected possibility.

[7] If, although the actuality of *das Nichtige* is not eternal, God's knowledge and rejection of it are eternal and hence prior to creation, it is necessary to ask if God's triumph of this rejected possibility is also eternal and hence prior to time. If this latter point is also true then two questions immediately arise: (1) Did *das Nichtige* ever have any reality or was it always a defeated possibility lacking reality and therefore always a semblance? and (2) If the triumph is eternal and as such prior to our time then does the temporal historical action of Jesus Christ have any significance or function other than as an illustration or revelation of that which has already taken place apart from the creaturely realm? Berkouwer (*Triumph of Grace*, 250) is acutely aware of this latter question and states that Barth's claim of what he takes to be the eternal triumph of grace seriously calls into question the significance of history: "His conception leaves the impression that everything has already been done, all decisions have been taken, so that one can hardly say that the *historical reconciliation* are at issue, but only the *revelation* of redemption in history the *revelation* of the definitive Yes of God's grace"

Such a claim appears at once to contradict all that Barth has set forth. First it would make God the author of evil and hence ultimately responsible for it. As such it would call into question Barth's central conviction that God is the one who freely loves and would thereby undermine his association of love and power. Further, it would contradict Barth's assertion that God, as the ground and criterion of all genuine possibility, can only positively will that which affirms Godself. If God wills evil either God stands in contradiction of Godself or else that which is willed is not genuinely evil.

Barth attempts to circumvent this dilemma by introducing the idea of God's negative willing. Within this framework evil comes into being as an effect of this divine rejection. But does this Barthian solution really work? Once again the question of necessity is central. Could God have chosen not to exercise this negative will at all or have chosen to exercise it in a manner that did not result in the existence of this potent negative actuality? There are points where Barth appears to talk of this nonwilling and its objective effect as necessary: "It belongs necessarily and integrally to the creation which belongs with the creation of light that God rejects chaos" (CD 3. 1. 123). But, as we argued above, this necessity cannot be understood as external to or independent of God. There is, in the Barthian schema, no higher necessity to which God must correspond. Rather, if nonwilling is in any sense necessary in relation to the positive willing of creation, if God must exercise God's will in this twofold manner, it is a necessity whose ground is God's free self-determination; it is a product of God's free decision. For Barth, the only internal necessity God must conform to is the necessity not to contradict Godself. And since he offers no explicit arguments that it would involve such self-contradiction if God chose to will only positively or that God's rejection of all the possibilities that would not affirm God would result in self-contradiction if that rejection did not have as its effect this potent negative reality, it can legitimately be concluded that this double form of willing is purely the product of God's free self-constitution, and thus any strict internal necessity for such a choice is precluded. Further, the facts that God need not eternally will in a negative manner and that there need not be an eternal existent effect of this rejection both contribute to this conclusion that the divine nonwilling and its temporary product are not the result of the divine necessity not to contradict Godself but the result of God's free self-determination. And finally, because Barth does argue that God's free decisions are always God-affirming, then it might also be concluded that this decision for a double form of willing is more affirming of or appropriate to God than a single positive kind might be. Thus, although the end product, *das Nichtige,* of God's negative will might not be attributed to God in a positive or direct sense, nonetheless that there is such a negative will (and indirectly, therefore, its product) appears to be the outcome of God's free decision and choice.

If this observation is legitimate it leads to two further conclusions. On the one hand, the distinction between God's willing and nonwilling becomes somewhat obscured.[8] God's nonwilling is not only subordinate to but indeed a function of God's willing and self-determination. To say that *das Nichtige* is an effect of divine nonwilling rather than divine willing becomes, to some extent, merely a verbal distinction and one which ultimately does not mitigate God's responsibility for evil; the reality of divine nonwilling and the existence of its objects as potent, though negative, actually appear to be ultimately grounded in God's free and self-affirming decision, that is, in God's positive will. It will appear that Barth has not avoided the dilemma of God's omnipotence and God's responsibility and that finally Barth's God remains all-powerful but that divine omnipotence must take full responsibility for the existence of *das Nichtige.*

On the other hand, if God's nonwilling is to be seen as a freely chosen and not externally or internally necessitated corollary to God's willing, and as such ultimately in the service of that self-affirmation (as indeed all of God's choices are), then the status of *das Nichtige* as wholly evil comes into question. As the analysis has stressed, Barth denies that *das Nichtige* shares, in any form, in the goodness of creation; it is entirely and intrinsically evil. While Hartshorne rejects the claim that anything is only or solely evil, it is just such a thoroughly negative status Barth wants to maintain. However, if God could have prevented evil, if divine rejection did not need necessarily to issue forth in this potent negative reality, then can *das Nichtige* really be considered solely or even primarily in these negative terms? This suspicion that Barth's position ultimately leads to the rejection of *das Nichtige* as wholly evil is further supported by Barth's assertion that although God does not affirm *das Nichtige* nor give it a positive grounding, nonetheless God permits it to exist in its own peculiar menacing form. Barth is not very clear why this permission is granted, but the indications he does offer support this conclusion that *das Nichtige* is not wholly evil but rather it, too, serves God's purposes. On the one hand, *das Nichtige* becomes, albeit unwillingly, the instrument of God's creative purposes. Barth contends that the fact that *das Nichtige* can be pressed into such service does not indicate that it is therefore not evil, but rather it testifies that God is indeed all-powerful and can work God's loving purposes in all things. But this claim of serviceability, when coupled with the suggestion of its existence as somehow, even if indirectly, the effect of God's free choice, does indeed point to a possible reinterpretation of *das Nichtige* as at least instrumentally or functionally good. It too serves—and indeed perhaps exists to serve—a divinely determined purpose.[9]

---

[8] Both Griffin (*Evil and the God of Love,* 148) and Hick (*God, Power, and Evil,* 166–67) think that, in the end, such a distinction is merely verbal.

[9] Griffin (*God, Power and Evil,* 170) raises this question of whether *das Nichtige* is not in danger of being understood ultimately in positive terms. He asks if, from the perspective of evil's defeat, whether it is "*now* good that nothingness once existed? If the answer is Yes, this

And it must be asked finally if the purpose that *das Nichtige* serves is to testify to the power and love of God manifested in Jesus Christ.[10] Barth throughout his work insists that Jesus Christ is God's eternal decision to be with and for humanity and therefore must not be understood solely as a response to evil and sin. But it can be legitimately asked, I would suggest, if Jesus does not exist because of evil, whether evil, if it does not exist necessarily, exists rather for the purpose of God's self-revelation in Jesus Christ. That is, does *das Nichtige* not only come to serve God but does it also exist precisely for this reason? If this is so, not only does the character of *das Nichtige* become transformed but also Barth's close association of divine power and love is, if not sundered, in need of further elucidation.

Barth wants, as I suggested earlier, to maintain God's omnipotence, both as the power of self-determination and as the power of world-determination. He wants as well, however, to maintain the radical and genuinely evil character of *das Nichtige* and finally God's nonresponsibility for that evil. However, Barth finally cannot balance all these claims and instead must be interpreted as maintaining God's omnipotence at the expense of either or both of the latter claims. Thus, it can be argued that in the Barthian schema God is all-powerful and effects God's will always but as a result the solely negative character of *das Nichtige* is open for question; and divine responsibility for that evil which is no longer quite so radical becomes a clearly possible, and indeed perhaps necessary, implication of Barth's primary claim.

The Question of Sin

Much of what Barth says concerning human sin corresponds to and flows out of his broader understanding of *das Nichtige,* and to a great extent the structure of his analysis reflects the position outlined above. However, the examination of human sin within the Barthian schema provides as well a vantage point to see further implications from which to explore new, if parallel, difficulties with it.

Barth asserts that true knowledge of sin, as the concrete manifestation of evil within the creaturely realm, is revealed only in Jesus Christ. Humans

---

would mean that nothingness never was genuinely evil. For, if the world is finally better than it would have otherwise been because nothingness once existed and was then defeated, then nothingness cannot be judged in the final analysis as having been genuinely evil."

[10] Hick (*Evil and the God of Love,* 145) asserts that there is the possibility, though he thinks Barth does not explicitly go this way, of arguing in this manner. He states: "If the whole of creation centers upon this great event, is it not implied that man's need for salvation was envisaged in God's creative plan, the presence of evil being a necessary pre-condition of redemption, and the fall accordingly serving ultimately the high purpose of setting God as Saviour at the centre of His creation? Thus instead of 'O felix culpa . . . we might sing O felix Nihil, quae talem ac tantum meruit habere redemptorem!'" See also Hartwell, *Theology of Karl Barth,* 122–23.

cannot know or recognize sin as real evil because our participation in it obscures its true nature. It is therefore only in faith, through God's action not ours, that this ignorance is overcome and the gravity and depravity of sin is made clear (CD 4. 2. 379).

In Jesus Christ sin is revealed as the dynamic and visible manifestation of opposition to and hostility toward God and God's loving purpose. In the form of sin, of human rejection of divine grace, *das Nichtige* no longer lurks at the frontier of creation but crosses the boundary into that good creation. And by so doing it corrupts and alienates it, especially humanity from its true source and goal. In sin, the rejected possibility is no longer denied but embraced. Several important claims both underlie and flow from this definition of sin as the concrete form of *das Nichtige*.

First, as *das Nichtige* could not be understood either as an element in or even a possibility of God's good creation, so too sin must be rejected as a genuine possibility for humanity. Human beings, as part of God's good creation, possess no innate potentiality for sin (CD 3. 3. 356; 4. 1. 409). This means explicitly that, for Barth, sin cannot be understood, as it is for Hartshorne, either as the unfortunate result or the necessary by-product of good freedom. Human freedom does not mean the neutral capacity to choose between alternative possibilities, between good and evil, God and *das Nichtige*. Rather, freedom indicates the capacity to choose and affirm God; it is the potentiality to be obedient to the divine purposes:

> And man's freedom to decide, as it is given to man by God, is not a free-dom to decide between good and evil. Man is not made to be Hercules at the crossroads. Evil does not lie in the possibilities of the God-created creature. Freedom to decide means freedom to decide towards the Only One for whom God's creature can decide, for the affirmation of Him who has created it, for the accomplishment of His will; that is, for obedience.[11]

Freedom to be obedient to God is the only possibility inherent in creaturely reality. It is the only possibility whose ground and reason are God's affirming knowledge and will. The capacity of sin, to act counter to the divine purpose, is therefore an ontological impossibility; it has no basis in God and is pure contradiction of the scope and limits of possibility God has set forth for creation. Sin, consequently, must be understood as "that which is absurd, man's absurd choice and decision for that which is not" (CD 4. 1. 410). The result of such an imposssible, absurd choice is that sinful humanity exists not only in contradiction to God and the divine purpose but also in contradiction and alienation from its own true nature. Humanity, as sinful, is a stranger to itself (CD 4. 2. 93, 393, 411). This radical contradiction means several things for Barth.

---

[11] Barth, *Dogmatics in Outline*, 56.

First, he does not offer a doctrine of original sin which includes some notion of a sinless time, of some pristine primordial past. Rather, the idea of the Fall points to the all-encompassing reality of sin. It indicates that we are dealing with the "original and radical and therefore the comprehensive and total act of man, with the imprisonment of his existence in that circle of evil being and evil activity" (CD 4. 1. 500). Nor is there any way to get behind this sin with a backward glance to pre-Fall times. For Barth, any understanding of sinless humanity must take its point of departure not from an idea of primordial humanity but from Jesus Christ. Here and only here are made known both the radical and total corruption of humanity and the possibility of sinless humanity (CD 3. 2. 31).

Second, Barth asserts that although *das Nichtige* takes concrete form in sin it is not exhausted in this sin. That is, in sin humanity becomes the agent of *das Nichtige* but by so doing it also becomes its victim. Humanity, as sinful, stands in contradiction to its nature and that alienation has concrete and destructive ramifications as well—most notably death and physical suffering. Barth considers the facts of death, age, and loss to be part of God's good creation and not, in themselves, destructive or evil. However, because humanity exists in an alienated and corrupted state these realities become forms of *das Nichtige* and are therefore experienced as wholly negative. Death, which for Barth is by nature the "natural termination of life" (CD 3. 3. 310), becomes the "life-destroying thing to which all suffering hastens as its goal, as the ultimate irruption and triumph of that alien power which annihilates creaturely existence" (ibid., 310). Thus, *das Nichtige* not only corrupts and distorts human existence in the form of sin and hence morally, but also "physically and totally" (ibid.). *Das Nichtige*, in all its forms, is the "comprehensive negation of the creature and its nature" (ibid.).

And finally, and equally importantly, it must be stated that although *das Nichtige* takes all these forms of sin, suffering, and death and thereby totally alienates humanity from itself and God, Barth also insists that *das Nichtige*, in these forms, does not take creation and humanity outside the scope of God's purpose and control. Barth adamantly rejects any idea that through sin *das Nichtige* has somehow created a second and independent creation (CD 3. 2. 28). Even as sinners, human beings remain God's creature under God's all-determining control (CD 4. 1. 480, 489, 492; 3. 2. 27, 58).

Thus, stated succinctly, sin is a dynamic and concrete manifestation of *das Nichtige* in the intrinsically good creation. As such it is a potentiality not grounded in God's will but an absurd and indeed ontologically impossible possibility. It results not only in the complete alienation of humanity from itself but its profound repercussions include as well the transformation of death and physical decline and suffering from natural creaturely limitations into forms of destruction and negativity. And finally, all this occurs not outside the realm of God's purpose and power but, although in opposition to it, nonetheless under the control of God's rule.

Having set forth what sin is and its relation to the negative reality *das Nichtige,* we must now ask why and how sin can come to be at all. If creation is good and the possibilities intrinsic to it are all positive and oriented toward God, why do humans sin? Even if *das Nichtige* must exist (itself an uncertain claim) why must and indeed how can humanity decide against itself and God, for that which is not?

The first thing that must be stated is that Barth, having denied any positive potentiality in human nature for *das Nichtige,* nonetheless qualifies this denial by seeing in that good nature a certain vulnerability in relation to this negative force. That is, God as the omnipotent source and ruler of all reality, is opposed by *das Nichtige* but is not thereby ultimately threatened or challenged by this power. Therefore, "to God it is no problem . . . in face of God it has no power" (CD 3. 3. 77). God is utterly superior to it. But this superiority is God's alone and does not extend to God's creatures. Human beings, as nondivine, are mortally threatened by *das Nichtige.* And humanity, as only relatively powerful, is no match for the onslaught of this wholly negative power. As creaturely reality, humanity is defenseless against *das Nichtige.* Barth asserts:

> Even in a Christian doctrine of sin, although there can be no question of an innate potentiality for evil in accordance with creation, we have to reckon with the fact that, unlike God, man is indeed exposed to the assault of chaos by reason of this creatureliness, that he confronts the nothingness which is intrinsically alien to him, not with the superiority of God, but—although no possibility in this direction can be ascribed to him—with a certain revisionary tendency. (CD 4. 2. 398)

Thus, while on the one hand Barth maintains that creatures possess no positive capacity for evil, he on the other hand qualifies his claim in such a way to allow for, if not a propensity toward *das Nichtige,* at least a vulnerability in relation to this negative force. But now we must inquire why this vulnerability is permitted to exist and whether its existence does not call into question the earlier stated interpretation of creation as intrinsically and wholly good.

Barth's first response to such concerns is that creaturely defenselessness is not to be understood in negative terms. As we noted concerning the shadowside of existence, this vulnerability flows from humanity's creaturely status and reflects the good and proper need for and dependence upon God that corresponds to that status; to be human is to be derived from God and hence absolutely dependent upon God. A certain precariousness is fitting to this creaturely reality; it distinguishes the creature from God and demonstrates God's powerful but always gracious relation to that creature. Barth points out that

> the fact that the creature can fall away from God and perish does not

imply any imperfection on the part of creation or the Creator. What it does mean positively is that it is something created and is therefore dependent on preserving grace, just as it owes its very existence simply to the grace of its Creator. A creature freed from the possibility of falling away would not really be living as a creature. It could only be a second God—and as no second God exists, it could only be God Himself. (CD 2. 1. 503)

Barth adds as well another qualification of his understanding of God's creation and its intrinsically good possibilities which, if it does not explain the actual fact of sin, does suggest how it is possible. This qualification concerns human freedom. It can only be understood as freedom *for* God, as the capacity or ability for obedience. But Barth also wants to claim that obedience which is coerced is not true obedience; freedom which is compelled is slavery not liberty. Hence, although Barth insists that obedience to God is the good possibility God sets forth for creation and that such a possibility is the primary meaning of human freedom, he also wants to maintain that choice among alternatives, and hence freedom in another secondary sense, is also present. God, in order to preserve the noncoercive nature of obedience, does not therefore hinder human choice but rather permits the possibility, if not the positive grounding, for sin. Barth maintains that "because this is His will, He gives him *freedom* to obey, and has not therefore made obedience necessary or disobedience physically impossible" (CD 3. 1. 266). Thus, although Barth does not want to say freedom positively involves choices between alternatives, he does seem to claim that freedom, as decision and not just capacity, entails at least the negative possibility for sin. Or stated otherwise, it involves the absence of impossibility. But with such a claim it must be noted that Barth has indeed widened and somewhat altered his conception of human freedom to include not only the notion of freedom as capacity for something but as decision which intrinsically involves choice among alternatives. It is just such a widened conception of nondivine freedom for which Hartshorne will be seen to argue. He asserts that there is no freedom where there is no choice of action. Therefore, while Barth seems to speak reluctantly of such alternatives and sees them as secondary to the primary meaning of freedom as obedience, Hartshorne declares them to be indispensible and central to the meaning of freedom itself.

But where has Barth brought us with these explanations? Once more he seems to want to maintain a variety of not easily integrated claims. First, he asserts that creation is good and hence only possesses positive possibilities, including freedom from God. But next he qualifies that statement by claiming, on the one hand, that *das Nichtige*, although not part of creation, nonetheless exists as a menacing force against which humans are, by themselves, defenseless. On the other hand, he claims that human freedom, though oriented towards God, entails nonetheless the negative possibility of sin. With these explanations of the essential vulnerability of creaturely

existence and at least structural possibility of sin Barth has given some indication of how sin can be possible. However, although these give some
rationale for the how of sin, we must still inquire further concerning the why
of sin.

Given these qualifications we must conclude that in order not to fall prey
to this negative power but to actualize the inherently good possibilities of
creation, including freedom, humans need God and God's grace. That is,
humans need God's presence/grace/support in order not to sin. Without
God the vulnerability of creaturehood issues forth in sin. Obedience, not
disobedience, becomes impossible without God. Barth agrees to all this:

> Man *in abstracto,* i.e., apart from the merciful will of his Creator pri-
> marily directed towards him, would be a being hopelessly exposed to
> the threat of surrounding non-being. In his fall there would take place
> only something to which he was predestined as a being already aban-
> donded and lost. (CD 3. 2. 146)

But Barth also insists that there is no humanity *in abstracto,* there is no
humanity without God. In Jesus Christ it is revealed that humanity is and
always has been the covenant partner of a faithful and ever present God.
Barth concludes that all this leads to human guilt and responsibility for sin.
For if there is no abstract humanity but only humanity coexisting with a
gracious God then "man cannot now appeal to his defencelessness, to the
natural weakness of all being and justify himself as a sinner on the ground
that he is inevitably delivered up to the forces of evil" (ibid.). Instead Barth
claims:

> If man actually decides against God, he does so neither on the basis of a
> possibility rooted in his own being, nor because he is prevented from
> choosing his legitimate possibility by the superior power of evil pressing
> upon him from without. On the contrary, when he chooses evil he
> grasps that which is made impossible for him and from which he is
> preserved. (Ibid., 147)

Barth's final word on how this wrongly directed choice takes place is one
that points not to divine responsibility but to the absurdity and
incomprehensibility of sin, that is, to the mystery of sin. He states concerning humanity's participation in *das Nichtige,* "He is not forced to commit this
sin. As we have seen there is no reason for it. All that we can say is that he
does commit it" (CD 4. 1. 484–85). For Barth, all theological thought
reaches its limit here.

This is the final word. But for those who analyze Barth's position it is not
clear that his fundamental assertions concerning the scope of God's power
do not ultimately lead to other conclusions. Barth also insists that the will
of this divine covenant partner is done in all things and that God's gracious

presence is irresistible and triumphant, although nonoppressive and non-coercive, wherever it is operative. How does one mediate between the fact of God's irresistible and gracious presence and the fact of sin? Barth's recourse was to appeal to the mystery and incomprehensibility of sin. But taking all the above claims together, it is possible to argue that Barth, albeit unwillingly, has laid the foundation for concluding that if humans can sin only through the absence of God's presence and grace—and indeed must sin in its absence—then the fact of sin points not to some incomprehensible human choice and responsibility but to the absence of God. It is legitimate at least to ask if humanity can be considered truly and solely responsible for sin or whether God is not only responsible for the negative existence of *das Nichtige* but also, in God's Barthian omnipotence, ultimately for humanity's sinful participation in it.

Barth, throughout his analysis, has been concerned to maintain the scope of divine omnipotence while at the same time maintaining its gracious character. The union of power and love has been perhaps his primary concern. However, when the questions of evil and sin are examined it is not clear that Barth has effectively maintained this union nor that he has overcome the traditional difficulties concerning the relation of omnipotence and divine responsibility for evil and sin, and divine nonresponsibility for that reality. However, the conclusion emerging is that Barth finally cannot hold all these claims together in a consistent manner and that as long as he maintains his understanding of omnipotence in such all-determining and causative terms, questions will arise concerning divine responsibility for evil and sin, and the status and integrity of creaturely decisions and activity will remain unclear.

3.2 Divine Power and Human Activity

It is now necessary to turn our attention to what Barth perceives as the positive relationship between divine activity and human activity. To state his position in summary form, Barth makes two major claims: first, he adamantly asserts that God's activity is all-determining and all-controlling in relation to every creaturely activity; and second, he contends in an equally insistent manner that humans are nonetheless true agents posessing their own integrity, independence, and hence responsibility. It is our present task to consider what Barth means by each of these claims and how he holds them together.

Divine Providence

It is in Barth's conception of divine providence that we find his most extensive and fruitful treatment of this relation between divine and human agency. God does not abandon creaturely reality in a deistic manner once it has been brought into being. God does not set the world on its course and

leave it to its own devices. Rather, as God carried out the divine eternal
decision in creation, so too does God continue to execute divine purposes in
all creaturely happenings. And it is under the rubric of divine providence
that Barth attempts to convey the fact and the character of this continued
presence. By providence "is meant the superior dealings of the Creator with
His creation, the wisdom, omnipotence and goodness with which He maintains and governs in time this distinct reality according to the counsel of His
own will" (CD 3. 3. 3).

Barth reminds us from the outset, as he did concerning the Creator and
creation, that any true understanding of how the power of God acts in and
through all creaturely reality can be ascertained only from the perspective of
faith, that is, only as guided by knowledge of the one who has eternally
chosen to be with and for that creation. The meaning and character of the
divine power which is operative in the world must not be disassociated or
interpreted in separation from the power of God made known on the cross.
Such a point of departure in Jesus Christ precludes the idea of providence as
some form of "philosophy of history" (ibid., 23–24). Rather, from the point
of view of salvation history, all creaturely history, though not simply
identified with the realm of covenant relations, comes to be understood as
the arena in which that special history takes place and as existing precisely
to be that arena, and as such under the determination and direction of God
(ibid., 42–43, 53–54). Thus, the God who controls and guides the world is
first and foremost the God who in Jesus Christ eternally chose humanity to
be God's covenant partner and hence to exist in loving fellowship with God.

Because the interpretation of God's activity within the creaturely sphere
must always be grounded by this central claim that the God who works and
rules here is first the gracious God revealed in Jesus Christ, certain conceptions of that divine agency must be rejected as inappropriate, and, as will be
clearly seen, Barth's analysis here closely parallels his delineation of the
scope and character of divine power set forth in the preceding chapter. On
the one hand, Barth contends that any understanding of divine activity, of
divine knowing and willing as effectively active in the creaturely sphere in
terms of mechanical, blind, or impersonal force is absolutely ruled out (ibid.,
20–22). Although God may work through or in unconscious forces within
the world (e.g., the laws of nature) to shape and condition creaturely experience, God's activity is not to be merely identified with or reduced to these
factors. Hartshorne, for his part, identifies God's activity directly with such
worldly forces as the laws of nature and sees them as the form of God's personal action upon the world. Barth, however, insists that while God may
utilize these factors, God must never be merely identified with them but
rather they must be interpreted as the instruments of God's conscious and
willed purpose.

On the other hand, any understanding of God's activity in relation to
worldly activity must reject, if it is grounded in revelation of the gracious

God, all interpretations of God as a tyrant. The personal, conscious, and purposeful God revealed in Jesus Christ is also and always the gracious and loving God. Therefore, all of God's activity in the creaturely sphere must be understood to have this gracious character as well. Thus Barth, while maintaining God's absolute power, reiterates continuously that God's omnipotent presence is not the "presence of a dictator and tyrant brutalising the world he controls" (CD 3. 2. 148).

Hence, the God operative in the creaturely sphere must be identified with the God revealed in Jesus Christ, and the divine activity in both arenas must be seen as one in a gracious purpose and character. But Barth also contends that just as God is understood as omnipotent even and especially on the cross, so too must God's power in relation to the whole of creaturely reality and history be understood as all-determining. No element in or aspect of that history, either in general or in specific, takes place outside of God's awareness, permission, and rule. In relation to the sphere of creaturely occurrence and human agency the determination of God is absolute. Barth declares that in relation to creaturely history,

> whatever occurs, whatever it does and whatever happens to it, will take place not only in the sphere and on the ground of the lordship of God, not only under a kind of oversight and final disposal of God, and not only generally in His direct presence, but concretely, in virtue of His directly effective will to preserve, under His direct and superior co-operation and according to His immediate direction. In this history, therefore, we need not expect turns and events which have nothing to do with His lordship and are not directly in some sense acts of His lordship. This Lord is never absent, passive, non-responsible or impotent, but always present, active, responsible and omnipotent. He is never dead but always living; never sleeping but always awake; never uninterested, but always concerned; never merely waiting in any repsect but even where He seems to wait, even where He permits, always holding the initiative. In this consists His coexistence with the creature. This is the range of the fact that in the act of making it He has associated Himself with the creature. He co-exists with it actively in an action which never ceases and does not leave any loopholes. (CD 3. 3. 13)

Under the broad rubric of providence, Barth sets forth his interpretation of the "directly effective will" in terms of what he designates the divine preserving, the divine accompanying, and the divine ruling of creaturely reality. We must now examine how Barth understands these forms of divine activity and how he coordinates such divine operation with human activity.

A. *God's Preservation of the World*

Barth asserts first that God is active and determining in relation to creation in that God preserves this earthly reality. That is, God does not merely create a reality distinct from Godself which is then self-sufficient. Rather, it is God alone who continues to uphold and sustain individual creaturely existence and the context for that existence itself—that is, the world within which that existence takes place. Several factors are involved in such claims for Barth.

First, he understands God's preserving activity to mean that God maintains creaturely reality as creaturely, as a reality distinct from God exhibiting those characteristics appropriate to creaturely nature: dependency, nonself-sufficiency, and temporal limitations. In no way does divine preserving entail the divinization or eternalizing of creaturely existence (ibid., 61).

Second, Barth suggests that God's preserving activity can be understood as "indirect" activity in the sense that God utilizes the worldly context and the interdependent relationship within that context as the medium of divine activity. Creaturely reality itself becomes the means of God's preserving work. However, Barth insists that although God acts through the world, this continuance of creation is solely and wholly God's work and cannot be attributed to any capacity for preservation or self-sufficiency on the part of creaturely reality (ibid., 65).

Third, Barth maintains that this act of divine preservation cannot be understood as necessary or as owed to the creature in some manner. Rather, it must be conceived as God's gracious and free determination to be faithful to and stand by God's decision for the creature. And it is because and only because the creature is preserved by this free and gracious will of God that its preservation has a secure and trustworthy grounding.

And finally, Barth suggests that this understanding of preservation underscores the need of the creature to be preserved. As was stated in the earlier section of *das Nichtige,* without God's continual presence *das Nichtige* would overwhelm and destroy all creaturely reality. Only God, not the creature itself, is able to maintain creaturely existence in the face of this threat. *Das Nichtige*

> continually calls this cosmos into question. . . . If only for a moment God were to turn away His face from the creature, the offensive would break loose with deadly power. In its relation to God chaos is always an absolutely subordinate factor, but it is always absolutely superior in relation to the creature. (Ibid., 76)

B. *Divine Accompaniment of Worldly Activity*

The second form under which Barth interprets divine providence is that which he labels divine accompanying. It is in relation to this divine accompanying that we see raised most explicitly the question of how divine and human agency are to be coordinated. For it is in this form of accompanying that divine activity is said to "co exist" with human action and that in such coexistence both divine and human activity have integrity and independence.

The notion of divine accompanying involves three central claims. The first is that the activity of the creature, and in this case human action, does not take place in isolation from God's own life and action but in its presence. "Alongside the act of the creature there is always the act of the divine wisdom and omnipotence. . . . It is not alone on the way, but as it goes it is accompanied by God, by the God who is this Lord" (ibid., 92). The second claim Barth puts forth is that part of the idea of divine accompanying is that God acknowledges and affirms the independence and integrity of that creaturely activity. God's own activity does not destroy or denigrate human action. Rather, God's accompanying humanity means that God "affirms and approves and recognizes and respects the autonomous actuality and therefore the autonomous activity of the creature as such" (ibid., 92–93). And thirdly, divine accompanying means that God rules over that creaturely reality. This divine control in relation to creaturely activity does not signify however, for Barth, a rejection of the preceding claim. God rules absolutely but in such a manner as to insure, instead of deny, this creaturely autonomy. Divine determination of creaturely activity means

> the creature does not belong and is not subject to Him like a puppet or a tool or dead matter—that would not be the Lordship of the living God—but in the autonomy in which it was created, in the activity which God made possible for it and permitted to it. . . . God rules in and over a world of freedom. (Ibid., 93)

Barth attempts to develop and to explicate the relationship among these general claims by analyzing divine accompanying under three guises: God's activity as preceding, as going along with, and as following human activity. In the first instance, Barth asserts divine activity (divine knowing and willing) must be understood as preceding all human action and as such totally conditioning it. Barth acknowledges that other creaturely factors condition human activity and at least relatively determine its shape and content. But as the previous chapter argued, God's preceding activity conditions in an absolute manner, and in this sense it must be said to foreordain this human action. It is not simply that God's knowledge and will precede human decision and action and, so to speak, set the general or even specific conditions within which creaturely activity then occurs. Nor does God, in this preceding action, envision a variety of possibilities among which humans then pick and choose. (Ibid., 120). Nor is it the case that God merely knows in advance these human decisions. Rather, God's independent and superior knowledge and will are the ground of, and thereby absolute determiners of, all that follows them. For Barth, divine activity's preceding human action means the "individual no less than the totality of creaturely activity is wholly and utterly at the disposal of the divine foreordination" (ibid., 122).

But finally it must be stated that, for Barth, this preceding knowledge and will of God, this foreordaining divine activity, does not constitute a constraining or humiliating or weakening of the creature (ibid., 130). Rather, in and through this divine knowing and willing humanity is determined for freedom though we must always keep in mind Barth's particular understanding of freedom as capacity to respond to God; in and through divine foreordaining activity creatures are determined for the freedom which consists in the capacity to be with and for God (ibid.).

In the second instance, and here we reach another claim which is difficult to comprehend, God's activity must be understood as going along with or accompanying all human activity as it occurs. Barth asserts several very important things in relation to this claim. For Barth, God's accompanying of or coexistence with creaturely activity does not mean either separation of the two actions or mutual conditioning of either by the other. Rather, in this form divine activity must be understood to effect creaturely activity. That is, God's activity determines the fact, the content, and the character of all human occurrence in an absolute manner. Barth contends that the coexistence of divine and human activity means the following:

> It is God who effects creaturely occurrence, that is, He is the living basis of its occurrence as such, and the living basis of its order and form. Both the fact that it happens and the way in which it happens derive from Him; they are decreed and brought to pass by Him. . . . The Fact that God is with us even as creatures as such means that He is so as sovereign and almighty Lord. It means that His activity determines our activity even to its most intimate depths, even to its most direct origins. It means that always and in all circumstances our activity is under His decision. (Ibid., 132)

In order to insure our recognition of the all-embracing and radical extent of this divine determination, we must elaborate a bit further what Barth means and does not mean by such a claim. He does not mean by his assertion (that God's activity is with human activity) that God's action merely elicits human response, with the human being deciding the ultimate configuration of that response and in that sense God determining human activity as a potent catalyst. (We shall see that this is in part Hartshorne's claim, but it is an assertion Barth thoroughly rejects.) Nor does Barth understand God's activity to be only the first in a series of actions which sets in motion a whole sequence of events. Nor is God's action simply a stronger or more powerful action which bends and subjugates separate human decision and activity to itself (ibid., 136). Rather, Barth argues, God's activity is one with human activity, the two actions are "a single action" (ibid., 132). The claim that God accompanies and by so doing determines creaturely occurrence must be understood to mean that God "is so present in the activity of the creature, and present with such sovereignty and almighty power, that His own action takes place in and with and over the activity of the creature" (ibid.).

This coincidence of divine and human activity thus means that it is only as and how God acts that humans act (ibid., 133). But this does not involve a collapse of the two actions. God neither becomes a creature nor the creature divine (ibid., 136). Somehow — though the how is not clear — divine activity inheres in human action and yet each still exists as itself with its own integrity and independence. Thus, there is conjunction but not collapse; there is union but not comingling. And in that coincidence there is always a definite order, a superiority and inferiority which can never be reversed.

In the third instance, Barth asserts that God's activity follows all creaturely activity. By this Barth does not mean that God, so to speak, makes the best out of what the creature has done, harmonizing to the greatest extent the results of human choice. Such harmonization is precisely what Hartshorne's God will be seen to do. But for Barth's God this is not so. Rather, God's following means that God determines the effect or consequence of all creaturely actions. The effect, just as the activity itself, exists under the Lordship and hence under the determining knowledge and will of God. For Barth,

> God accompanies the activity of the creature as its Creator and Lord. And this means that even the effects of this activity, even the changes brought about by it, are still subject to His disposing and control. There is no withdrawal on the part of God. (Ibid., 152)

C. *God's Ruling of Creaturely Activity*

Barth explicates a third and final form of God's providence under the designation of God's ruling or government. In speaking of divine ruling or governing Barth presupposes all that has preceded but wishes to emphasize in this context the purposeful nature of God's determining action. God rules by ordering (ibid., 164). All that takes place in the creaturely realm occurs according to a specific plan and is oriented toward and takes place in the service of a definite goal. All creaturely occurrences, whether they appear to us as contingent or necessary, as random or purposeful, are embraced by God's transcendent intention. And as such human activity can be understood to participate in and be part of God's own divine operation; it is that through which God carries out the divine purposes (ibid.).

D. *The Form of God's Providential Activity*

Thus, God's activity is related to creaturely activity in all its aspects and is related in such a manner that all worldly occurrences take place under and according to the determination of the divine purpose. God's preserving activity insures the very continuance of creation and its creatures, and God's accompanying activity precedes all creaturely occurrence. This is so for several reasons. First, God's eternal knowledge and will foreordain its content and character, and secondly God's own activity takes place in and with creaturely action as it occurs. Thirdly, God's activity determines the consequences resulting from each creaturely happening, and finally, this all occurs in accordance to the divine vision and intention. There is no human decision or action that takes place outside of the wider context of divine decision and action. And yet Barth also asserts that this determining character of divine knowledge and decision does not take away from the genuine individuality or autonomy of creaturely and especially human activity. According to Barth, "Its activity is still free, contingent and autonomous. . . . Between the sovereignty of God and the freedom of the creature there is no contradiction" (ibid., 65–66). And this is so, not despite God's controlling action, but because of it. God's presence is the basis for this autonomy. But has Barth really given any adequate explanation of how these two claims are held together or does he merely assert that it is so? How indeed can these two forms of activity be coordinated in the manner in which Barth suggests?[12]

As must be concluded from the above, Barth rules out several ways of understanding the relationship between divine and human activity. First, it is clear that any explanation of this relationship in dualistic terms is rejected from the start. The relationship between God and humanity, between divine activity and creaturely activity cannot be conceived as one between two intrinsically separate and independent entities. Creaturely reality does not, in this schema, exist over against divine reality but as a product of divine knowledge and will, as an issuance of divine power. Second, it may be argued that Barth also denies that this relationship can be conceived in monistic terms. Although Barth speaks of the divine activity as one with human action, he is adamant that he does not mean that by that union any identification of or collapse of the two activities into one another; each remains what it is according to its nature. This rejection of monism is further supported by Barth's other claims that God's action precedes and follows creaturely occurrence and hence cannot be understood as exhausted in it. And third, it can be seen, though with less clarity, that Barth rejects as well any way of understanding this relationship in terms of a synergism or cooperation between the two activities.[13] They coexist but in such a way

[12] Duthie ("Providence," 69) points out as well that "while Barth keeps affirming the coincidence of divine and human action, he leaves his statement on the level of generalization and does not show how this coincidence works out in practice in daily life."

[13] Duthie (ibid., 68) asks concerning Barth's opposition to any form of synergism "whether he himself has not such an anxiety complex with regard to synergism that he fails to do justice to the reality and freedom of man."

that God's activity has absolute priority and controls and determines human action, while creaturely activity does not condition or determine God's action; the two activites can only be said to cooperate insofar as human action corresponds to God's knowledge, decision, and will.

Having eliminated these ways of understanding the relationship set forth, what does Barth leave us? Barth attempts in several ways, other than pure assertion, to demonstrate how this relationship can be coherently conceived. He suggests at one point that the notion of causation developed by Aristotle and further utilized by Thomas Aquinas might be helpful.[14] In this schema God is understood as the *causa prima* and as such the "source of all causae, the basis and starting-point of the whole causal series" (CD 3. 3. 98). No other cause exists prior to or in superiority to the divine cause. And as this first cause God both posits and conditions all other causes. Creatures, in their own terms, are then understood as *causa secunda*. They are subjects who act and hence bring about effects within their own creaturely realm, but they are such agents only in a secondary and derived sense. The "divine causare" are understood as the primary causes that function through, in, and with these "creaturely causare," but without denying that these creaturely causes also occur. Barth suggests that this notion of primary and secondary causation can allow for the absolute priority of divine activity while at the same time not eliminating the fact and function of human agency.

However, when Barth fills out this notion of causation from the perspective of everything stated above, the model appears less helpful. For, Barth appears to have a far more extensive and intensive conception of divine activity that this idea can accommodate. Further, though utilizing the notion of causation, Barth does so in a more circumscribed and qualified manner than many of its more obvious proponents. He insists that causation cannot be understood as a genus under which both God and humanity fall as fellow agents. In a move parallel to his rejection of *analogia entis*, he asserts there is no *analogia causae*. God and creatures are not subjects and causes in any corresponding or analogical sense; they are, for Barth, utterly unlike (ibid., 102–3). God is a self-posited, self-conditioned cause, while all creaturely causes are externally grounded and determined. God posits and conditions absolutely and in a complete sense, while creatures never posit at all and only condition one another relatively and God not at all. God, thereby, "bends their activity to the execution of His will" and subordinates their operation to God's own (ibid., 105).

---

[14] This utilization of the notion of causation is a good example of how Barth envisions the relation of philosophy and theology. He does not, as is sometimes claimed, totally reject any connection between theology and philosophy. Instead, he envisions theology's relation to philosophy as one in which theology can use philosophy's concepts but at the same time does not subjugate itself to presuppositions or principles of any particular philosophy.

Thus, Barth's explication of divine causation does not significantly illumine our problem concerning the relation between divine and human activity. On the one hand, the notion does not seem to be adequate to the full scope and depth of Barth's idea of divine activity, and, on the other hand, the very use of the term "cause," when circumscribed from Barth's perspective, is difficult to apply to both God and creatures. When divine causation is understood as not only the prior basis of but also the controlling factor within all creaturely activity, it is still not clear in what sense creatures are truly agents. The idea of causation, utilized as Barth does, finally does not resolve the dilemma of how to speak of creaturely autonomy, integrity, and independence while also maintaining complete determination. Hartshorne, for his part, will be seen to argue that the only way to understand divine and creaturely activity in a noncontradictory fashion is to see them as indeed belonging to the same genus, that is, that both God and creatures are causes in parallel ways. However, the result of such a move is that the notion of all-determining power must be foregone. And this move is one that Barth refuses to make.

Barth, at another juncture, suggests that the problem of the relation of these two activites can be alleviated by recognizing that the two agents involved here belong to completely separate orders. That is, we are not dealing with two comparable subjects both executing the same action at once—an impossibility Barth admits. Rather, in relation to God and humans we are concerned with two incomparable subjects who "belong to two different, two totally different orders and confront each other in a necessary relation of superiority and subordination" (ibid., 133). However, this suggestion does not unquestionably mitigate the difficulty either. On the one hand, the example in relation to which he discusses this two-agent theory is Quenstedt's example of writing where the "hand guides and the pen is guided" (ibid., 134). Such an illustration, however, instead of supporting his intention calls into question Barth's very assertion that humanity is not a puppet, tool, or mere instrument of God but a true subject and agent. In this instance we do not have two agents in separate orders but one agent and an instrument to whom agency is only dubiously and finally improperly applied. And on the other hand, Barth himself reasserts that even in this explanation it must be fundamentally understood that "it is God who has called forth this action of the creature, and in and with this action He Himself is at work in sovereign power" (ibid.).

Although he suggests the above notions might be fruitful ways to conceive of the relationship between God and God's creatures, he contends however that the major obstacle or difficulty in acknowledging the fact and content of this relation is not finally intellectual but ultimately spiritual. That is, all the rational or logical explanations of how the divine and creaturely realities coexist will have no compelling power so long as human beings perceive God as a mechanical or tyrannical force which is not for humanity but over against and hostile to human needs and interests. Barth states:

> The basic condition for a perception and understanding of this proposition is not intellectual but spiritual, that of overcoming and removing the fear-complex which suggests that God is a kind of stranger or alien or even enemy to the creature; that it is better for the freedom and claim and honour and dignity of the creature the more it can call its own sphere marked off from God and guaranteed against Him and the worse for it if this sphere is restricted and worst of all if it is completely taken away; that it may be and necessarily is a legitimate interest to defend the claim of the creature in the face of an unjustified and dangerous claim on the part of God. (Ibid., 146)

And, this fear-complex that imagines it is better to be without God than with God is only done away with when the relation between God and humanity is viewed from the perspective of revelation, that is, within the context of faith. When the divine operation and its creaturely counterpart are viewed from this perspective, they can no longer be conceived, and hence feared, as mechanical or tyrannical operations but only in terms of the personal Word of God and its human response, that is, in terms of address and answer (CD 3. 2. 147–48). For Barth, when this divine operation is understood in these terms of personal address and response, it need no longer be feared as that which denies or annihilates creaturely freedom and agency but as that which constitutes it. "Where the Word and Spirit are at work unconditionally and irresistibly, the effect of their operation is not bondage but freedom" (CD 3. 3. 150). And from the perspective of revelation it can be seen that this is the nature and character of all of God's operations, both in covenant history and creaturely history as a whole. There is no other divine operation than this address and response.

Thus, we come full circle to where we began in Chapter 1. We end our analysis where we commenced it, with knowledge of God and God's activity understood only as faith-knowledge. Faith plays a dual role at this juncture. On the one hand, it is from this perspective alone that the proper understanding of divine activity in general is gained and, on the other hand, faith itself is the preeminent example of God's activity in relation to human activity. It is here that all Barth's claims of God's determination and human integrity are finally focused.

Divine Power and Faith

For Barth, the object of faith, that which addresses humanity and calls forth this faithful response, is the Word of God, God Godself revealed in and as Jesus Christ. As such, this Word is the objective basis upon which and in relation to which faith takes place. But human beings, as creatures and sinners, have no capacity to hear and respond to this gracious address of God in Jesus Christ. There is "no human awareness corresponding to this divine utterance" (CD 1. 1. 149).

And yet, despite this lack of appropriate disposition in humanity, some humans do respond to and acknowledge this divine address. But they do so, according to Barth, not through their own capacity but only as the Spirit of this Word acts in and through them in faith; the operation of the Spirit, not human decision or ability, is the subjective basis of true hearing of God's Word. Thus, not only the Word, the address, but also the effect of the Word is God's action.

It is this latter claim that the Spirit is the subjective basis for any and all response to Jesus Christ that is of special interest here, for it is perhaps Barth's most important example of the coincidence of divine and creaturely activity and hence highlights both the claim and the difficulties which emerge from it. Barth is not claiming that the Word of God as it is addressed to humanity merely elicits a believing response and as such is the occasion or the catalyst for that response. Rather, he is asserting that the Spirit initiates, establishes, and controls the response to this address of God. And further, this determination of humanity for God cannot be understood as an external determination but rather the Spirit must be understood as God present in the creature and its work. Faith must be conceived as the simultaneous activity of the Spirit and the creature. If, however, the internal presence of the Spirit and the activity of the human coincide, how are they to be understood?

First, the Spirit, as God, and the human, as creature, must never be confused, must never be identified. The Spirit is the Spirit of Jesus Christ, not in any sense the "human spirit"; it is present in human decision, but it is not to be collapsed into a human component of that decision and action (CD 4. 1. 646).

Second, as God present in human decision and action, the Spirit must be understood as present in an unconditional and irresistible way. It is the Spirit who inaugurates, controls and supports human faith. Therefore, the Spirit and its activity, although coinciding with creaturely decision, must be understood to be completely superior to and have priority over the human aspect of that activity; the Spirit is the all-determining factor in the human response to God.

Barth wants to claim, thirdly, however that this priority of divine activity in faith is not to be interpreted to mean that faith is not a human decision or action. Faith, although based upon and finally controlled by the presence of the Spirit, is nonetheless a human decision; faith is the creature's own act (ibid., 757–59). Barth, with this claim that faith is simultaneously the work of God and the work of the creature with the former preceding and determining the latter, once more brings us to the point of asking if the introduction of the Spirit as the mode of God's all-powerful determination truly overcomes the difficulties entailed in understanding divine operation's relation to creaturely activity. The structure in relation to faith is essentially the same as we have been examining up to this point, and it must be asked if the terminology of address and response makes any significant contribution to illuminating how that relationship can be coherently conceived.

Barth, in response to the above concerns, insists that the Spirit's presence and its determination of the creature for faith does not involve the obliteration of freedom but rather its constitution. Indeed, faith is freedom; in faith, and only in faith, is the creature given true freedom, the capacity to be both from and to God (CD 1. 2. 270). Such a claim involves several implications, and with these implications several questions arise that are not only relevant here but also in relation to our previous analysis.

By asserting that human freedom is not destroyed but established by the work of the Spirit, Barth is maintaining once more his claim that real freedom is freedom to be *for* God. And this freedom for, as earlier, is interpreted as capacity or ability to be something or to do something. Hence, in faith the Spirit determines the creature to be able to be obedient to God, to be able to conform to God's purpose. On the one hand, this means that determination by the Spirit doesn't eliminate creaturely ˙self-determination but really consists in the establishing of the capacity to determine itself for God. And on the other hand, this interpretation of freedom as capacity does not involve the conclusion that creaturely freedom and obedience or submission to the will of God contradict each other. Rather, when freedom is conceived of as this capacity, then "subordination is not opposed to freedom" (ibid., 715). Instead, it is the ultimate exercise of this freedom to acknowledge and submit oneself to the will of God.

Thus, Barth claims that where the Spirit is active this faith and its attendant freedom result. But he claims as well that where the Spirit is present it is present irresistibly and unconditionally, that is, as Lord; where the Spirit acts it does so omnipotently, and the creature must respond. Freedom does not involve the capacity to be unfaithful. As recipient of the Word of God the creature "*must* pass from a well-known past to a future. . . . There is necessarily a compulsion. No question of a choice can enter in" (CD 4. 2. 578). Hence, God's presence, and it alone, allows this type of freedom and also must be said to compel it irresistibly in some manner.

But does not this interpretation involve as well the conclusion that just as faith and its attendant freedom are solely the results of God's decision and presence, then so too must unbelief and its lack of freedom be understood as the outcome of that divine decision and subsequent absence of divine presence? If unbelief is real and not just an illusion, must God not be held responsible for it as well as for true belief? This is a somewhat difficult and problematic conclusion, but it is one that follows from Barth's own position. For, according to Barth, "not all men are free. Freedom is not a matter of course and is not simply a predicate of human existence."[15] Humans do not of themselves have the capacity to be for God, and therefore Barth admits, "It is not for man to chose first whether he himself will decide (what an illusion!) for faith or for unbelief" (CD 4. 1. 746). Confronted with these claims of radical human need of God's presence, of grace, and the irresistible and omnipotent nature of that presence, we must conclude that unbelief just as belief is not a decision first made by humans but a human activity determined, as is faith, by God.

These claims can be seen to entail the same problematic conclusions that we encountered in relation to sin. First, by denying any human capacity for faith, Barth thereby must also deny any ultimate human responsibility for unbelief. If God's presence is irresistible and omnipotent and brings with it this freedom, then unbelief if we accept it as real, points not only to the lack of capacity for God but also and more fundamentally to the absence of the divine presence which would make it possible. This conclusion, in turn, raises profound questions concerning God's graciousness toward humanity. Barth maintains that God, revealed in Jesus Christ and present through the Holy Spirit, is a gracious God. And yet if God is ultimately responsible both for faith, with its freedom, and unbelief, with its lack of freedom, then does this latter fact not at least raise questions about the graciousness and benevolent character of this God? In the face of the realities of faith and unbelief can Barth maintain his connection between divine love and power?

Barth recognizes but does not resolve this dilemma in relation to the idea of *apokatastasis,* universal salvation or restoration. Barth consistently rejects any necessary claim of universalism, maintaining that his doing so does not call into question divine graciousness but rather emphasizes the free and independent character of that decision. Nonetheless, despite this appeal to divine freedom, Barth fails to harmonize such rejection with his fundamental claim that in Jesus Christ God has eternally decided to be for humanity.[16] The fact of unbelief and the future possibility of eternal rejection stand as challenges to either divine omnipotence or divine graciousness when they are defined in the Barthian manner.[17] If God's presence is irresistible and

[15] Barth, *Dogmatics in Outline,* 138.

[16] Berkouwer (*Triumph and Grace,* 116) states: "There is no alternative to concluding that Barth's refusal to accept the apokatastasis cannot be harmonized with the fundamental structure of his doctrine of election."

[17] Hartwell states:

> "Barth has no satisfactory answer to the question of why some hear the Word of God and believe whilst others fail to do so. If the rejection of God's Word is the impossible and inexplicable behaviour on the part of some men, there must be something in those who accept it by virtue of their own free choice and decision which constrains them to act in this way; in other words, there must be in them a will to good. To counter this by saying that man's faith is the exclusive work of the Holy Spirit in man is begging the question since in that case the

God is truly gracious, then the question of why some believe, why some can recognize that presence and others do not, will always raise questions about either the irresistibility of divine grace (i.e., its power to be effectively present) or the graciousness of a God who would deny creatures God's presence.

This analysis of Barth's interpretation of faith also raises questions concerning the activity of God and the activity of the creature in general. Barth insists that this latter general activity must always be understood from the perspective of this particular activity, that is, revelation and faith. And further, when understood in light of that primary activity, God's all-determining action in the creaturely sphere will be understood to take place only for the purposes of God's loving decision to be for and with humanity. However, certain questions also arise when God's activity in the creaturely realm is understood from the point of view of salvation history. One such concern is whether freedom, in the way in which Barth has defined it, is an appropriate notion to apply at all to creaturely existence. For, Barth has, in the latter analysis of faith, tied freedom solely to faith, and faith consists in the explicit and conscious recognition, acknowledgment, and confession of the Word of God. Now if true freedom, as freedom for God, takes place only in the context of faith, in what way can we understand creaturely reality outside of the sphere of faith to be free? Is all activity outside this sphere unfree? Barth earlier wanted to maintain that God determines and rules all creaturely action, not only in the explicit context of salvation history but in the general creaturely sphere as well, and yet he also wanted to maintain that God determines these creatures for freedom. However, if freedom is connected to the explicit acceptance of the Word of God, it is difficult to conceive of how this acknowledgment takes place. Are we to assume that outside of the Christian circle of faith this acknowledgment of and submission to God takes place but in a way that is really tied to Jesus Christ yet unconscious that this is the God it recognizes? Is Barth proposing some form of anonymous Christianity in which unbelief is an illusion? Or is he really finally suggesting that acknowledgment, and with it its attendant freedom, is only possible in this particular sphere and only in this manner, and hence, outside of this small circle, God does indeed precede, accompany, and follow all human action but creatures do not know this and cannot acknowledge it and hence remain forever unfree with no true capacity for God? Is Barth ultimately saying that outside of Christian faith the omnipotent divine determination is ever present but the corresponding

---

question arises: why then do not all men believe? To assume that God gives faith to some but not to others contradicts the truth of His love to all men." (*Theology of Karl Barth*, 186–87.)

See also Berkouwer, *Triumph of Grace*, 266–67.

creaturely freedom is not? Or is Barth really simply once more eqivocating on his meaning of freedom—is freedom in the creaturely sphere a question of choice between alternatives (though not consciously of God) instead of freedom for God? All these are questions that arise from the premises Barth sets forth, but they are, unfortunately, dilemmas he chose not to resolve and, more seriously, they are dilemmas not easily resolved within the framework he has set forth.

And finally, in closing we must return once more to the question of how all this takes place. In the previous section the question arose as to how divine and human activity could be understood to coincide in a manner which maintained the reality and integrity of both activities. Barth, as a means of explaining this "how," finally pointed to faith as that point from which we can understand that it is as Spirit that God acts in and through creaturely decisions and action. But once having said this Barth does not help us much further in understanding how this exactly occurs; his explanation remains at a very general level. He does suggest, and this is really the most explicit he gets, that the most fruitful way of conceiving of the Spirit's work is to understand it as giving direction. For Barth the German word for "direction," *die Weisung,* is particularly helpful because it comes from the same root as *weise* which means "wise" and *die Weisheit* meaning "wisdom." For Barth, the work of the Spirit involves this imparting of wisdom, and the images he utilizes to convey what he interprets as the Spirit's action include awakening, renewal, and illumination. Barth does not, by use of these images, want to minimize the determining and controlling character of that direction; he wants to indicate the character of the direction and how it might take place. Rather than minimizing the sense of control, Barth contends that this direction

> falls, as it were, vertically into the lives to whom it is given. It is thus effective with divine power. It is the sowing and developing seed of new life. It crushes and breaks and destroys that which resists it. It constitutes itself the ruling and determinative factor in the whole being of those to whom it is given. (CD 4. 2. 523)

Thus, Barth suggests that the operation of the Spirit be conceived as divine direction. However, he does not offer any precise analysis of the step-by-step process by which this all occurs. Rather, he finally asserts that how this all happens cannot be fully analyzed or understood, even from the perspective of faith, and that we must simply affirm the fact that it does so occur. Barth declares, "It is strange but true that fundamentally and in general practice we cannot say more of the Holy Spirit and His work than that He is the power in which Jesus Christ attests Himself, attests Himself effectively creating in man response and obedience" (CD 4. 1. 648). Barth leaves us finally with the claim that we know this is all so because, within the circle of faith, it is experienced thus but that faith only affirms that it does take place; it does not illuminate the process by which it occurs.

3.3 Summary Remarks

In closing, it is possible to draw certain conclusions. On the one hand, Barth has asserted that from the perspective of faith God's operations in the creaturely realm as a whole might be recognized and better understood. However, we have seen, by analyzing the faith process, that the very same questions of how this divine operation takes place and, if it does take place, whether creaturely action is not jeopardized again, only this time in relation to faith. We have also seen that Barth does not resolve the difficulties in terms of faith any more adequately than in terms of providence. And, on the other hand, his appeal to faith, rather than resolving the dilemmas, can be seen to raise new difficulties in terms of the status of human activity outside the sphere of faith. Given the above analysis, it is possible to conclude that Barth leaves us with the same two claims with which he began: that God's knowledge and will, God's omnipotent activity, determines irresistibly and absolutely all creaturely decision and action; and that the activity of the creatures, especially humans, is their own and as such characterized by autonomy, integrity, and responsibility. However, it is not at all clear at this concluding point, any more than at our departure point , that Barth holds these together in any way other than pure assertion. In fact, the development of the first claim eventually involves if not the rejection of the second at least its serious undermining.[18] And we must finally ask, therefore, if theology by assertion is adequate or acceptable, or must we turn elsewhere?

The analysis of Barth is completed, and through this exploration a number of elements of the Barthian vision have become clearer. His concern to make the God-world relationship of central importance for understanding God's nature and character and his insistence that that relation be understood as gracious and loving have been evident throughout. However, the analysis also revealed the problems that emerge when such a relation is interpreted from the perspective of all-determining power, and with the recognition of these problems, grave doubts have arisen as well concerning the viability of the Barthian position. It is now time to turn to the understanding of God developed by philosopher Charles Hartshorne and to explore his way of conceiving of divine power and the implications of that

---

[18] Duthie states: "Convinced of the all-embracing Lordship of God and compelled to recognize the reality of human actions within the same world he simply puts the two things together and affirms their unity while holding fast to the transcendent character of the activity of God. The junction between God's action and man's is mysterious and unfathomable." ("Providence," 72)

conception for his vision of the God-world relation. This examination of Hartshorne's position will have as its intention not only the analysis of his vision over against Barth's but it will seek to determine whether indeed he offers an alternative to this position which overcomes the Barthian dilemmas while avoiding problems of its own.

4

HARTSHORNE'S GUIDING PRINCIPLES AND METHODOLOGICAL APPROACH

The analysis of the idea of divine power expressed in the thought of Karl Barth was carried out through the exploration of Barth's understanding of the status, source, and means of knowledge of God, an explication of Barth's conception of divine power, and finally an examination of the repercussions of such a conception in relation to human freedom and the problem of evil. A parallel analysis of the conception of divine power developed by Charles Hartshorne will now be undertaken, along with an exploration of the differences in approach, content, and implications that such a position offers.

Charles Hartshorne approaches the questions of knowledge, reality, and God from the perspective of a secular philosopher, and as a representative of such a perspective, he works out of a conceptual framework widely divergent from the one developed by Karl Barth. Barth understands himself to be a church theologian, working within a circle of faith and speaking primarily neither for nor to the general secular world, but rather to those within the circle of Christian faith experience.[1] Speaking from his understanding of this perspective, Barth argued that there is but one source of knowledge for both God and the world, and that source is God's self-revelation in Jesus Christ. Human reason and imagination have no capacity whatsoever to attain a valid understanding of the reality and nature of God. At most, human reason can reach an idea of Supreme Being or perfection, but such ideas only indicate the outermost limits of human cognitive power, and as such, they represent human idols, not divine reality. Any natural knowledge of God is therefore unilaterally rejected by Barth.

Barth argues as well that it is only from the perspective of God's self-revelation that true knowledge concerning the nature of nondivine reality and particularly of human nature is to be obtained. True knowledge of the world follows after and presupposes knowledge of God. Thus, although

---

[1] See above, 1.2 and 1.3.

humans can know much about the world through natural means, true insight into the nature and purpose of the world cannot be reached in this manner. Not only God but also the world is finally not interpretable by human reason and imagination.

Thus Barth, from his revelational perspective, has severely circumscribed the limits of human cognitive capacities. Humanity's creaturely status and sinful condition foreclose the possibility of human reason attaining to true knowledge. Only reason shaped by and subordinated to revelation and the faith experience can have access to true reality; without that input humanity maintains a truncated and misdirected perception of it.

Charles Hartshorne, as a secular philosopher, grounds his position in presuppositions that differ significantly from, and indeed contradict, those of Karl Barth. Hartshorne is, from beginning to end, a rationalist who is convinced of the capacity of human reason to grasp adequately and truly the general nature of reality on its multiple levels, divine and nondivine alike. This basic trust in human cognitive capacity underlies and provides the foundation for Hartshorne's entire philosophical schema. All of his positions reflect the conviction and determination, reached at the age of seventeen after reading Emerson's *Essays*, "to trust reason to the end."[2] There are several aspects of this confidence in reason's capacities that are important to note. First, this rationalistic orientation assumes that reality has an intelligible and coherent structure and that there is no reality that fails to exhibit this structure. Going along with this is the assumption that not only has reality such a structure but that human reason has the capacity to penetrate reality, to grasp this intelligible constitution.[3] Human thought has the capacity to know reality, at least its generic nature, as it is. This means as well that there is, or can be, a basic congruence between reality or what is the case and human ideas of it. Human ideas concerning reality are not merely the invention of human imaginative processes imposed upon a basically unknowable reality but rather there is a basic correspondence between the nature of reality and human ideas of it. The structure of thought and the structure of reality correspond to one another.[4] This is not to say that all

[2] Charles Hartshorne, *The Logic of Perfection* (LaSalle, Illinois: Open Court, 1962) viii; hereafter cited as LP.

[3] Langdon Gilkey (*Naming the Whirlwind* [New York: Bobbs-Merrill, 1969] 227–28) rejects these rationalistic assumptions and argues that present-day theology and philosophy can no longer assume a coherent structure of reality nor human capacity to reach that structure. He states, including Hartshorne in this remark, "The Whiteheadian must ask himself why he believes, in the first place, in the objective rationality and coherence of process, and the power of speculative thought to reach beyond immediate experience, and how he might defend those beliefs intelligibly to the modern philosophical mind that finds both almost incredible."

[4] Gunton (*Becoming and Being*, 87) states that this structural congruence between thought and reality indicates why for Hartshorne realism and idealism are not opposed but rather idealism is "equated with it as a form of conceptual realism."

ideas reflect reality correctly. Many human conceptions are mistaken or misguided. But the very fact that we can speak of mistakes and errors in thought indicates the possibility of correct and valid knowledge.[5] To say that there is not a basic relationship between reality and human ideas of it is to deny that any ideas are more valid or adequate than others. In this case, human ideas would reflect not knowledge but mere preference.

And further, these assumptions also presuppose that the nature of reality is a public affair, accessible to all who can reflect carefully enough. Contrary to Barth for whom knowledge of reality cannot be ascertained in any public or general fashion, Hartshorne claims that the structure of reality is everywhere and in everything accessible, and the task is to conceive and understand it in an adequate manner. Knowledge of the nature of reality is not the province of a chosen few but a possibility for all who choose to think.

These convictions are axiomatic for Hartshorne and as such they are accepted, not proved. They are foundational assumptions behind which one cannot go. Thus, they are in a sense expressions of faith. Rationalism depends upon the assumption that both reason and reality are trustworthy.[6] Faith, as he understands it, is therefore not opposed to reason, but is ultimately confidence in reason and trust in the reality reason seeks to know.[7] And finally, it must be stated that this fundamental confidence in the knowable and trustworthy nature of reality does not entail reality as, so to speak, domesticated by or subjugated to reason. Reason, in its metaphysical form, is an access to the structure or generic nature of reality, but concrete, particular reality must be encountered; it can only be known either by the intuition or direct awareness that is prior to all conscious reasoning or by the empirical a posteriori reason that concerns itself with the particular and the concrete. This distinction between metaphysical and empirical ways of knowing is of immense importance to Hartshorne's schema.

4.1 The Nature of Metaphysics

According to Hartshorne there are different kinds or levels of reality, and as those levels vary, so too must the kind of knowledge that corresponds to

---

[5] Perhaps it is more accurate to say there is a congruence between experience and reality. Hartshorne (*Creative Synthesis and Philosophic Method* [LaSalle, Illinois: Open Court, 1970] 79–80, 94–95; hereafter cited as CSPM) asserts that high level forms of rationality and verbalization often distorted their objects whereas sublinguistic experience is both more immediate and accurate. However, he nonetheless asserts that truth is possible, even if it is difficult to ascertain.

[6] Hartshorne, *Reality as a Social Process* (New York: Hafner, 1971) 164; hereafter cited as RSP.

[7] Ibid.

them and the method for obtaining and assessing such knowledge. As the logical type differs, so too must the methodological approach. For Hartshorne it is "an axiom that every logical difference in subject matter implies a methodological difference."[8]

In Hartshorne's view, the philosopher, or more precisely the metaphysician, is concerned with a very particular logical class of entities (RSP, 174). The metaphysician is concerned not with particular or concrete facts but with the common or generic features embodied in and displayed by every fact whatsoever. That is, the metaphysician seeks to discern the general character of reality and to formulate those ideas which will be applicable universally to all conceivable and all actual situations. Metaphysics is "an attempt to describe the most general aspects of experience, to abstract from all that is special in our awareness, and to report as clearly and accurately as possible upon the residuum" (ibid., 175).

Thus, metaphysics seeks generality beyond any particular fact or specific case. And in so doing, metaphysics concerns itself not with what is contingent, particular, and discernible only a posteriori but rather with that which is universal, necessary, and knowable a priori. In order to better understand this universal, necessary, and a priori character of metaphysical ideas and their objects, as well as their distinct status in relation to all other ideas, it will be helpful to examine Hartshorne's claim that metaphysical statements must be understood as existential and nonrestrictive statements.[9]

Hartshorne distinguishes three general levels or types of existential statements: partially restrictive, completely restrictive, and completely nonrestrictive. (Hartshorne distinguishes mathematics from these kinds of statements by arguing that it is unrestricted but not existential and it deals only with possible worlds rather than actual worlds.) The first type refers to ordinary factual statements dealing with contingent facts, that is, empirical claims. Contingent facts always involve the possibility of alternatives. The contingent is always a decision among possibilities, the clash of the positive with the positive.[10] As such it is exclusive—rather than inclusive—and competitive; insofar as a contingent fact is what it is, it excludes other possibilities from being realized (LP, 281). By affirming one thing it denies another (CSPM, 159). Contingent means "that what is asserted selects among the

---

[8] Hartshorne, "God's Existence: A Conceptual Problem," in Sidney Hook, ed., *Religious Experience and Truth* (New York: New York University Press, 1961) 212; see also RSP, 173.

[9] Hartshorne builds on Karl Popper's classification of existential statements set forth in *The Logic of Scientific Discovery* (New York: Basic Books, 1959) 633–35. The best places for looking at Hartshorne's position are CSPM, chap. 8, and "Metaphysics and the Modality of Existential Judgments," in Ivor Leclerc, ed., *The Relevance of Whitehead* (New York: Macmillan, 1961) 107–21.

[10] Hartshorne, "Could There Have Been Nothing?: A Reply," *Process Studies* 1 (1971) 26. For Hartshorne, there is no such thing as either a purely negative fact (every fact is at least partially positive) or a purely positive fact (every fact excludes or denies something).

conceivable possibilities, affirming some individuals and excluding others. To say that some individuals are elephants excludes a world consisting entirely of individuals other than elephants."[11] Thus, these statements are always a mixture of the positive and the negative, affirming the actualization of some possibilities while denying others. Because this is so, Hartshorne, adopting Karl Popper's principle of falsification, argues that such empirical statements can be identified as such by virtue of the fact that they can always be falsified or refuted by some conceivable alternative.[12] According to Popper's criterion, the "empirical" equals the "conceivably falsifiable"; it is that which is "capable of being contradicted by some, but not all, conceivable observation statements."[13] This means that empirical statements and the realities they refer to can never be conceived of as necessary, but are always "merely facts." And finally, for Hartshorne, the exploration of such restricted and refutable facts and the formulation of adequate ideas concerning them are the task and responsibility of the natural and social sciences. That is, contingent facts can only be known by reason in its empirical mode.

Now, all concrete, actual entities and the ideas that refer to them are of this nonnecessary, contingent type. And up to this point in his analysis Hartshorne is in fairly large company. It is "commonplace in logic that ordinary existential statements are contingent."[14] It is, however, further commonplace to many thinkers (including many logicians as well as those working from the perspective of historical relativism) that such contingent statements are the only possible ones. Hartshorne rejects this conclusion and argues that we must also examine the meaning and status of completely restrictive and completely nonrestrictive existential statements. The former are utterly negative statements and the latter are completely positive, or, in Hartshorne's schema, metaphysical statements. Simply to generalize the contingency of ordinary existential statements to all statements does not settle the question through true analysis but merely resolves it by question begging and dogmatic assertion. Rather, in order to adjudicate this matter their full meaning must be examined.

According to Hartshorne, completely restrictive existential statements are those that contradict every and any positive existential assertion. "Nothing exists" is Hartshorne's favorite example of such a statement. It is a purely negative claim denying that any positive possibility is realized. Hartshorne, however, argues that such a statement is verbal only, and when closely

---

[11] Hartshorne, "Metaphysics and the Modality of Existential Judgments," 110.

[12] Hartshorne, "The Development of My Philosophy," in John E. Smith, ed., *Contemporary American Philosophy* (New York: Humanities, 1970) 219.

[13] Hartshorne, *Anselm's Discovery* (LaSalle, Illinois: Open Court, 1965) 62–63; hereafter cited as AD.

[14] Hartshorne, "Metaphysics and the Modality of Metaphysical Judgments," 110.

examined, it can be seen to be nonsensical.[15] There are two central reasons
for Hartshorne's rejection of such statements.[16] The first is that a purely
negative statement can never be verified.[17] "Blank nothing is not a
datum."[18] In order for it to be verified, something (i.e., the verifying experience itself) would have to exist (CSPM, 159). Hence, completely restrictive
existential statements, excluding all positive assertions, can never be known
to be true. Second, any experience whatsoever will negate or falsify this
claim. If it is true that "anything exists," then "nothing exists" must be
false. Thus, purely negative existential statements can never be verified but
are always being falsified. This leads Hartshorne to claim that such statements are verbal nonsense with no extralingual significance or reference.
Why "something exists" rather than "nothing" is, despite Heidegger, a
pseudo and merely verbal question without intelligible content.

Further, the falsity of such a statement is of a special kind for Hartshorne.
Empirical statements are always true or false contingently depending upon
factual conditions. But a purely negative statement such as "nothing exists"
is false unconditionally and necessarily. Referring to this type of statement,
Hartshorne states:

> Can such a statement be false in the merely factual or contingent sense?
> Is it not rather a statement which is bound to be false: If nothing were
> to exist, what would make this true? Bare nothing? And what would
> "existence" mean, if it were wholly unexemplified? Would the idea or
> possibility of "existence" still remain in some Platonic heaven of forms?
> I submit that the more plausible view is that a completely restrictive or
> wholly negative statement expresses an impossibility, not a conceivable
> but unrealized fact. (Ibid.)

Thus, completely negative statements are false a priori, that is, necessarily
and without alternative possibility. As empirical statements are contingently true or false, merely negative statements are false without exception; they are, for Hartshorne, verbal nonsense.

This brings us to the center of Hartshorne's concern: the possibility of
completely nonrestrictive existential statements. For Hartshorne, such

[15] Hartshorne, *A Natural Theology for Our Time* (LaSalle, Illinois: Open Court, 1967) 83;
hereafter cited as NTOT.

[16] For an extended discussion of Hartshorne's position, see Eugene H. Peters, *Hartshorne and
Neoclassical Metaphysics* (Lincoln: University of Nebraska Press, 1970) 22–24.

[17] Hartshorne, "Metaphysics and the Modality of Existential Judgments," 111. Hartshorne
claims that only something that is at least partly positive can be known; the purely negative is
unknowable. He states, "To know is to know something positive and the knowledge itself
must be something positive" (ibid.).

[18] Hartshorne, "The Structure of Metaphysics: A Criticism of Lazerowitz's Theory," *Philosophy and Phenomenological Research* 19 (1958) 236.

statements are entirely nonrestrictive in the sense that they exclude no alternative possibilities but are compatible with any and all possibilities or actualities. They are not exclusive, affirming some possibility while denying others, but would be pertinent to all situations. They are equally applicable to both sides of any contingent fact. As such they are wholly positive, noncompetitive, and inclusive of all possibility. It is important to unpack Hartshorne's meaning concerning this matter while keeping in mind that he has argued adamantly that the purely negative ("Nothing exists") is not possible.

First, such statements could never be falsified but only verified. No positive alternative or meaning could refute statements for they are equally compatible with any actual or possible state of affairs. Thus, Hartshorne suggests that nonrestrictive existential statements can be identified by virtue of the fact that they can never be falsified (in distinction from contingent claims) but only verified (in distinction from completely negative claims).

This impossibility of falsification and its corollary possibility of verification lead Hartshorne to claim that such statements are necessarily true, that is, without possible alternative (LP, 149). This is so because they are true no matter what possibility is actualized, and they are thus neutral to all real possibilities. In Hartshorne's words,

> Absolute necessity is that which requires no special assumptions or conditions rather than any others. Thus the notion that "necessary" means necessitated *by* something in particular is groundless. To be necessary is merely to be common to all possibilities, hence neutral as to which possibilities may be actualized. (AD, 80)

To state Hartshorne's position a bit differently, this neutrality to alternative means that every possible and actual state of affairs will exemplify or affirm such nonrestrictive existential statements. That is, they are universally true, verified by the actualization or possible actualization of anything.

Thus, nonrestrictive existential statements are necessary, universal in applicability, nonfalsifiable, and wholly positive. They are, succinctly put, the subject matter of metaphysical inquiry which seeks the general, necessary features exemplified by reality. As Hartshorne puts it,

> Metaphysics . . . studies nonrestrictive existential affirmations. . . . Metaphysics tries to express what *all* possibilities to existence have in common, excluding blank nonexistence as an impossibility. It searches for the common element of all positive existential possibilities, some of which *must* be actualized—if not this, then that; if not that, then still another—but at any rate something. Metaphysics, in the old phrase, explores "being *qua* being," or reality *qua* reality, meaning by this, the

strictly universal features of existential possibility, those which cannot
be unexemplified.[19]

It can be seen that Hartshorne agrees for the possibility of necessary statements that deal not with particular facts but with that which is common to
all contingent reality, to "facts-as-such" or "reality-as-such." And he further
suggests that these statements and that to which they refer are the providence of metaphysical inquiry and the metaphysical method. Hartshorne
labels this metaphysical method as the a priori method, in distinction from
the empirical or a posteriori method. It is important to note just what
Hartshorne means by "a priori." He does not mean having nothing to do
with experience of concrete reality. For Hartshorne, all ideas, metaphysical
no less than empirical, are grounded in experience. In his words, "Basic
ideas derive somehow from direct experience or intuition, life as constantly
lived" (NTOT, 2). However, metaphysical ideas, being necessary and
universal, are exemplified by all experiences and thus not by any experience
more than others. Metaphysical inquiry does not need any specific fact but
merely any fact; no fact is any more important to metaphysical inquiry than
any other. It is the "common quality," not the "uncommon quality," which
is of concern. Thus a priori does not mean in distinction from all experience, but in distinction from the particularity and the uniqueness of individual experiences. Thus, although a priori statements are nonempirical, they
nonetheless have existential and experiential reference.

This claim for existential and experiential import, though not empirical
importance, can be stated somewhat differently. Because metaphysical ideas
refer not to the particular but to the common aspects of all particular facts,
they do not yield any specific information concerning reality (LP, 291–92;
CSPM, 93; AD, 171–72). They are nonhistorical, or perhaps better, they
are transhistorical. Specific information is the task of empirical inquiry, not
metaphysical analysis. However, Hartshorne wishes to emphasize that
although no concrete, specific information about particulars is conveyed by
metaphysical ideas, nonetheless, general truths are indeed elucidated. Metaphysical ideas, as necessary and universal, affirm "that about the world
which would be real no matter what possibilities were actualized and which
therefore cannot be denied except by impossible formulae."[20] But in order
to function in this manner, metaphysical ideas must be of the utmost

---

[19] CSPM, 162. Hartshorne (LP, 283) also argues that there are conditionally necessary
statements as well as unconditionally or metaphysically necessary ones. Such conditionally
necessary statements are necessary if certain conditions prevail but not necessary in any and
every situation. An example of this conditional necessity is the statement "Two apples and
two apples are four apples." Such a statement is necessarily true only if apples exist. And
hence, the claim is only conditionally necessary, while the statement "Two and two are four"
is always and in any circumstance true, and hence is unconditionally true.

[20] Hartshorne, "Metaphysics and the Modality of Existential Judgments," 112.

generality and infinitely flexible so that they might be applicable in all instances. They are, therefore, extreme abstractions, devoid of all reference to the particular that gives empirical ideas their specific content and importance (CSPM, 164–65).

But how does one discern these "common" features of reality? What specific methodology does Hartshorne suggest for uncovering the necessary and the universal aspects of experience? Hartshorne appears to suggest what are, for him, two complementary approaches to the problem. The first is more usually associated with a priori claims, that is, logical analysis.[21] We must seek ideas as general and abstract as possible and then subject them to the most careful scrutiny in order to arrive at the highest level of consistency and coherency. Hartshorne suggests that the best method for attaining this consistency and coherency is to set forth all possible alternatives and analyze them in relation to each other.[22] And because he is convinced that metaphysical ideas are necessary and universal, he asserts that their denial will, if properly understood, be recognized as self-contradictory.[23] He states:

> Truths can be necessary only if their denial is absurd, and this can only mean if insight into the meaning of the denial suffices to exhibit it as self-contradictory. In short, the assumptions of philosophy are self-evident upon careful inspection of the terms involved. (MVG, 70)

Thus, there is a sense in which metaphysics has meaning and linguistic

---

[21] Hartshorne, *Man's Vision of God* (Hamden, Connecticut: Archon Books, 1964) 80–81; hereafter cited as MVG. Hartshorne (*The Divine Relativity: A Social Conception of God* [New Haven: Yale University Press, 1948] xvi; hereafter cited as DR) is not sure if there should even be a distinction between logic and metaphysics and suggests, for certain purposes, they are the same.

[22] MVG, x. There are a number of commentators on Hartshorne's work who do not think Hartshorne has been nearly so exhaustive in his analysis as he claims to be, especially concerning the possibility of an empirical or naturalistic philosophy which he rejects without a thoroughgoing analysis. See E. S. Brightman, Review of MVG, *JR* 22 (1942) 97; Bernard E. Meland, Review of MVG, The Christian Century 59 (1942) 1290; P. H. Phenix, Review of DR, *Journal of Philosophy* 46 (1949) 594; and Gene Reeves, "Whitehead and Hartshorne," *JR* 55 (1975) 127.

[23] This method of eliminating rival views through the procedure of reducing them to absurdity or self-contradiction is central to Hartshorne's method. If a metaphysical idea is necessary, positive, and universal, ideas that contradict it cannot also have this status but must be impossible and finally incoherent. For discussion of this negative method, see Eugene H. Peters, *Hartshorne and Neoclassical Metaphysics,* chap. 2; and Lewis S. Ford ("Whitehead's Differences from Hartshorne," in idem, ed., *Two Process Philosophers* [Tallahassee,: American Academy of Religion, 1973] 71) who states: "Now there can only be one set of consistently conceivable principles which are both nonrestrictive and affirmatively existential. Hartshorne therefore argues that all other proposed metaphysical systems must be inconsistent."

expression as a central concern.[24] However, in Hartshorne's view all basic ideas derive from experience. Therefore, Hartshorne's metaphysical method also includes an experiential approach. That is, he suggests that we examine specific experiences or known realities in search of the generic features exhibited by all reality.[25] And he suggests that the place where we must begin is with what is known best, that is, human experience. The method to be utilized is two-pronged: first, we must abstract from all that is particular, we must remove the limitations which qualify the experience as uniquely human; and second, we must generalize those features to be expressive of all reality. Thus, we begin with our own human experience and extrapolate outward toward an understanding of reality and its nature in general. In Hartshorne's words, "The aim of metaphysics is to generalize the generic traits of human experience so as to arrive at the generic traits of all experience and so of all possible objects of experience, to discover the eternal character of the cosmos."[26]

Hartshorne recognizes the arguments against such a method of generalization as sheer and unjustified anthropomorphism.[27] Nonetheless, he defends his position for two reasons. First, he assumes that all of reality really does have a common character, that all levels of reality, though distinct, are nonetheless akin to each other. "Every individual in nature is in some degree akin to man, either as inferior or as superior to him" (BH, 50–51). This principle of continuity is for him the "supreme law of rationality" (ibid., 50). And second, he argues that there is no escape from some form of anthropomorphism but only the capacity (and the necessity) to guard against crude and unjustified forms of it. He declares:

> Yet the alternatives to a legitimate, limited analogy between human and non-human are an illegitimate, inaccurate analogy, or an unintelligible dualism. The purely (unknowable) is, as Peirce said, the sole (and

[24] David A. Parker ("Neville's Critique of Hartshorne," *Process Studies* 4 [1974] 190) raises the question of whether meaning and language are all that metaphysical ideas tell us about: "A basic problem with any proposed a priori truths . . . concerns their reference. Do they tell us, that is, about the actual structure of reality (as Hartshorne apparently presupposes they must) or only about the ultimate structure of our understanding of reality?"

[25] MVG, 80–81. Hartshorne is often—and mistakenly, I think—thought to ignore experience for the analysis of concepts. However, there are a growing number of commentators who agree that Hartshorne also has an equally strong experiential basis for his position. See William O'Meara, "Hartshorne's Interpretation of Whitehead's Methodology," in *Two Process Philosophers*, 86–87; and Griffin, "Hartshorne's Differences from Whitehead," in ibid., 46.

[26] Hartshorne, *Beyond Humanism* (Lincoln: University of Nebraska Press, 1937) 268–69; hereafter cited as BH.

[27] Bryant C. Keeling ("Feeling as a Metaphysical Category: Hartshorne from an Analytical View," *Process Studies* 6 [1976] 56) voices just such criticism, arguing that Hartshorne's method of generalization yanks categories out of their contexts of meaning and use and thereby compromises their meanings.

illusory) escape from the task of finding a reasonable anthropomorphism.[28]

It is now possible to summarize briefly Hartshorne's claims and to move toward the examination of what he takes to be the central metaphysical ideas. It can be stated that Hartshorne sets himself in opposition to those who claim that all existential statements are contingent and the only truth we are capable of apprehending is empirical (to say nothing of being in opposition to Barth, who not only rejects the validity of metaphysics as defined by Hartshorne but also calls into question the status of contingent knowledge). Instead, Hartshorne argues for the possibility and validity of necessary existential truth and metaphysical knowledge. He argues as well, however, that such metaphysical knowledge is general and abstract, telling us nothing about concrete actuality except its generic nature. And he further suggests that we uncover such methodological truth through the double approach of logical analysis and analogical generalization.

In claiming all this Hartshorne aligns himself with a long tradition of metaphysical thought.[29] However, although he affirms metaphysical truth in general, he wants clearly to differentiate himself from much of the metaphysical tradition. He wants to distinguish himself because he is convinced that much of what he terms classical metaphysics has misinterpreted fundamental ideas and experiences. Metaphysics, to be valid, must be able to account for the widest range of experience and possibility and to do this not by simply denying any experience but by synthesizing or assimilating it within its general categories. It is possible to understand Hartshorne's concern here by explicating his conception of polar contrasts.[30] Hartshorne, building on Morris Cohen's "Law of Polarity," argues that all basic metaphysical ideas come in pairs of contraries.[31] That is, every basic metaphysical idea has an equally basic metaphysical contrary. Such contraries are inseparable and mutually imply one another. Examples of such ultimate contraries are concrete—abstract, relative—absolute, becoming—being, and effect—cause. Traditionally, according to Hartshorne, one side of each of these metaphysical contraries was taken as ultimate while the other was often denied

---

[28] Hartshorne, "Anthropomorphism," *An Encyclopedia of Religion* (New York: The Philosophical Library, 1945) 27; see also MVG, 88.

[29] Gunton (*Becoming and Being*, 11), as a sympathetic interpreter of Barth, states that Hartshorne "is a philosopher with a traditional, pre-twentieth century conception of the philosopher's function . . . He is what Strawson would classify as a revisionary metaphysician."

[30] Peters (*Hartshorne and Neoclassical Metaphysics*, 93) suggests that Hartshorne's conception of polar contrasts is one with his aesthetic interpretation of reality in that it represents the harmonization of contrasting elements.

[31] Hartshorne and William E. Reese, eds., *Philosophers Speak of God* (Chicago: University of Chicago Press, 1953) 2; hereafter cited as PSG; CSPM, 89, 99.

completely (being was taken as real, and becoming was interpreted as an illusion), or alternately one side was applied exclusively to one aspect of reality while the other was assigned exclusively to another level of reality (God was identified with absoluteness, creatures with relativity). That is, classical metaphysics played favorites among the metaphysical categories. Hartshorne argues, however, that these contrasting ideas go together; to neglect one side of the contrast is to deny any meaning to the other. "The two poles of each contrast stand or fall together, neither is simply to be denied or explained away, or called 'unreal.' For if either pole is real the contrast itself, including both poles, is so" (CSPM, 99). Thus, for Hartshorne any valid metaphysics must account for both sides of the contrast and apply both poles to every instance of reality.

However, although both poles of ultimate contrasts are real and each implies the other, they are not equal in status (ibid.). Hartshorne suggests, in what has been called his "Law of Inclusive Contrast," that one side of each of the contrasts is more inclusive and can include and account for its contrary while the other side cannot.[32] In Hartshorne's words,

> Though the polarities are ultimate, it does not follow that the two poles are in every sense on an equal status. As mere abstract concepts they are indeed correlatives each requiring the other for its own meaning. But if not the concepts but their examples or instances are considered on the one side are the dependent, inclusive entities, on the other the independent, included ones. One side forms, in the given context, the total reality, the other consists of mere though independent constituents or aspects. Thus the admission of ultimate dualities is one doctrine, dualism is quite another. The concept expressing the total reality is the entire truth, not because the correlative contrary can be dismissed or negated but because the referents of the latter are included in those of the former, while the converse inclusion does not obtain. Thus a basic asymmetry is involved. (CSPM, 99)

As we explicate Hartshorne's conception of metaphysical reality it will be important to keep these two principles in mind; metaphysical ultimates come in contrasting pairs and one side of each pair can be understood to take account of and include its polar contrast. One of Hartshorne's tests for metaphysical validity is how well any metaphysical idea can be said to exemplify these principles, and, to his mind, it was precisely by failing to do so that classical metaphysics was invalid.

We may now turn to the explicit treatment of Hartshorne's metaphysical vision, for it is necessary to have an overall sense of it if his understanding of God's place within this schema and, in particular, his conception of divine

---

[32] George L. Goodwin, *The Ontological Argument of Charles Hartshorne* (Missoula: Scholars, 1978) 32.

power are to be clearly and thoroughly explicated.

4.2 Creationist Metaphysics

In Hartshorne's view, the philosophy which is most adequate is the one which both accounts for the concerns of its rivals and offers something more besides. [33] And it his conviction that the metaphysical schema he terms neoclassical, process, or creationist philosophy offers just such a new and inclusive vision. [34] In his understanding, this new philosophy is the philosophy of the twentieth century in that it fulfills the requirements of metaphysical truth as set forth above and manages as well to give full attention to both aspects of the ultimate contrasts: [35]

> It is my belief that our age has the privilege of producing a neglected alternative both to the old speculative theology or metaphysics, and to the mere rejection of all metaphysics and theology, an alternative as significantly new as relativity physics or quantum mechanics, yet attractive not simply in that it is new, but because it renders substantial justice to both parties in many an old battle. In other words, there is a novel 'higher synthesis' which offers promise of being not merely one more doctrine to fight over, but, to some extent at least, a transcending of the causes of conflict. [36]

"Something Exists"

It was argued above that all metaphysical truths or statements must be, according to Hartshorne, completely nonrestrictive. It became clear that this meant that metaphysical ideas must be inclusive, necessary, and universal; they must not conflict with any real possibility but indeed be exemplified by all possibilities and actualities. The idea which Hartshorne

[33] Hartshorne, "The Modern World and A Modern View of God," in Norbert O. Shedler, ed., *Philosophy of Religion: Contemporary Perspectives* (New York: Macmillan, 1974) 478.

[34] Hartshorne calls his metaphysical vision by a variety of labels, among them: naturalistic theism, neoclassical theism, societal realism, creationist metaphysics, panentheism, surrelativism, and process philosophy or theism.

[35] Hartshorne, *Aquinas to Whitehead: Seven Centuries of Metaphysics of Religion* (Milwaukee: Marquette University Publications, 1976) 11; hereafter cited as AW.

[36] RSP, 18; although Hartshorne came to many of these convictions on his own and has developed them in his own unique manner, much of his position regarding these matters corresponds to and appropriates the philosophical vision proposed by Alfred North Whitehead (*Process and Reality* [New York: MacMillan, 1929]). Therefore, for those readers who wish to pursue more detailed analysis it is suggested that they examine the works of Whitehead as well as the Hartshornian corpus.

argues most clearly and irrefutably fulfills these requirements is "Something exists" (CSPM, 161–62). This statement is unfalsifiable (hence not contingent), yet verified by every moment (hence not completely negative; ibid., 162). Further, it is implied in the meaning of every other possible statement (ibid.). The statements "Elephants exist," "Atoms exist," and "God exists" involve, necessarily and without exception, the truth that "Something exists."[37] Hence, for Hartshorne, "Something exists" is the metaphysical idea par excellence, and it is by means of understanding it and all it implies that we come to the metaphysical truth (CSPM, 163). For Hartshorne, "Something exists," finally embraces within its meaning all metaphysical truth—including whatever truth concerning divine reality is accessible to metaphysical reasoning.

Hartshorne's metaphysical vision can be interpreted, therefore, as the explication of what he takes to be the meaning of this primary statement, "Something exists." All the claims that will presently be set forth, Hartshorne contends, are implied by this foundational statement. This includes, as the next section will demonstrate, the claim "God exists." On the one hand, Hartshorne argues that he has uncovered these implications through his twofold method of logical and meaning analysis and the generalization to all of reality of what he takes to be the basic dimensions of human experience. He does not take them to be purely speculative notions but to be grounded in phenomenological and logical analysis. And, on the other hand, Hartshorne asserts these implications of "Something exists" have the same metaphysical status as that general truth; they are, in this schema, necessary and universal, applicable to all reality whatsoever. This means, as this thesis demonstrates, that every reality, both divine and nondivine alike, must be understood to exemplify these metaphysical categories. They are the basic notions through which we must interpret all that is.

The general and overarching meaning that Hartshorne elicits from "Something exists" is that it is concrete reality that exists. Hartshorne argues that the fundamental form of reality is concrete actuality, not abstract entities, ideas, or forms. (At this juncture, Hartshorne is strongly anti-Platonic; concrete reality, not ideas nor universals, are the "final real thing.") The Aristotelian conviction that the abstract is neither real nor existent apart from concrete reality is axiomatic. In his view, concrete is the basic and inclusive form of reality, and the abstract is real only as a constituent in or an abstraction from concrete actuality.[38]

Hartshorne argues further that this fundamental concrete reality is social,

---

[37] This is equally true for partially negative statements such as "Elephants do not exist," for they always imply that "Something else does exist."

[38] CSPM, 22, 27. Hence Hartshorne (CSPM, 22, 25, 32) can state that metaphysics seeks to discern what it means to be a concrete entity. It does not seek to explain or describe any particular concrete reality but rather to understand "concreteness" itself.

creative, sentient, and temporal. It is necessary to unpack each of these claims, for they represent the basic groundwork of the Hartshornian position. First, and in many ways foremost, to be a concrete actual reality is to be an experiencing subject existing in relation to other such experiencing subjects; it is to be a thoroughly and intrinsically social being, coexisting in interdependent fashion with other equally social entities, acting and reacting, relating and being related to. "In a thoroughly social view of reality, nothing can be 'wholly other,' without affinity to other things and nothing can be immune to action and reaction with other things."[39] This social interpretation of concrete reality has a number of implications for Hartshorne.

To begin with, he conceives of this socially defined concrete reality to be ultimately composed of distinct, individual, momentary units of experience.[40] "Neoclassicism takes a momentary experience as the model or paradigm for concrete reality" (CSPM, 128–29). However, in this social vision, such individual entities must never be understood as either bits of dead matter or self-enclosed spirit. Rather, each instance of concrete reality is to be conceived as a unit of process, a dynamic experience which is a product of social interaction.

Hartshorne captures the social character of these concrete units of experience by asserting that they are best understood as processes of creative synthesis whereby moments of experience synthesize and integrate the data of their social world into new reality. This means, for Hartshorne, that there is not first a subject that then experiences or relates to other realities. The concrete reality, the subject is the experience, the synthesis of its data; there is no changeless ego or substance or being lurking behind the process. Rather, "our view affirms the contrary, that becoming is reality itself."[41]

Hence, concrete reality is synthesis or becoming, not substance or being. That concrete reality is creative synthesis can be stated in another way: each moment of process or unit of experience is what it is by virtue of its relation with its world. Every unit of experience, including divine experience, is internally related to its objects or data and it is constituted by these relations; it depends upon, is affected by, and finally is determined by those realities it experiences. Social relativity is, therefore, a metaphysical category, universally exemplified by every reality.

Hartshorne, however, interprets this social relativity in a very particular manner. The structure of social relation is a thoroughly temporal one. The relation between a becoming, experiencing subject and its social world is

---

[39] Hartshorne, "Philosophy of Creative Synthesis," *The Journal of Philosophy* 55 (1958) 948.

[40] Hartshorne, "Interrogation of Charles Hartshorne," in Sydney and Beatrice Rome, eds., *Philosophical Interrogations* (New York: Rinehart & Winston, 1964) 328; LP, 271.

[41] Hartshorne, "Philosophy of Creative Synthesis," 946.

always a temporal relation. [42] The social structure of all experience intrinsically involves distinctions among past, present, and future (RSP, 134). This claim entails several things. First, it means that there is no "purely timeless or immutable existent" (ibid.). To be actual, whether as divine or nondivine, is to be a social experience, and social experience is irrevocably temporal. Second, the meaning of subject and object, or of experiencing unit of process and its social world, can be essentially explicated in terms of their temporal status. Stated succinctly, to be an experiencing, becoming subject is to be present, while to be an object or data for creative synthesis is to be past. For Hartshorne, each momentary unit of process comes into being by taking account of, appropriating, and integrating its past world into a unified integrity, and having reached this unity, it thereby ceases to be an active, experiencing subject; upon achieving this integrated determinateness, the unit becomes available as a stimulus, object, or datum for future experiencing subjects. Once it has reached this point, it cannot change, be affected, nor influenced. And it is finally this facticity, this settledness that constitutes the very meaning of the past.

The subject, for its part, is present reality, reality in the process of coming to be. As such, Hartshorne argues it must take account of its past world, and that world is therefore determining of the present in a significant manner. Although the past does not fully determine the present, it does set limits to its possibility. It is, in other words, a causal determinant in relation to the present. [43] Every instance of reality, once it becomes past, is a causal factor for its successors, including God. The temporal relationship is therefore finally, the relationship between cause and effect. Further, this relationship is asymmetrical, one-directional, and wholly irreversible. The present takes into account the past and indeed is constituted and conditioned by that past; it is internally related to it. The past, however, is externally related to the present, data for its experience but unaffected by that status. Temporality is a one-way movement. [44]

Hartshorne suggests that this process by which the present appropriates and is influenced by the past is best understood along the lines suggested by Whitehead's idea of prehension. [45] Hartshorne states: "Prehension is a part or aspect of the more or less complex whole which is an act of awareness. It is the element of pure givenness in this act; experience as the having of an

---

[42] LP, 149. For a very good discussion of temporality in Hartshorne's metaphysical vision, see Goodwin, *Ontological Argument*, 34–45.

[43] Hartshorne, *Whitehead's Philosophy* (Lincoln: University of Nebraska Press, 1972) 175; hereafter cited as WP.

[44] Hartshorne,"Personal Identity from A to Z," *Process Studies* 2 (1972) 210; see AW, 29.

[45] Although Hartshorne disagrees with Whitehead on a number of important points, he wholeheartedly embraces his theory of "prehension" which he calls "one of the finest contributions ever made to epistemology" (WP, 125).

object" (WP, 125). That is, prehension involves the immediate intuition or awareness of object by subject. It is accordingly the "feeling of feelings," the experience of experience, the echo of one experience in another (RSP, 34). It is, finally, the direct sympathetic participation of one experience of other experiences.[46]

One of the important aspects of this Hartshornian claim which will be seen to have serious repercussions concerning Hartshorne's conception of God is that the relation of present experience to past experience, through the prehensive activity, entails the past as truly and literally ingredient in the present. To prehend the past is to include that past in the present. Hartshorne states:

> As many idealists and some realists have held, in becoming datum for an experience or unit-subject, an entity becomes constituent of the subject. Subjects inlcude their objects. Thus an actual entity must "house" its actual (meaning its past) world, must embrace the latter in the "synthesis" forming its own unity. [47]

If being present means to prehend and take into account the past, it involves as well being a potential contributor to the future. If becoming entails knowing or feeling the past, being actual, as past, involves being prehended or felt by successive experiences. Actuality involves therefore both retrospective and prospective relationship. This prospective necessity Hartshorne terms his principle of contributionism. "Individual existence is nothing more or less than contribution to the future world society."[48]

Two further implications of this temporal structure, with its asymmetrical movement, entail the status of contemporaries and that of the future. Both will receive greater attention in subsequent chapters, but their status must be briefly elucidated in this context. For Hartshorne, if the past is settled and determined actuality, and the present is coming to be actuality, then the future is not actual at all but rather is the realm of possibility. As such it has neither the status of concrete cause or concrete effect that past and

---

[46] Ibid., 21. Hartshorne ("Religion in Process Philosophy," in J. Clayton Feaver and William Horosz, eds., *Religion in Philosophical and Cultural Perspective* [Princeton, New Jersey: Van Nostrand, 1967] 252–53; "The Development of My Philosophy," in John E. Smith, ed., *Contemporary American Philosophy* [New York: Humanities, 1970] 223; and WP, 181) further suggests that the two forms of prehensive activity that can be discerned with the most clarity by human beings are memory and perception. Memory and perception are the fundamental ways that the present synthesizes and unifies the multiplicity of data that is its past. Both involve inheritance of past reality by present experiencing subjects. The only difference is that memory has as its objects one's personal sequence of experiences, while perception has as its material the sequences constituting "one's body, and less directly, environment."

[47] Hartshorne, "Personal Identity from A to Z," 210.

[48] Hartshorne, "Development of Process Philosophy," in Ewert H. Cousins, ed., *Process Theology* (New York: Newman, 1971) 61.

present have; it is that unsettled and indeterminate realm to which all past and present actualities will contribute themselves as data to be prehended and experienced. And finally, contemporaries are coming to be actualities, but because the causal relation is asymmetrically defined as the relation of past to present, Hartshorne, as fellow process thinker Alfred North Whitehead before him, argues that contemporary experiences exist side by side, so to speak, but do not experience or influence one another. The status of contemporaries will be seen to present profound difficulties for Hartshorne's vision of divine knowledge, but at this juncture it is enough to confirm that the social relation is fundamentally a relation of present to past. Hence, as social relativity is a metaphysical truism for Hartshorne, so too is the temporal character of that relativity and with it the causal relation between past and present.

If Hartshorne argues that reality is social and temporal, he contends as well that every entity, excluding none, is or once was such an experiencing subject. That is, he argues for a universal subjectivity. Any individual unit of reality that has internal unity and coherence is not entirely without experience of its own. Hartshorne denies the validity of both a materialistic monism and a dualism that asserts a fundamental split between matter and mind or spirit (RSP, 139). This is Hartshorne's famous panpsychism or principle of universal subjectivity or experience (ibid., 70). By it he claims that every individual unit of reality, from the least subatomic particle, to human beings, to the universe as a whole, is or once was a sentient, feeling, experiencing, active reality.

Several points must be elucidated at this point. On the one hand, Hartshorne's claim does not mean everything feels or experiences. There are entities that are not sentient or experiencing at all, such as stones or tables. But, Hartshorne argues, these unfeeling entities are not individual units with internal unity and coherence but are rather collections and aggregates of individuals who in their own turn do experience (CSPM, 141–42). Thus, there are indeed inanimate things, but these are not the basic units of reality but rather are composed of these more fundamental entities. Therefore, the things we take to be dead matter (e.g., stones or tables) are merely a particular organization or configuration of ultimately living and feeling units (LP, 217).

On the other hand, Hartshorne extends the applicability of terms such as feeling, experiencing, and, as he often says, "mind," to cover all unified integrated units of experience, from subatomic particles to the universe as an integrated individual. [49] Every individual experiences, has a subjective immediacy whereby it literally feels and is aware of the world in a manner

---

[49] A number of critics, while sympathetic to other Hartshornian positions, part company with him on the question of panpsychism. See Brightman, Review of MVG, *JR* 22 (1942) 98; and D. C. Mackintosh, Review of MVG, *Review of Religion* 6 (1942) 443.

unique to itself. Although there are levels of this subjectivity, there is no sheer absence of it in any individual; subjectivity and individuality are one. And while Hartshorne acknowledges these varying levels of intensity and scope of feeling—a molecule does not experience as the universe does—he nonetheless adamantly maintains that all forms of individual reality experience in some analogous manner.[50] Subjectivity or feeling, just as social relativity and temporality, are universal, metaphysical categories.

Along with the three major metaphysical categories of social relativity, temporality, and feeling, Hartshorne suggests creativity or freedom as another universal aspect of all concrete reality. He states that although each experiencing subject must take account of its past world and that this past world influences the present and sets the limits of its possibilities, the past does not completely determine the present. Each moment of experience creatively synthesizes the multiple data or stimuli presented by the past into a new emergent whole. Thus, while each subject depends upon, indeed is somehow constituted by, its past data, how it takes account of it or synthesizes it is a matter of self-determination (WP, 132; CSPM, 1–3). All experience is a form of creative self-determination; it is emergent out of, but neither entirely determined by nor deducible from, its data (WP, 163). If temporal progression is a movement marked by casual determination, it is also a process that is equally marked by intrinsic freedom and creativity; the transition from past to present is one of creative growth, novelty, and "additions to the definiteness of reality" (CSPM, 3; see also, RSP, 201; WP, 163). And such creative freedom is present on every level of individual actuality whether the level be that of divine reality or subatomic reality. Thus, creativity or freedom is also a metaphysical principle applicable to all reality.

We can see that Hartshorne has managed to elicit a great deal from his initial assertion, "Something exists." Starting from that primary claim, he has concluded that concrete actuality, experience, time, causality, and creative freedom are all metaphysical principles. They are exemplified by all reality, and it is further necessary that some entities exhibiting these characteristics do exist. "Something exists" means that necessarily and without alternative something temporal, creative, feeling filled, and social exists. In short, it means that finite, contingent entities characterized by both the power or capacity to prehend and be influenced by the past world and the power or capacity, in turn, to effect and condition all future worlds cannot fail to occur. That there are contingent and finite entities and that they have this twofold power is the basic metaphysical meaning to be placed

---

[50] LP, 310. Keeling ("Feeling as a Metaphysical Category," 60) adamantly disputes this claim, arguing that "there is no possible behavior on the part of an electron or the universe as a whole which is sufficiently analogous to human behavior to make it possible to apply the word 'feel' in its ordinary sense to either."

upon "Something exists"; to be at all is to possess the power of social relation, the power to receive from the past and to give to the future. In
Chapters 5 and 6 we shall examine what this double power means in terms
of divine reality, but before turning to this question it is necessary to ask
how Hartshorne's vision takes account of the contrasts to the categories that
have been set forth, how he includes those polar opposites he deems so
important.

Polar Contrasts

Hartshorne contends that a valid philosophy must not only be able to
argue its own perspectives but must also be able to take account of its rivals'
concerns and to do this not merely by denying these concerns but by
somehow incorporating them within its framework. He is convinced, as in
his own way was Barth, that classical metaphysics with its concentration
upon independent , self-sufficient, timeless being or substance did not—
indeed could not—adequately deal with temporal and relative process.
However, he is equally convinced that the reverse is not true. That is, he
maintains that actuality understood as process, creative becoming, or experience can take account of its opposite—that which does not change, is permanent and nonrelative:

> Becoming or process can be so conceived that it entirely includes its
> own contrast with being, while being cannot be conceived to include its
> contrast with becoming. More precisely, what becomes and what does
> not become (but simply is) together constitute a total reality which
> becomes.[51]

Thus, process or creative experience is the inclusive reality, and all that is
not process is an abstraction from this creative reality.[52]

We have already seen one way in which this is true for Hartshorne. The
past, as such, does not change: it is independent from (i.e., externally
related to) the present and yet is a constituent in the present experiencing
moment. The past, in a very literal sense, is not relative to but absolute in
relation to the present (WP, 116). Yet the present process or the relative
mode of actuality is the inclusive one, including the past and being relative
to it.

Another way in which the concrete process can be understood to be
inclusive is in that the concrete always includes the abstract. This Aristotelian dictum is one Hartshorne wholeheartedly and frequently cites. An
example of this (though only one among many, for this distinction covers or

---

[51] Hartshorne, "Interrogation," 321.
[52] Ibid.

has pertinence to all the others) is that every moment of process embodies the abstract principle of process itself. This principle does not have reality apart from its concrete illustration, but nonetheless it does not change. Thus, the principle of change is unchanging and permanent. In Hartshorne's words,

> Constants are abstract aspects of concrete, particular happenings. Every becoming, for instance, contains the generic trait of becoming-as-such, which does not become but simply is. The generic becoming is not more, but less, than any concrete becoming.[53]

There is a related sense in which the important contrast concrete—abstract has application for Hartshorne; it concerns the question of personal identity through time. If discrete momentary experience is the basic unit of reality, what becomes of identity through successive changes? Hartshorne contends that the older metaphysics posited an enduring entity, an ego or soul which was self-identical through all successive changes.[54] Change was incidental to that which was permanent. The opposite is the case in Hartshorne's view. Each moment of experience is numerically new, and it is a different and novel actuality.[55] Nonetheless, there is such a thing as enduring individuality or identity. Such identity consists, in this schema, of a common character that a successive line of individual momentary experiences share. That is, a succession of concrete acts or events share, through memory and anticipation, "abiding personality traits, fixed purpose and continuity of memories."[56] The units are still momentary process, but they can be understood to be identified or associated in a significant way that we call the "self."

And finally there is one last distinction, closely related to the preceding one and falling equally under the rubric of the concrete—abstract contrast, that must be examined. This is the distinction between actuality and existence. To state it succinctly, existence and actuality are not the same; existence refers to the fact that a possibility, an alternative, or a nature are somehow concretely actualized, while actuality is how it is concretized in all

[53] Hartshorne, "Divine Relativity and Absoluteness: A Reply," *Review of Metaphysics* 4 (1950) 32–33.

[54] Hartshorne, "Strict and Genetic Identity: An Illustration of the Relations of Logic to Metaphysics," in P. Henle, et al., eds., *Structure, Method and Meaning: Essays in Honor of Henry M. Sheffer* (New York: Liberal Arts, 1951) 252.

[55] A number of critics have raised questions concerning Hartshorne's conception of personal identity arguing that it does not offer a strong enough sense of self. See John Clifford Robertson, "The Concept of Person in the Thought of Charles Hartshorne and Karl Barth" (PhD. diss., Yale University, 1967) 115–19, 123; Peter A. Bertocci, "Hartshorne on Personal Identity: A Personalistic Critique," *Process Studies* 2 (1972) 216–21.

[56] Hartshorne, "Religion in Process Philosophy."

its particularity and definiteness. [57] Hartshorne states it as follows:

> The existence of a person (or of an individual "thing" in the every-day meaning) is to be contrasted with his (or its) actuality. . . . According to common usage, a person exists if his personal essence is now actualized in *any* appropriate accidents, e.g., in any appropriate concrete experiences.[58]

This distinction entails several aspects for Hartshorne. Combined with the preceding distinction, it allows Hartshorne to explain how "I exist" is true both yesterday and today, while also claiming that the final and basic mode of reality consists of momentary units of process. The particular actual moment is concrete, and existence is but an abstract feature of it. It refers only to the fact that something is, not how or what it is. A further all-important implication of this distinction is that Hartshorne claims that while "actuality can in no case be necessary" existence can indeed be necessary (CSPM, 254). He argues, that actuality is always and on all levels, divine and nondivine alike, contingent. How a possibility is actualized, the particular configuration of its emergent synthesis, is always a matter of contingent fact. But that an essence or nature is actualized might be either necessary or contingent.

In this section, it has been argued that Hartshorne asserts that "Something exists" is the fundamental metaphysical idea and, as such, it is a necessary truth, never falsifiable but universally applicable to all situations. It was further argued that when this statement, "Something exists," is interpreted within the Hartshornian schema it is seen to involve the statements that creative, temporal, determined, and determining actualities exist; that is, individuals possessing the power to be in social relation exist. And it was concluded that, according to Hartshorne, these basic ideas incorporate and make sense of their contrasting ideas. Thus, actuality and with it the capacity for social relationship, freedom, time, and causality are all metaphysical truths or ultimates. That is, it is necessary that process or creative becoming take place and that it has this character. As Hartshorne puts it,

> Becoming or creativity itself is necessary and external because it has nothing more general or ultimate above it. The contingent is that for which there is an alternative, and this always implies some more general conception embracing the alternatives. But *creativity embraces all alternatives and is indeed alternativeness itself; therefore, although particular becomings or instances of creation are contingent, that something or other becomes or is created is necessary.* (Ibid., 14)

---

[57] AD, x, 131; RSP, 205–6.
[58] Hartshorne, "Divine Relativity and Absoluteness," 40.

4.3 God and Creationist Metaphysics

Hartshorne has argued that when the metaphysical truth "Something exists" is properly explicated, it can be understood to mean creative synthesis or process necessarily exists and that all the various categories set forth above are legitimate implications or aspects of such creative synthesis. But Hartshorne wishes to make further and more far-reaching claims concerning the existence and nature of this creative process. Stated bluntly, he claims that creative process or synthesis has two contrasting forms: divine or eminent process and nondivine or ordinary process. In accord with his deeply held conviction that fundamental concepts come in pairs and receive their intrinsic meaning only through contrast with their counterparts, Hartshorne argues that

> synthesis is held to be essentially a two aspect affair; it is always and necessarily both divine and non-divine. [59]

> The necessarily existent abstraction "something" divides *a priori* into two correlative abstractions, divine or unsurpassable something and non-divine or surpassable something, or creator and creature. Both sides are equally abstract. If, then, abstraction implies necessity, "God" and "not God" must both be necessary. (CSPM, 250–51; see also, AD, 285)

There are several preliminary implications involved in these statements. The first is that both God and nondivine reality or world are metaphysical ideas for Hartshorne. That is, they are nonrestrictive, nonexclusive, clashing with no possibility or actuality. This means that they both, insofar as they are metaphysical ideas, can be known and understood by reason. Thus, Hartshorne argues, contra all Barthian assumptions, that knowledge of God is within reach of human cognitive capacities. Although specific concrete states of experience can never be known solely through metaphysical reasoning, knowledge that such states must occur and must embody a definite character or nature is possible for reason. While for Barth no valid knowledge of God is possible outside the milieu of revelation and faith experience, according to Hartshorne there is indeed legitimate and valid knowledge available to reason; knowledge of God is, on a metaphysical level, a universal possibility.

A further implication of Hartshorne's claim that both God and the world have a metaphysical status is that they are both necessary. Divine and nondivine experience are correlates, and neither can be denied without destroying the meaning of the other. This assertion also runs counter to all of Barth's assumptions, for while he could concur that God could not fail to

---

[59] Hartshorne, "Philosophy of Creative Synthesis," *The Journal of Philosophy* 55 (1958) 951.

exist, he adamantly insists that the world is not the result of any necessity but rather the product of God's entirely gratuitous decision. God and the world do indeed go together in the Barthian schema, but this is because of the free act on God's part and reflects no primordial necessity whatsoever. For Barth, God could have remained alone with no creation at all; God would have been different but no less God. For Hartshorne, this is not so. The status of necessary existence applies equally to divine and nondivine reality. How God and world differ will be discussed at a later point in the analysis, but at this juncture it will suffice to say that God and world, as contrasting forms of creative synthesis, metaphysically imply one another. Therefore Hartshorne concludes the following:

> Many theologians have taken it for granted that if God is free to create this or that he must be free to create nothing at all, i.e., not to create. But this is, to me at least, counter intuitive. For a creative being not to create at all is for it not to exist as creator. . . . Moreover, since any world is better than none at all (there is no value in nonentity), it would be wrong or be foolish of God not to create. But God cannot do wrong or be foolish. I conclude that not only does divine freedom imply contingency both in God and in the world, but that if there is necessity in God there is necessity in the world.[60]

Another all-important ramification of Hartshorne's claim that God and world are further specifications of "creative synthesis" is that any understanding of either of them will reflect the understanding of creative process set forth in the preceding section. That is, as contrasting aspects of creative synthesis or social process, both God and world exemplify, though in qualitatively distinct manners, the categories developed above. This means, on the one hand, that God must be interpreted according to the categories of creative process but, on the other hand, that such interpretation permits analogical comparison between divine and nondivine forms of creative experience. Thus, Hartshorne, unlike Barth, has a natural basis for analogical language concerning God and the world. As will be clear subsequently, there are differences in principle between the two but as contrasting aspects of creative process, similar though carefully qualified language is legitimate in relation to God and the world; they are not, in this schema, "wholly other."

Divine Perfection

It is not my intention in the present context to articulate Hartshorne's

---

[60] Ibid., 264–65; see also, Hartshorne, "Process and the Nature of God," in George F. McLean, ed., *Traces of God in a Secular Culture* (Staten Island, New York: Alba House, 1973) 127–28.

numerous proofs for the existence of God but rather at this juncture merely to indicate how he thinks the idea of preeminent process or God arises. As has been argued above, for Hartshorne the ideas of divine and nondivine experience are intrinsically and irrevocably correlative to one another. The basic and often-voiced rationale that he gives for such a claim is simply that every basic idea implies an equally basic contrasting form and that such ideas are given their meaning and significance within the context of this contrast. And the idea of eminent divine process emerges through the simple, though necessary, contrast of surpassable or ordinary or limited social experience with its opposite form of *un*surpassable social process. Reflection on the former leads inevitably to the idea of the latter; from a clear understanding of "surpassable by others" is derived the idea of "unsurpassable by others."[61] In Hartshorne's words, "The recognition of ourselves as beings surpassed by others in power, wisdom, duration, and other positive traits yields, by simple contrast, that of the being unsurpassable by others" (NTOT, 128). Hence, the conception of eminent social process is the natural and necessary corollary to the idea of ordinary social experience.

Further, it is precisely such a notion of "unsurpassable being" that is meant by the idea of God. "'God' is the name," according to Hartshorne, "for the one who is unsurpassable by any conceivable being other than himself" (ibid.). "God" signifies that reality which is uniquely excellent and superior in relation to all others (PSG, 7). And he asserts that this philosophical definition of deity as unsurpassable in excellence and superiority is exactly what is entailed in the religious conception of God as the reality who is worthy of devotion and worship. For Hartshorne, the very ideas of worship, devotion, and love that are at the heart of the religious vision entail that their object be beyond all rivalry and competition (NTOT, 129). "That God surpasses all is implied . . . by his being the proper object of worship. If he could have a rival we should not know whether to worship him or some other" (CSPM, 261). Thus, the religious idea of a worshipful being is not opposed to or different than his philosophical conception of deity. Rather, Hartshorne is convinced that a sufficiently reflective understanding of the religious object and the philosophical one will yield the conviction that they are really the same. Finally, in contrast to Barth, both secular and religious thinking lead him to similar conclusions.[62]

The idea of God refers to that reality which is unsurpassable and has no rivals. But, Hartshorne claims, this superiority and excellence must not be

---

[61] NTOT, 40, 128, 129; CSPM, 261. For Hartshorne the opposite procedure is also possible; that is, one could begin with the idea of unsurpassable being and, by contrast, reach the idea of surpassable or nondivine being.

[62] CSPM, 261; NTOT, 129–30. Hartshorne treats the religious vision as universally the same. Although he acknowledges the different rituals and detailed beliefs or dogmas of the various historical religions, they ultimately have the same object of experience.

understood as merely an "unusually high degree of merit" (PSG, 7). This excellence is not only a matter of difference in degree. Unsurpassability must designate a difference in kind; it is a categorical superiority, a "superiority in principle, a definite conceptual divergence from every other being" (ibid.). Unsurpassability refers not only to quantitative distinction between the superior and the inferior forms of reality but to qualitative and categorical differences. And "perfection" is the term used by Hartshorne to indicate this categorical difference between that unsurpassable reality, God, and all other realities.

Hartshorne contends that he and the classical tradition that he rejects both understand that a perfect reality is to be understood as intrinsically superior to all else (ibid.). However, he also contends that the classical tradition conceived of this perfection in a one-sided or single-polar manner. Perfection, in most theological and philosophical thought, meant only immutable, complete, and absolute unsurpassability or excellence. In this tradition change was an indication of inferiority, and God, being superior, was understood as unsurpassable by virtue of the fact of being one complete essence/existence/act which was the actualization of all values, complete in perfection and incapable of growth or alteration of any kind. That is, God has been conceived, for the most part, to exemplify only one side of the basic categorical contrast while nondivine realities were relegated to the other, so-called inferior, side. Hartshorne thoroughly rejects this manner of construing perfection. According to the tenets of Hartshorne's metaphysics of creative synthesis, God exemplifies—indeed is—both sides of all metaphysical or categorical contrasts.[63] In a social perspective, Hartshorne asserts:

> God is not merely on one side only of categorical contrasts, he is not merely infinite or merely finite, merely absolute or merely relative, merely cause or merely effect, merely agent or merely patient, merely actual or merely potential, but in all cases both, each in suitable respects or aspects of his living reality, and in such a manner as to make him unsurpassable by another. (NTOT, 74–75)

Stated succinctly, Hartshorne argues that traditionally perfection, defined within the context of a substance metaphysics, was identified with that which is absolute, unchanging, and utterly independent. However, his conviction, developed according to the tenets of a metaphysics of creative becoming, is that social relation, and with it process and dependence, admit

---

[63] Hartshorne, "The God of Religion and the God of Philosophy," in *Talk of God, Royal Institute of Philosophy Lectures, vol. 2, 1967–68* (London: Macmillan, 1969) 162; PSG, 24; NTOT, 74–75, 128; AW, 22. As will be seen later in the analysis, God also includes within Godself the contrast of unsurpassable—surpassable by virtue of the fact that God includes within Godself all nondivine reality.

equally superior forms (CSPM, 231). And he is further convinced that this claim is not simply the imposition of his speculative notions upon the idea of perfection but that just as the analysis of "Something exists" yielded a social and dynamic interpretation, so too will the analysis of perfection.

Hartshorne suggests that the idea of unsurpassability or superiority-to-all-others involves a certain ambiguity; it can mean either unsurpassed both by other individuals and by Godself in any divine state whatsoever, or it can mean unsurpassed by all other but self-surpassing in each subsequent moment of experience (PSG, 105; RSP, 112; MVG, 158). The classical tradition, with its basically static conception of being, accepted the first interpretation of perfection as axiomatic, while Hartshorne, with his conception of dynamic and progressive experience, argues for the second. In his view, superiority-to-all-others "admits of two profoundly contrasting though analogous forms," (RSP, 112) unsurpassable superiority and self-surpassing superiority. These two forms he labels variously as "Absolute" or "Static Perfection" and "Relative" or "Dynamic Perfection."

Hartshorne wholeheartedly agrees with the tradition—and with, I think, Barth as well—that there is a sense in which perfection is absolute, sheerly maximal, and incapable of increase. But he suggests that such absolute perfection is comprehensible, within a dynamic and social vision, only in terms of those values or categories that can be understood, without contradiction, to admit upper limits of realization. Such categories or values are, according to Hartshorne, only those which are *"neutral to the distinction between actual and possible"* (ibid., 121). That is, God is perfect in an absolute and static sense only in terms of those dimensions of experience to which changing, concrete conditions make no difference whatsoever. And Hartshorne argues that in a social vision such neutrality to conditions refers not to the content of actual relations but to the types or kinds of relation:

> Now some ways of measuring value which are proper in theology have the required neutrality; for they refer to a *type of relation* (between a being and other actual or possible beings) that can be at its best regardless of how many of which possible other beings are actual. This type of relation may be called "adequacy." (Ibid.)

This adequacy of relation, or static perfection, means that no matter what conditions prevail, no matter with whom God interacts, God will be related to those situations and social partners in a perfect and unvarying manner. Omniscience, as an absolute type of relation, means that whatever is actual or possible God will know perfectly and fully. Or alternatively, whatever situations occur, God will respond with a never-changing righteousness or ethical purpose (NTOT, 19). As types of relation, knowledge, power, will, and love can all be understood as maximal, inflexible, and admitting of no alternative (MVG, 35; NTOT, 44).

The result of such absoluteness is that God has a certain independence of any particular world. Because God is related always and in a never-varying manner of adequacy to any and every world, there is a sense in which it makes no difference whatsoever what world does in fact occur. Hence, in this schema, independence signifies a neutrality or indifference to alternatives (DR, 72). God, insofar as God is absolute, is tolerant of all alternatives or possibilities; the divine adequacy of relation entails that God's existence is compatible with any and every actuality and possibility and that the manner of divine relation to such actuality and possibility will be of an unchanging and fixed character.

What this absoluteness does not imply is nonrelationship. Within the context of a metaphysics that defines actuality in terms of social relationship, absolute perfection cannot mean lack of social connectedness but only a tolerance toward and a uniform mode of relating to all situations. According to Hartshorne, "The absoluteness of God need not imply his nonrelationship to the creation *as such*, but only to the contingent alternatives of creation" (ibid., 73–74).

Furthermore, perfection interpreted according to the tenets of a philosophy of creative synthesis, has as well another form, and indeed the very understanding of absolute perfection as adequacy of relation indicates or points to a way in which God is neither absolute nor independent but relative and dependent. For, according to Hartshorne, if God always relates to the world in an adequate manner, then the content or concrete instances of such relationship will necessarily change as the world changes. God, in order to relate perfectly, will need to adapt to all changing conditions. Absoluteness, interpreted as a fixed relational mode, therefore, has as its necessary corollary the relativity of each instance of divine experience that exemplifies the relational adequacy.

Hartshorne argues that there are other insights growing out of his social vision that support this claim. In the classical tradition divine perfection, as never varying and always absolute, entailed that God could not increase in value but rather God possessed, as actual, all value in the one unchanging divine experience. However, Hartshorne argues, on the one hand, that not all values are compossible; there are positive alternatives that conflict and cannot be actualized at the same moment. Therefore it is impossible for one being, even God, to possess all values at once (RSP, 203). Only a vision that admits a dynamic dimension of perfection can account for this. On the other hand, further support for this conviction concerning dynamic perfection arises from the recognition that certain dimensions of value can indeed admit no sheer maximal unit (CSPM, 242–43). For a dynamic vision that affirms the progressive, creative, and growing character of experience, there are dimensions of experience that are open-ended, always capable of increase, and hence, no maximal case is ever possible in relation to these (MVG, 35). God as preeminent creative experience no less than creaturely experience cannot reach a completed and finished state with reference to them. Hartshorne suggests that such open dimensions include happiness, aesthetic experience or beauty, and knowledge as concretely experienced (RSP, 121). Each of these aspects of experience are not neutral to the social world but depend upon the particular entities in that world; the content and contour of divine happiness, aesthetic enjoyment, and knowledge all depend upon the world as God's relational partner, and as that world alters, so too does God's own experience. There are several further aspects concerning this claim of relative or dynamic perfection.

First, such relationship between God and the world does not indicate that God might have a possible rival. Rather, because God's mode of relating is always perfect in adequacy, then in each moment of experience God possesses the maximal amount of value that is possible. God, as the perfect prehender of the world, experiences and includes in Godself all that is, both actual and possible. No other being could possibly rival God in value for every possible rival could represent but a fragment of the value possessed by God and would be intrinsically inferior. However, because certain dimensions of value admit increase and reality is ever changing and growing, God can indeed surpass Godself in each succeeding state of experience. In this sense God is self-contrasting (PSG, 10; RSP, 116, 124). In any state, God is always superior to all other realities, but in God's own subsequent states God can admit growth. God is, thus, the self-surpassing surpasser of all or the reflexively superior being.[64]

Second, although God changes in every moment, Hartshorne maintains that there is still continuity throughout such changes. Working along the lines set forth in the previous section concerning personal identity through time, Hartshorne argues that each successive state, though different in experiential content, will nonetheless embody perfection in both its absolute and relative forms; each new moment will exemplify the divine character and identity and thus be identifiable as the experience of the one God (LP, 41; see also AD, 293).

Third, the assertion that God grows, in certain aspects, in value, and changes as the world changes entails the assumption, that God, as a social experiencer, is literally related to and dependent upon the world as God's social partner. In a social vision, relation, both preeminent and ordinary, entails dependence. But God's relativity or dependence, just as God's independence, is of a categorically superior sort. Whereas the tradition understood dependence as a mark of inferiority, Hartshorne argues that dependence or the power of social relativity, in its superior, divine form, is an excellence beyond all rivalry. That is, all other entities are related to and dependent upon a fragment of the existing realities, while God, as perfect in

---

[64] DR, 19–22. Gunton (*Becoming and Being,* 16, 24–25) criticizes Hartshorne's vision of dynamic perfection as being too "quantitative" and argues that God's superiority, in this schema, can only be judged by the amount of God's experience.

social power, is literally and adequately related to all. According to Hartshorne's view,

> To be relative in the eminent sense will (accordingly) be to enjoy rela-
> tions to all that is in all its aspects. Supreme dependence will thus
> reflect all influences—with infinite sensitivity registering relationship to
> the last and least item of events. Is this not genuinely something
> eminent and supreme? (DR, 76)

Therefore, God's relativity is universal in scope and sensitivity. But beyond this universal range of dependence there is also a sense in which relative or reflective superiority is absolute. According to Hartshorne, it is true that God, as the preeminent social reality, will be literally related to every nondivine reality no matter what circumstances prevail; just as God's independence signified a certain indifference to all particular alternatives, so too does God's preeminent relativity:

> God is relative, but what we may call the extent of his relativity is
> wholly independent of circumstances, wholly non-relative. Regardless
> of circumstances, of what happens anywhere and when, God will enjoy
> unrestricted cognitive relativity to all that coexists with him. . . . God is
> not, it is true, *simpliciter* "independent," but the generic manner or
> universal extent of his dependence is his unique and wholly indepen-
> dent possession. (Ibid., 82)

Hartshorne, thus, argues that perfection is a more complex notion than the classical tradition has understood it to be. He rejects the traditional identification of absoluteness and perfection and instead suggests, from the perspective of a philosophy of creative synthesis, perfection must be conceived of both statically or absolutely, and dynamically or relatively. God is superior or transcendent in a dual fashion. On the one hand, God as abso-
lute and unvarying surpasses all other entities and is unself-surpassing as well. In this aspect God is omnitolerant of all other realities, and hence both the fact of God's existence and the divine character which is exemplified in all divine relationships are absolute and indifferent to the conditions of the world; God always exists and always exists as Godself. On the other hand, Hartshorne argues that God as supremely relative surpasses all nondivine entities and also is self-surpassing and capable of increase, growth, and change. In this aspect God is supremely sensitive and responsive and changes as God's worldly counterpart changes.

Hartshorne holds these two distinct aspects of divine perfection together by invoking the distinction between abstract and concrete. God, as relative and internally related to all, is God as actual and concrete, God as the supreme instance of creative process who will subsequently become available for the world to experience in its turn. God as concrete both receives the world and in turn offers Godself to the world just as any noneminent

form of creative synthesis does, but on a preeminent scale. The absolute and unvarying dimension of perfection refers to an abstract aspect of that concrete reality. God as absolute and independent is but an abstraction from the primary divine concrete actuality. Further, the concrete is always inclusive of the abstract, not vice versa. Therefore, it is divine relativity that includes and makes sense of divine independence. Thus, Hartshorne declares:

> The Absolute is God with something left out of account. . . . I am argu-ing that the absolute is . . . an abstract feature of the inclusive and supreme reality which is precisely the personal God. . . . The absolute is not more, but less, than God—in the obvious sense in which the abstract is less than the concrete. (Ibid., 83)

Divine Necessary Existence

Another way of stating this distinction was suggested in the preceding section and has also been implicitly assumed throughout the present analysis: that is, the distinction between existence/essence and concrete actuality. Hartshorne's argument is that existence and essence refer to the fact that something occurs while actuality refers to how it takes place, to the concrete reality in all its uniqueness and particularity. Hartshorne also argued that all such actuality, divine and nondivine alike, as social and tem-poral, is always contingent and never necessary. Hence, it cannot be known by reason in any a priori or metaphysical sense, but can only be encountered after the fact; that is, it can only be an object for a posteriori knowledge. However, existence/essence concerns a different level of reality and of knowledge. According to Hartshorne, it is not self-evident that existence can only be contingent. In ordinary cases it is indeed contingent; certain conditions or the occurrence (or nonoccurrence) of other events could mean I or any other nondivine reality might not exist in any state of actuality at all. Existence for nondivine individuals is as precarious and contingent as is actuality. However, and this is one of Hartshorne's most adamantly argued points, in relation to divine reality existence is not contingent but rather is uniquely necessary.

Necessity, in Hartshorne's view, signifies a neutrality toward alternatives, an indifference toward varying conditions. And according to this view, when such neutrality toward alternatives is explicated to its fullest it means that no matter what conditions prevail, God will always be in some concrete state or other. To exist means to Hartshorne to be actualized in some con-crete state or momentary experience; to exist necessarily entails that some such actualization will take place. However, although some such actualiza-tion always occurs, just which particular divine event does take place in any given moment is a contingent matter, a question answered only by the moment-by-moment interaction of God and the world. Thus, for God as for all other reality, existence/essence and actuality are distinct; the former is abstract and the latter concrete. And while necessity of existence indicated that divine actuality or creative synthesis is necessary and will inevitably have a certain character, it yields no information concerning the explicit how of that synthesis (AD, 235).

With this claim of necessary existence and its distinction from divine actuality we have come full circle to where this section commenced; that is, we have reached once more the Hartshornian assertion that the idea of God (at least as it pertains to divine existence), or alternatively, that the concept of perfection has the status of metaphysical truth. As was argued in 4.2 above, the mark of metaphysical ideas is their nonrestrictive, nonexclusive nature. And divine existence, as omniflexible and universally relative, has just this nature. "The concept of perfection is non-specific, non-exclusive, non-restrictive, its exemplification being compatible with the existence of any positively conceivable state of affairs" (LP, 70). Further, because it is thus compatible with any conditions whatever, no conditions could therefore falsify it. And as Hartshorne argued above, it is the sign of contingent truth that it can be falsified and the intrinsic trait of metaphysical or necessary truth that it cannot be so contradicted. Thus, insofar as divine existence is universally tolerant, it can be understood to be necessary and as such a proper object of metaphysical inquiry. According to Hartshorne, therefore, divine existence or the existence of perfection are metaphysical ideas capable of elucidation a priori and apart from the specifics of any contingent reality. They are a matter for metaphysical analysis, not empirical or a posteriori inquiry. They are logical or philosophical questions, not historical ones. Concerning the question of divine existence, Hartshorne declares, "Not warm emotions but cold logic and intense intellectuality alone can ever resolve it. Here I am an ultra-rationalist."[65] Thus, while God's actual states, which are incomparably richer, elude all a priori reasoning, that there are such states can be known by all who analyze the meaning of unsurpassability or perfection.

Hartshorne has spent much of his intellectual effort in the elucidation of this metaphysical or a priori approach to divine existence through his formulation of a neoclassical version of the ontological argument.[66] It is beyond

---

[65] Hartshorne, "Is God's Existence a State of Affairs?," in John Hick, ed., *Faith and the Philosophers* (London: Macmillan, 1964) 32.

[66] There are numerous places to examine Hartshorne's position concerning the argument. See esp. LP, passim; AD, passim; "What did Anselm Discover?," in John Hick and Arthur C. McGill, eds., *The Many Faced Argument* (New York: Macmillan, 1967), 321–33; "The Formal Validity and Real Significance of the Ontological Argument," *The Philosophical Review* 53 (1944) 225–45; and "Introduction to the Second Edition," *Saint Anselm: Basic Writings* (LaSalle, Illinois: Open Court, 1962) 1–19. The secondary sources on this topic are also numerous. See esp. Goodwin, *Ontological Argument*, passim; Peters, *Hartshorne and Neoclassical Metaphysics*, chap. 5; Robert D. Shofner, *Anselm Revisited* (Leiden: Brill, 1974) passim; J. N.

the scope of this thesis to examine thoroughly Hartshorne's version of the age-old proof for God's existence. Nonetheless, it is important to make explicit several of the central features of this Hartshornian proof (most of which were part of the preceding analysis).

Hartshorne asserts that Anselm of Cantebury, in his famous attempt to formulate an ontological proof, actually developed two arguments instead of the ordinarily assumed one.[67] The first formula argued that since existence is better than nonexistence, God, as the perfect being, must exist. However, this seemed to make existence a predicate, a possibility logicians have long disputed; and it seemed to have argued from a concept or abstraction to a concrete reality, another move long considered philosophically illegitimate. Hartshorne is in full agreement with the argument's critics that this version of the proof fails (NTOT, 29). However, he asserts that Anselm also developed a second far stronger version. In this form, existence is not contrasted with nonexistence, but contingent existence is contrasted with necessary existence, and, it is argued, perfection entails the latter, not the former (AD, 156). That is, Hartshorne argues that while existence is not a predicate, the modality of existence is (LP, 50). This claim requires elucidation.

Hartshorne argues that something can exist as possible (it does not exist but might), as contingent (it does exist but might not), as impossible (it does not exist and never could), and as necessary (it exists and cannot fail to exist). Ordinary contingent entities form the first two modes of existence; their possible or actual existence is contingent, dependent upon circumstances. And as such that contingency or mode of existence, is necessary; a contingent entity could only have that modality. Completely negative or, for Hartshorne, self-contradictory entities entail the second mode; their existence is impossible and not only contingently so but by necessity. And finally, divine existence or perfection entails the mode of necessary existence; it is neither impossible nor contingent. Its mode of existence is thereby necessary. Hartshorne concludes from this that the modality, the way an entity exists, as contingent or necessary, is knowable and provable from an understanding of what that entity is; the definition will tell us the mode of existence proper to any entity. In Hartshorne's words, "*Modality of existence is always a property* and is always deducible from the definition of a thing. By modality I mean the kind of existence appropriate to a definition,

---

Findlay, "Some Reflections on Necessary Existence," in William Reese and Eugene Freeman, eds., *Process and Divinity* (LaSalle, Illinois: Open Court, 1964) 515–27; John B. Cobb, Jr., "'Perfection Exists': A Critique of Charles Hartshorne," *Religion in Life* 32 (1963) 294–304.

[67] LP, 24–27; AD, passim; Hartshorne (AD, 11, 13), who disagrees with Barth's interpretation of the arguments, has high praise, nonetheless, for Barth's recognition that there were two forms of the argument.

whether contingent, necessary or impossible existence."[68] And Hartshorne argues that perfection, as he has conceived it, involves the necessary, not contingent, mode of existence; only its existence, not its alternative, is conceivable. Therefore, for him, the status of perfection can only be "that of necessary exemplification in reality" (LP, 50). Thus, the true contrast is not between existence and nonexistence, but contingent and necessary modes of existence.[69] And hence, he argues, the difficulties surrounding the claim that existence is a property are circumvented by asserting that the modality of existence is what is the property. Thus, Hartshorne believes he has salvaged the ontological argument on that disputed point.

However, Hartshorne also argues that this ontological argument is only valid in relation to neoclassical or creationist metaphysics which makes the distinction between existence and actuality. For, he concurs with the proof's critics that the concrete cannot be adduced from the abstract and argues that a metaphysics that distinguishes existence and actuality is all that can avoid this dilemma.[70] Neoclassical metaphysics, contrary to classical metaphysics, argues from the idea of perfection, an abstraction, to the existence of perfection, equally an abstraction. This latter abstraction implies that there must be some actuality, but it does not specify anything concrete about such actual states. Thus Hartshorne can state:

> The whole point of what Anselm discovered, if anything, was that the mere "existence" of God is entirely metaphysical, not factual. Findlay draws the plausible conclusion that God is therefore no conceivable actuality, but only an empty or absurd abstraction. Classical theism cannot, I hold, fairly rebut this charge. Neoclassical theism, however, distinguishes existence and actuality, and does this in reference not only to God but to all things. What is exceptional about God is that in Him alone is it possible to treat existence as not only different, but different *modally*, from actuality, i.e., so that the one is necessary, the other contingent. The "actualized somehow" here covers such an absolute infinity of variability in the particular possible hows of actualization that all possibility is included, and hence there can be no possibility that the divine existence will be simply unactualized. (AD, 78–79)

Thus, from the idea of perfection or deity, we cannot deduce God's concrete actuality, the particular social experience that constitute's God's life, but we can argue from the idea to the conclusion that perfection, by its nature, must be necessarily exemplified or actualized in some concrete state or other. That is, the idea of God or divine perfection can lead us to infer

---

[68] Hartshorne, "What Did Anselm Discover?," 326.

[69] Goodwin (*Ontological Argument*, passim) offers an excellent treatment of the modal character of Hartshorne's argument.

[70] Hartshorne, "Introduction," 13; LP, 27.

that a perfect being exists while not yielding any concrete information concerning how.[71]

Therefore, Hartshorne's general conclusions are that divine existence is a logical, a priori question and never a factual one and that, further, all proofs relating to divine reality are a priori in character (CSPM, 258, 279; MVG, 29). There are no a posteriori proofs arguing from contingent particularities to necessary truth. This means that empirical theism and empirical atheism alike are "logical blunders" or "logical monstrosities" (NTOT, x). Empirical facts, contingent in nature, prove nothing for or against a divine existence which is omnitolerant of all alternatives (AD, 4). The only question which is truly relevant is whether the idea of perfection or of a perfect being makes any sense or has any meaning at all.[72] It is here that the true challenge comes for Hartshorne, not from empirical atheism or theism but from a positivism which argues that the idea of perfection from which the proof proceeds is, when examined, nonsensical. Hence, Hartshorne's two real choices concerning the question of divine reality are a priori theism, or a priori atheism or positivism. In this view, "Positivism and theism taken as necessarily true: these exhaust the reasonable views: and the choice between them is no question of fact but of meaning, whether the definition of deity makes sense."[73]

God and the World: Distinction and Identification

This section began by stating that Hartshorne argues that the metaphysical idea "Something exists" can be further specified to mean "Something divine exists" and "Something nondivine exists." It has been the purpose of the present analysis to elucidate this claim for divine reality through the explication of the idea of divine perfection according to the tenets of Hartshorne's social metaphysics. Through this inquiry it was possible to see how and why Hartshorne claims metaphysical status for the idea of divine perfection, and also how he safeguards, through his steadfast distinction of existence/essence and actuality, the character of creative synthesis in relation to divine actuality. But he also, as was stated at the outset, argued that

---

[71] Goodwin (*Ontological Argument*, passim) once more offers an excellent examination of the relation between the abstract and concrete in this issue.

[72] Cobb ("Perfection Exists," 298–301) argues that while Hartshorne avoids a number of the logical difficulties traditionally connected with the ontological argument, he nonetheless has not truly established it, for, Cobb argues, Hartshorne's position depends upon the prior acceptance of a creationist ontology. And while Hartshorne asserts this is the only acceptable ontology, Cobb believes other ontologies might also be possible and with them different assessments of the status and meaning of "existence" and "perfection." Thus the question is not just whether perfection makes sense, but what kind of perfection and what kind of ontology are being considered.

[73] Hartshorne, "What Did Anselm Discover?," 327–28.

"surpassable" (i.e., imperfect) reality also exist by necessity, that God and some world are equally necessary correlates; in a socially defined philosophy they imply one another. We must ask how God can be said to be different than the world which is God's, so to speak, social counterpart.

Hartshorne's answer is that God is an individual and the world is a class of entities. He argues that some world must exist but that this does not mean some specific individual. It only entails that the class of contingent, nondivine entities must not be null or empty. Necessary existence refers only, on the nondivine level, to the class, not to the nondivine entities which instantiate that necessary existence. However, in relation to God this is not so, and God's unique status is reflected in several ways. First, God necessarily exists and each state of divine experience must embody the divine character or essence. Each divine social experience or creative synthesis instantiates the same divine individuality (AD, 291).

Second, God is the only individual with universal functions. Only God is related to everything that exists or could exist. God alone prehends all actuality and all possibility, and only God becomes the universal object for all subsequent prehensions. God alone is universal subject and object. The sphere of interaction for all nondivine realities is severely limited. Only God, as the preeminent form of creative synthesis, of perfect social power, is coextensive with all reality. Hartshorne argues that as coextensive with reality as both actual and possible, God is the measure of all that is and finally as well, the ground of possibility for that which might be (LP, 38, 137; NTOT, 71–72; AD, 123). God as preeminent social process is both an individual, unified and internally coherent, and finally reality itself. In Hartshorne's words,

> If I have called God an "individual" this is with the understanding that, as the unique because unsurpassable individual, he is absolutely cosmic or universal in his capacities, interacting with *all* others, relevant to *all* contexts, and in this sense absolutely universal—the only strictly universal individual or individual universal. (NTOT, 136; see also LP, 92–93, 115; AD, 58)

And finally, it must be stated that because of such necessary existence and corresponding universal functions, divine individuality is the only individuality that can be specified through concepts alone and hence a priori. Such individuality is thoroughly abstract and hence requires no reference to facts to give it meaning. According to Hartshorne, "God is the only individual identifiable by abstractions alone. This does not imply that God is merely abstract entity, but only that what makes him God and no other individual is abstract" (CSPM, 246). All other realities need factual material or information to specify their individuality while only the most general conceptions, such as perfect power or knowledge, are needed to "individuate" God (DR, 31).

Hence, while the world is necessary, such necessity refers only to a class of multiple possibilities, none of which is necessary in itself. Only God as preeminent reality must exist as a unified, integrated individual. That is the mark of the unique status of unsurpassable perfection: to be individual, necessary, and universal all at once.

In closing this section it can be stated that for Hartshorne the world consists of the plurality of nondivine, contingent events to which God as the preemeinent social individual is related. As the subsequent chapter of this study will explicate, Hartshorne comes to understand this relation between God, as the universal individual related to all reality, to mean finally that God is the cosmic synthesis of that plurality; that is, God, as preeminent process, is the integration and unification of all reality. The world and God are, in the end, contrasting forms of the creative process which is reality— the one being the multiplicity of fragmented and noninclusive experiences and the other the creative unification of all localized and contingent events. The world and God are different ways of looking at (or perhaps different levels of) the same creative activity which is finally reality interpreted as social, temporal, creative, and sentient.

This intimate connection between the two forms of creative synthesis means finally that metaphysics and natural theology are the same. A thorough explication of either one leads Hartshorne to the other. It is his conviction that " 'neoclassical metaphysics,' when its ideas are adequately explicated, is neoclassical natural theology and vice versa" (CSPM, 40).

Thus finally, metaphysics and natural theology yield the same truth to Hartshorne: both God and some world exist necessarily. Knowledge that they are actualized somehow and that such actualization is best understood as creative, progressive synthesis is within the capacity of human cognitive power. Nonetheless, concrete and particular actuality, on both divine and nondivine levels, is always beyond the grasp of a priori reason; to know that truth, it must in the end be encountered not as a general, nonrestrictive truth but the living, unique reality it is.

4.4 Summary Remarks

It is now possible to set forth and examine in detail Hartshorne's conception of what divine power means within the context of his process metaphysics. But prior to turning to that task, it is important to summarize the contrast that has been emerging in the foregoing analysis between Hartshorne and Barth.

In agreement with Barth, Hartshorne has argued that God is such that relationship is primary. In contrast to much of the classical tradition, both Hartshorne and Barth begin with the notion of relationship and each attempts to develop a consistently relational interpretation of divine reality. However, for Barth, while the internal trinitarian relationship may be a necessary one, God's relationship with the world is purely gratuitous and the existence of creaturely reality at all is a product of God's free and gracious act. Hartshorne argues, on the other hand, that relationship is central to the meaning of reality itself. To be is to be related, and this is true, in Hartshorne's view, for every entity from minute molecules to the cosmic whole. Thus, while both argue for the centrality and fundamental importance of the divine-world relation, Hartshorne and Barth interpret such relation in radically different ways.

Hartshorne's position also concurs with the one developed by Barth in that for both, God's concrete acts of relationship are not rationally deducible but can only be encountered. This concrete relationship transcends reason and can only, be experienced, according to Hartshorne, as sheer fact. However, once more the interpretation of this transcendent character of divine actuality is radically divergent for Hartshorne and Barth. On the one hand, all actuality, nondivine as well as divine, has this transcendent nature. All particular concrete reality can only be known a posteriori. On the other hand, while God as concrete must be encountered, such an encounter is, for Hartshorne, a universal possibility—indeed a necessity. That is, God as cosmic subject and object is the one certain and inevitable datum of experience for nondivine entities. For Barth, this is not the case; God is known, not as an inevitable datum of experience, but as the one who chooses to reveal Godself to certain, not all, creatures. For Barth, awareness of God is finally the result of divine free decision, while for Hartshorne, it is the nature of reality that God is known.

Furthermore, Hartshorne claims that not only is God, as actual, necessarily encountered a posteriori or empirically, but that, moreover, it can be known by reason alone that God exists and that God has a certain nature. For Barth knowledge of God's existence/essence and actuality are alike beyond human reason, while knowledge of the divine existence/essence is philosophically accessible for Hartshorne.

Hartshorne's convictions concerning these matters lead him to suggest that there are two different approaches to knowledge of God. The first is the one he has chosen to pursue and which this chapter has attempted to explicate. It is the philosophical or metaphysical analysis of experience which deals not with unique and novel aspects of reality but with the constant and necessary features of all experience. And God, as unsurpassable or perfect being, is precisely the most important and preeminent form of all such cosmic features. The second is the empirical approach, which is a posteriori in nature and concerns itself with the articulation of what might be termed the concrete encounter with God. But because God is a constituent of all experience this approach involves just about everything from the natural sciences to personal or communal revelatory experiences. On this level, all reality reveals the glory of God. For Barth, on the other hand, there is but one narrowly circumscribed approach to knowledge of God, and that is the revelation of God in Jesus Christ. All other experiences must be interpreted from this perspective. Knowledge gained from other sources can lead neither to true knowledge of God nor the world but only to the projection of the sinful and broken human image onto reality itself.

Thus, Hartshorne and Barth can be understood to offer distinct and contrasting approaches to knowledge of God which are grounded in fundamentally divergent principles. While they both develop significantly new positions in relation to the classical tradition, they stand in opposition to one another as well. Indeed, this opposition is so extreme that it is possible to conclude that these two thinkers are referring to very different realities when they speak of God; from Barth's perspective, the Hartshornian God appears to be that product of the human mind that indicates the limits of human cognitive capacities, while from a Hartshornian view, Barth's God might be a misinterpretation of that universally experienced deity that all humans encounter. And according to the principles each has set forth the only way either thinker can deal with the other's position is to understand it as, at best, a misguided interpretation or, at worst, a human idol made in the image of a distorted human vision of itself. And not only do these positions result in the denial of the validity of the other but they do so while at the same time claiming a status of universal truth and certainty concerning their own positions; while relativizing all other views, they understand their own visions to have a validity and certitude that escapes all others. The Conclusion of this dissertation will return to this tendency toward absolutizing that Barth and Hartshorne share, but it is sufficient to say at this juncture that the principles that each set forth and the fundamental conception of God each thinker presupposes stand as radical challenges to the meaning and validity of the other's vision.

5

DIVINE POWER
ACCORDING TO HARTSHORNE

The preceding chapter carried out the explication of Charles Hartshorne's metaphysical framework and the philosophical principles that guide and ground that intellectual vision. It has been possible to arrive at several general conclusions. Fundamentally, Hartshorne asserts, with the tradition and Barth as well, that God is the one perfect being. Perfection and deity are synonymous. However, he also contends that perfection must be interpreted according to the principles of creative synthesis. And when divine perfection is so conceived, a conception of perfection emerges that is radically distinct from the one espoused by the so-called classical tradition and equally alien to the Barthian alternative. In the first place such an interpretation results in a dual notion of perfection; God is to be conceived as perfect both in a static and absolute sense and in a dynamic and relative sense. God always exists, and the divine character is stable and fixed; but God's concrete states are ever changing, growing, and acquiring new value. In the second place, and corresponding to this recognition of the dynamic dimension of perfection, the interpretation of perfection according to the tenets of a creationist metaphysics entails the assertion that God, as perfect, is not thereby wholly other than or alien to nondivine and imperfect entities. Rather, God is understood as the supreme individual exemplifying in the most perfect manner those attributes or categories exhibited in inferior form by all individuals whatsoever.[1] Hartshorne, therefore, introduces not only a dynamic element to divine perfection, but along with it a social dimension as well. The dynamic and the social are mutually implicative. However, it is important to highlight the implications that are involved in a social

---

[1] Hartshorne often seems to use attributes and categories interchangeably. When he does so, attributes can be interpreted to refer to those characteristics or qualities universally exhibited, not qualities that are unique to one segment of reality. An example of the difference is that while awareness is universally exemplified and is hence a category or general attribute, rational consciousness is a characteristic of only a small fraction of reality. In the present context, attributes are referring to the former qualities, not the narrowly exhibited latter ones.

interpretation of perfection while also noting as the analysis proceeds the repercussions of the dynamic conception.

It is metaphysically true, in the Hartshornian framework, that everything that is actual and individual, from atoms to deity, is an instance of creative becoming and thereby instantiates the categories or attributes set forth in Chapter 4 above. God, as the perfect individual, is therefore not beyond such categories but is the preeminent exemplification of the universally present categories. However, it must be stated unequivocally that the universal exhibition of these categories does not, according to Hartshorne, call into question the unique and supreme status of deity. For preeminence entails that God is not merely greater in degree but in principle is superior to all nondivine realities. On the one hand, this means that other entities only partake or share in the categories, while God is these categories (DR, 34). That is, the metaphysical categories, though exhibited by all reality, coincide with God's essence and nature. "Thus he is the literal instance (because the original one) of the categories; they are himself in his individual essence, though not . . . in his total actuality" (ibid., 36). An important implication of this coincidence of the metaphysical categories and the divine essence is that God is not subjugated to something external to Godself. God must, indeed, exemplify the metaphysical categories, but to do so is simply God's nature; it is an internal necessity not an external one.

On the other hand, the preeminent exemplification of the categories safeguards God's unique status by virtue of the fact that, in a very literal sense, God tells us what these categories mean; God, as the perfect example of these universal qualities, is thereby the sole norm by which their true meaning is elucidated. In a claim remarkably similar to Barth's position concerning this matter, Hartshorne claims that it is God who is truly creative, loving, free, and powerful and that creatures only display inferior and partial forms of these qualities.[2] Therefore, without knowledge of God, knowledge of the categories and their creaturely exemplification is incomplete and distorted. According to Hartshorne, "Self-knowledge and knowledge of God are apparently inseparable."[3] Barth would be in full agreement with such a claim. However, for Hartshorne knowledge of this divine standard is within the grasp of human cognitive capacities, while for Barth only God's self-revelation can yield true knowledge of the divine standard of excellence.

If, however, God is the preeminent and perfect exemplification of the metaphysical categories, this cannot and does not mean that God is the sole instance of any of these attributes (AD, 196). Hartshorne has argued that

---

[2] Ibid., 39, 77; Hartshorne, "Tillich's Doctrine of God," in Charles W. Kegley and Robert W. Bretall, eds., *The Theology of Paul Tillich* (New York: Macmillan, 1964) 179. Here Hartshorne even refers to Barth.

[3] Hartshorne, "The Idea of God—Literal or Analogical," *The Christian Scholar* 39 (1956) 136.

the categories entailed in creative synthesis are universally applicable, and this means every nondivine entity displays, though in a creaturely and thereby imperfect manner, those very attributes God exemplifies in a perfect fashion. Barth rejected the term "attributes" in favor of "perfections" for he was convinced that the former indicated some quality or character shared in common.[4] It is, however, precisely this shared quality or universal exemplification that Hartshorne wants to affirm. Eminence is a distinct form of exemplification, but it does not thereby deny the reality of lesser forms. In Hartshorne's words, "Divine attributes can only be eminent forms of universal or categorical aspects of reality in general."[5] Therefore, divine eminence must be interpreted in such a manner that both perfect and imperfect forms of the metaphysical categories are upheld. The interpretation of divine preeminence must always take as axiomatic this principle of the social distribution of metaphysical characteristics.

The purpose of this chapter is to develop this Hartshornian claim of the universal exemplification or social distribution of the metaphysical categories in relation to the idea of divine power. That is, I shall examine what meaning divine omnipotence can have within the framework of a philosophy which asserts that God is the chief, but not sole, instance of power. By way of accomplishing this task, I shall first explicate Hartshorne's social conception of power in general and broad terms and then develop his claims through a more specific analysis of divine power as, on the one hand, the capacity to receive influence and as, on the other hand, the power to influence and determine the world.

5.1 Divine Power as Social Power

Hartshorne develops his social interpretation of divine power in contrast to what he understands to be the traditional or classical conception of God's omnipotence. He contends that for the most part, western philosophers and theologians have offered what he labels a "monopoly notion of power" (NTOT, 120). Traditionally, divine power has been conceived as a monopolistic concentration of all real power in the one divine agent. Omnipotence interpreted as the exclusive possession of power by God entails numerous repercussions, a number of which will emerge throughout this chapter as well as the next. However, for the present purposes, it is important to note several overarching aspects of this traditional claim.

Hartshorne contends that the traditional conception of omnipotence was developed primarily, and most often exclusively, in terms of God's capacity to act, to influence, and to determine. In this view, God as the all-powerful

---

[4] See above, 2.2.
[5] Hartshorne, "Process and the Nature of God," 134.

agent is always active, never passive, always influencing, never influenced.[6] Divine power refers to the capacity to be the all-determining cause, never the determined effect. In Hartshorne's words, "It was held that while ordinary individuals interact, God's superiority is that he acts only, and does not interact" (NTOT, 134). Divine power, thus interpreted, is unilateral power, one directional in nature, never social in character.[7]

The second broad element Hartshorne discerns in the traditional notion of power is the assumption that God possessed all real power. This sometimes has been interpreted to mean that all other entities besides God are utterly lacking in power. In other instances this claim has been taken to mean that there are indeed true powers besides God but such powers are grounded in God and are real insofar as God is their source and limit. It is this latter approach that Barth develops, arguing that only God has intrinsic power, while the power of all other entities is derived and as such remains under the control and determination of God. And, further, such creaturely power does not entail a capacity to affect or influence God in and of itself but only to work within the worldly sphere. Insofar as God is altered by the world's existence, this is first and foremost a matter of divine self-determination and only secondarily and never directly a question of creaturely determination.[8]

Thus, according to Hartshorne, most philosophers and theologians have conceived of God's power as absolute in nature rather than social in character. Hartshorne, however, argues that just such a conception of power is unacceptable; indeed, according to the tenets of the philosophy of creative synthesis, such a notion is logical absurdity. It denies the principle of universal exemplification and is therefore, from the perspective of creationist logic, "meaningless and contradictory."[9] But not only is absolute power a logical impossibility for a creationist metaphysics, it is as well a contradiction of what Hartshorne takes to be ethical, philosophical, and religious ideals of perfection. That is, a monopoly of power, even though it may be concentrated in a benevolent deity, is not an ideal to be admired or

---

[6] Hartshorne, "Omnipotence," *An Encyclopedia of Religion*, 545.

[7] Bernard M. Loomer ("Two Conceptions of Power," *Process Studies* 6 [1976] 5–32) offers an interesting analysis of the traditional conception of power from a process perspective. He suggests that the high estimation of one-directional linear power is closely connected with a nonsocial conception of the self which values the maximum of self-sufficiency and independence while denigrating dependence upon others and passivity. He further suggests that this is a particularly masculine way of conceiving of the self which emphasizes active agency rather than receptivity.

[8] See above, 2.2.

[9] Hartshorne, "Divine Absoluteness and Divine Relativity," in Herbert W. Richardson and Donald R. Cutler, eds., *Transcendence* (Boston: Beacon, 1969) 166; BH, 53; and CSPM, 292.

worshipped; rather, it is an ideal of tyranny worthy only of resistance.[10] He states:

> The point is not a vague, merely emotional one; nor is it simply a question of the nature of God's dealings with the world as just or merciful or otherwise. The point is metaphysical: a despot is one who wishes, so far as possible, to exert, but never suffer, power; who will be cause but not effect; who is a totally "independent" manipulator of things. This is the transcendentalized absolute negation of the principle of democratic rule, which is that ruler should in a sense also be subject and the subject in a sense also rules.[11]

Hartshorne, following the canons of his philosophy of social reality, argues that omnipotence conceived in this manner must be rejected if it is to escape the charge of tyranny and despotic rule as well as the accusation of logical incoherency. It must be noted from the outset that Karl Barth sought as well to free the notion of omnipotence from all association with despotism or brute force. But he did so in a manner that, while he emphasized the gracious and benevolent character of the divine rule, he did not call into question its absolute nature. While Barth interpreted the traditional view of omnipotence in light of his christological principles, it is not clear that he ever really rejected the notion of divine power as the only real power or the idea that power means being primarily an agent, a determining cause, rather than a conditioned effect.[12] In short, divine power, within the Barthian schema, remains essentially nonsocial in nature.

For his part, Hartshorne, working out of his philosophy of creative synthesis, urges a far more radical reinterpretation of the traditional tenets than the Barthian approach suggests. He argues that the traditional monopolistic notion of omnipotence must be replaced by a thoroughly social conception of divine power. Before stating Hartshorne's reinterpretation it is important to make several observations concerning his understanding of power in general. These assertions, as will be clear, follow after and flow out of the Hartshornian principles stated above but their enunciation will lay the foundation for his explicit treatment of power in its divine form.

---

[10] Hartshorne (AD, 201; CSPM, 292) states that in a social vision, the notion of absolute power is no ideal but a nightmare.

[11] WP, 184. Merold Westphal ("Temporality and Finitism in Hartshorne's Theism," *Review of Metaphysics* 12 [1966] 550–64) argues that a democracy of power is desirable only because on the human level wisdom and goodness are missing and hence it is wiser to share the responsibility of power. It is not, for him, clear that if a ruler were perfect in wisdom and goodness as well as absolute in power that a democracy would still be more beneficial than the benevolent despotism such a being could offer.

[12] For the discussion of whether the cross truly signals passivity on God's part or a unique form of causal power, see above, 2.3.

First, power, divine or otherwise, is relational in nature. Power, in any form, indicates relationship with other ontologically distinct indviduals. Its very nature is "social interaction."[13] Second, not only does power always indicate a social relationship but, of equal importance, such interaction is always with other entities that also have power. According to the principle of universal exemplifications, to be is to have power (PSG, 23). Power is always power in relation to other powers. Only nonentity or nothing lacks all power.[14] In Hartshorne's words, "Being is power, and any relation in which a thing was wholly powerless would be a relation in which the thing was nothing" (MVG, 198–99). Such inherent power is the mark of the lowest as well as the highest reality; the least of things, though its power may be slight, nonetheless possesses some degree of intrinsic power.

Thus, within the Hartshornian social vision, actuality and intrinsic power are inseparable, and power therefore always involves relation with other powers. This means that there is a genuine plurality of powers, that power is in principle shared. In a social vision, grounded in the conviction of the universal exemplification of categories, the division of power is an "analytic truth" (BH, 53). Now what does such division of power imply for Hartshorne's conception of divine power?

This assertion of the universal distribution of power entails foremost and by necessity the rejection of any understanding of divine omnipotence as absolute power or the possession of all power. "If there are beings besides God, there are powers other than the divine" (PSG, 436). Omipotence does not and cannot mean absolute power. Rather, divine power must be conceived as perfect, eminent and unsurpassable power. Such eminent and unsurpassable power means, on the one hand, all power that one social individual could conceivably possess; divine power is all possible power. In Hartshorne's words:

> Omnipotence (alas, our only word for perfection of power!) is power to the highest degree possible and over all that exists, it is "all" the power that *could* be exercised by *one* individual over "all" that is; but it remains to be shown how much power could be exercised in this fashion. (MVG, 30)

And on the other hand, divine power, as the highest degree of power, is unsurpassable, without rival or competition. As perfect power it is preeminent among powers, categorically superior to all lesser powers. "God's

[13] Hartshorne, "Omnipotence," 545.
[14] BH, 53; MVG, 89.

power is not absolute, but it is unsurpassable. No conceivable being could have more power." [15]

Thus, divine power as the "fullest possible extent of individual power" (BH, 54) is perfect power, and all other powers are infinitely inferior. However, in a social vision this perfect and unsurpassable power cannot be equated with an absoluteness of power. Rather, "omnipotence ... is *the ideal case of power assuming a division of power,* the maximal concentration of power that permits distribution of powers among a plurality of beings" (WP, 100).

Therefore, Hartshorne's social interpretation of power involves the rejection of what in his view is the traditional claim that God is the only real power. But Hartshorne's social version entails as well an equally adamant rejection of the traditional argument that power refers purely to the capacity to be an agent, to determine, and to cause rather than the ability to be open to influence, and to be affected. Hartshorne argues that for millenia thinkers working out of perspectives that failed to recognize the essentially social character of reality assumed the "superiority of agent to patient" and of cause to effect (NTOT, 134). And when this assumption was applied to the idea of divine power, the result was the equation of omnipotence with impassivity and immunity to all influence. God was pure agent, shaping the world, never being molded or conditioned by it. Even Barth, with his emphasis upon the centrality of relationship for God, was intent upon maintaining God's agential, determining status even in terms of the cross. For Hartshorne, the recognition that there exists a plurality of powers and that power is relational in nature, always involving mutual conditioning and interaction, leads to the conclusion that power has not only an agential form but also a receptive, responsive, patient form. Within a social vision, power is not only the capacity to be a cause but also the ability to be an effect. Power involves not only being a stimulus but equally a response.

Hartshorne argues as well that such capacity to be influenced is not a weakness or some lesser, inferior form of power but is equal to its agential counterpart (MVG, 105, 273). Passivity is not a form or species of powerlessness. Lack of power lies not in being influenced but only "in being influenced in the wrong direction, or disproportionately" (ibid., 106). It lies in being responsive to some, while excluding others from awareness. Further, the power to influence and determine others, if it is not to be despotic in nature, presupposes and depends upon such sensitivity to and awareness of the world it seeks to shape (ibid., 273). It is the inferior agent that seeks to determine others while escaping all influence, while the superior agent, open to the conditions of the world, acts with appropriateness and sensitivity. For Hartshorne, superior action always involves, as an essential

---

[15] Hartshorne, "Divine Absoluteness and Divine Relativity," 166.

component, reaction.

Thus, there are two equal forms of power: the capacity to be open to influence and the capacity in turn to influence. The two forms are not separable but imply one another. They are proportionately related: as one increases or decreases so too does the other.

When this recognition of the twofold nature of power is applied to the idea of divine power, the result is as radical as the rejection of the notion that God possessed all power. For, no longer can God be understood merely as agent but, in a social vision, must also be interpreted as patient. God is not only cause but also effect. And further, as the one individual perfect in power, God exemplifies both these forms to the highest degree. If divine influence is universal in scope and efficacy, so is God's openness to influence. Omnipotence is thus not, in a social schema, purely one-directional determination. Rather, it is both influence and susceptibility to influence "ideal in quality, degree, and scope." [16] God, as preeminent power, is the "perfection of action-and-passion" (MVG, 273).

In summary it can be stated that Hartshorne has rejected both the notion of divine power as all-power and the interpretation of such power solely in agential terms. Instead he has argued, on the one hand, that God is the eminent but not absolute power. God's power is the supreme form of that which is exhibited universally in inferior degrees or "resemblances." And, on the other hand, Hartshorne has argued that power, when explicated with this social philosophy, must be understood to have two equally important forms: the capacity to be influenced and the capacity to influence. It is now important to examine in more detail this double interpretation of power in order to understand its own unique content as well as the similarities and contrasts it offers to the Barthian position.

5.2 Divine Power as Receptive Power

Hartshorne, working out of his dynamic and creationist philosophy, does not interpret power as the capacity for influence in a simple or one-dimensional manner. Rather, he explicates this form of power in terms of the complex and multidimensional notions of creative synthesis and prehension. All concrete individuals are momentary units of experience or processes of creative synthesis whereby a multiplicity of past experiences are prehended, united, and integrated into a novel present actuality. Such creative synthesis entails, on the one hand, the fact that the past forms the data or raw material out of which the present emerges. As such it conditions the content and determines the limits of possibility for each succeeding experience. There is no present actuality that has not been influenced and conditioned

---

[16] Hartshorne, "Omnipotence," 546.

by the past. It is a product of and a response to that which is beyond its control. On the other hand, the present, as the novel unification of that multiple data, is creative and active in its response. Actuality, interpreted as prehensive experience or process, is the creative appropriation and integration of the past by the present. Hence, the power to be influenced turns out to be more richly textured than might have been assumed. It is creative receptivity, or active passivity. Hartshorne suggests that passivity might be interpreted as the "way in which an individual's activity takes account of, renders itself appropriate to, the activities of others" (PSG, 2). Hence, the capacity to be influenced entails both the dimension of determination by others and the dimension of self-determination. Power, in this form, consists in the "ability to use data to make new actualities" (WP, 195).

For their part, nondivine individuals are imperfect forms of such creative receptivity. On the one hand, their very existence is a matter of chance, dependent upon the precarious vicissitudes of the world. Too much of certain kinds of influence or lack of others could prevent or end the existence of any of the various types of creaturely entities. This is precisely the point of Hartshorne's claim that the existence of nondivine reality is always contingent, never necessary. On the other hand, every nondivine experience is always partial and fragmentary, influenced and conditioned only by a small segment of the past world in a vague and inadequate manner. Its inferiority lies not in its being influenced but in the narrowness of the scope of that influence and inadequacy with which such influence is received. God, however, as the one preeminent power, is the perfect instance of creative receptivity, open to all influences whatsoever and responsive in a manner possible only for deity.

It is under the rubric of perfect knowledge of omniscience that Hartshorne most fruitfully develops his interpretation of this divine form of receptive power. Indeed, receptive power and knowledge are the same thing for God; to speak of God's perfect power of receptivity is to speak of God's perfect knowledge. It is to this conception of perfect power interpreted as perfect knowledge that we now turn.

Receptive Power as Knowledge

Knowledge, for Hartshorne, is a high-level form of creative receptivity whereby an experiencing individual is aware of and reacts to its social environment.[17] It is the prehensive process, referred to in general terms in the preceding chapter, through which a present subject appropriates and is thence influenced by its past. Knowledge, interpreted as creative

---

[17] Hartshorne speaks, as did Whitehead before him, of the fundamental form of receptivity as prehension. Omniscience is the divine form of this direct awareness that, in the preceding chapter, was analyzed in terms of human memory and perception.

receptivity, follows after and is therefore relative to and dependent upon that which is known. That is, the knower, whether God or creature, conforms to and is the effect of its objects. "Awareness is essentially a response, an adaptation to others" (PSG, 22). Succinctly stated, Hartshorne espouses, in relation to God and creature alike, a thoroughly realistic epistemology.

Such a realistic epistemology offers a sharp contrast to the interpretation of the divine knowing process set forth by Karl Barth. Barth often sounds quite idealistic, taking full account of the active role the creaturely knower plays (at least in relation to fellow creatures) in interpreting its objects. But, in terms of creatures' knowledge of God, he espouses a radical realism in which the knower is completely shaped by its divine object.[18]

In relation to divine knowledge, however, Barth abandons any suggestion of such a realistic epistemology and thereby eliminates any ambiguity concerning the relation of knower to known. Omniscience is not the perfection of ordinary knowledge. Rather, the divine knowing process consists in the reversal of the cognitive process whereby creatures know God. God's knowledge is not responsive, even creatively responsive, in nature but causative in character. It is purely active. Several implications of this Barthian claim are especially pertinent to the present context and must be briefly reiterated.

First, Barth's conception of divine knowledge as purely active, along with his similar interpretation of divine will, allows him to understand God as self-constituting and self-sufficient apart from all relations with the world. God is self-causative, self-positing and as such is ontologically independent of all other realities. But if the Barthian interpretation of divine knowledge signifies an independent self-sufficiency, it entails as well the free capacity to create other realities besides Godself and to enter into relation with them. That is, God's causative knowing and willing, as omnipotent, can create and sustain the world. The important points here are two: first, concerning both self- and world-positing and determination, divine knowledge is creative and causative, not responsive, in nature; and second, the capacity of God to be self-causing entails that there is no necessity to enter into relationship with the world. World or no world are equal alternatives for a self-positing God. Divine self-sufficiency involves capacity for, but never necessity of, relationship with that which is ontologically distinct from Godself.

Hartshorne, working from his process perspective with its attendant realistic epistemology, adamantly rejects such a reversal of the cognitive process and its resultant interpretation of divine knowledge as absolutely self-creating and world creating; divine knowledge does not represent a reversal of the relationship of knower to known. Rather, as a form of preeminent power, it entails the perfection of the relationship; it is its ideal form. The

---

[18] See above, Chap. 2, n. 8.

implications of this Hartshornian claim are many and far-reaching and they must be elucidated with care.

First, Hartshorne (as well as Barth) links the content and contour of God's life to divine knowledge. God is, in a literal manner for both thinkers, constituted by God's knowledge. However, in the Hartshornian version, because divine knowledge is not causative but essentially responsive, the divine knower, no less than creaturely knowers, requires some, though no particular objects. This means that insofar as God is constituted by God's knowledge, God is essentially other-related, not merely self-related. God is God's creative response to the multiplicity of nondivine realities.

The responsive nature of divine knowledge requires as well a new definition of divine self-sufficiency. Barth, because of his causative notion of divine knowledge, could understand God's self-constituted existence and self-positing power apart from God's relations with the world. For Hartshorne this is not possible. Divine self-sufficiency cannot indicate independence from relationship with ontologically distinct others or the power to exist as self-related but not other-related. Rather, such power of self-sufficiency, interpreted noetically, is the power to know and hence adapt to and assimilate, every possible object of awareness. In Hartshorne's words, "God's absolute 'power to exist' is His ability to assimilate any and every causal condition, to *make* it 'favorable' to some appropriate responsive state of His own awareness" (AD, 176).

This capacity to know and adjust to all circumstances is, in essence, an interpretation of God's necessary existence in noetic terms. Understood noetically, which finally for Hartshorne is the only way to interpret it, necessary existence entails that God can know any and all possible alternatives and not be threatened but confirmed by them no matter how meager their value. And further, necessary existence means that while some world is indeed necessary as an object of divine knowledge, no particular world is required. God, as perfect knower, requires some world as object, but any world will do.

Moreover, Hartshorne's insistence upon the responsive and adaptive nature of knowledge corresponds to his distinction between existence/essence and actuality. For, while God's capacity to know all things and to know them perfectly (divine existence and essence) does not vary, the content of that knowledge and with it God's concrete life and actuality change and develop as its objects do.

Hartshorne contends that as a type of relation omniscience does not fluctuate or alter. Rather, this "generic abstract property of being-all-knowing is strictly absolute" (DR, 11). That is, God's knowledge is always adequate to that which is known no matter what that might be. And, further, it is always adequate to all objects. Nothing eludes or remains outside the scope of God's receptive and responsive knowledge. Its adequacy lies in its depth of clarity as well as its universality of scope (ibid., 122).

This perfect adequacy of divine knowledge can, I would suggest, be stated as follows: the perfection of divine knowledge lies in that it is conformal, inclusive, and preservative. Through an examination of God's receptive power as knowledge under these three rubrics the extent and boldness of the Hartshornian position will be brought to light as well as its clear opposition to Barth's. However, it must be stated at the outset that the Hartshornian program entails a number of internal difficulties that will be seen to be not easily surmounted, and as the analysis proceeds these will become evident.

A. *Knowledge as Conformal*

First, if knowledge in general means response or adaptation to its objects, omniscience means perfect correspondence between knower and known. It is perfect because it is in absolute agreement with reality. What is and what is known are one in God. "Infallible, certain, distinct, and complete knowledge of reality is knowledge in which something corresponds to and implies each and every item of reality" (ibid., 9). For Barth, divine knowledge and reality are in agreement because God's knowing and willing create that reality, while for Hartshorne they correspond because God's knowledge conforms itself to reality; for Barth, God's knowledge causes what is, while for Hartshorne it records what is.

This conformal aspect of divine knowledge means as well, for Hartshorne, that God must correspond to reality precisely as it is. That is, knowledge of all things "means, of each thing as it is, of the actual as actual, of the merely possible as merely possible, of the future as future, of the past as past" (WP, 74). The content of divine knowledge depends upon and is relative to its objects; their status as actual or possible, past or present determines how they are known. Perfect knowledge is therefore temporal in nature, corresponding to the temporal distinctions within the world.[19] It cannot be interpreted as above or beyond time. There are several important aspects to this claim. It involves the rejection of the traditional claim that God knows all things as actual, and it entails as well the denial of the Barthian claim that while God distinguishes past, present, and future, God still knows (and hence determines) the content of the future (MVG, 13). Hartshorne's reasons for dismissing the first claim are that God cannot know, and hence possess, all things as actual, for (1) not all values are compossible and (2) certain values admit no maximal realization. Hartshorne's rejection of the Barthian claim lies in his conviction that the future is not actual or determinable. As such it does not yet exist to be known, except in vague outline, and perfect knowledge can only know it as such a realm of potentialities.

---

[19] Hartshorne, "Omniscience," *An Encyclopedia of Religion*, 546.

The future is open and its details are beyond the grasp of God and creature alike. Retrospective knowledge is distinct, determinate, and exact, but prospective knowledge can only be general and indeterminate. In Hartshorne's words,

> Is it not the essence of the future that it consists of what may or may not exist, that is, of what is unsettled, indefinite, undecided? If so, then God, who knows things as they are, will know future events only in their character as indefinite, or more or less problematic, nebulous, incomplete as to details. (RSP, 158)

Hence, divine power of omniscience is not to be equated with foreknowledge (temporally or logically interpreted) or prediction.[20] This restriction of divine knowledge does not indicate weakness or a failure to know on God's part, but a correct correspondence between divine knowledge and the metaphysical status of its objects. To know temporally and therefore progressively and successively is no weakness or sign of inferiority but the perfect and ideal form of the cognitive process (MVG, 104).

A further implication, quite explicit already, of Hartshorne's interpretation of divine knowledge as conformal and receptive in nature is that this form of power cannot be equated with predestination (ibid., 104–5). To know is not to cause or determine, but to be caused and determined. In the following section I shall discuss how God indeed does affect, condition and influence the world, but at this juncture it will suffice to say that although God's influence upon the world depends upon the divine knowledge, the two cannot be equated in any simple manner.

Another ramification of Hartshorne's position is that divine knowledge is never complete but always growing and changing in content (RSP, 158). What is now unsettled may become fixed and determinate and, in so doing, come to contribute to and influence the divine life. It is precisely this divine capacity for change that Hartshorne's idea of relative or dynamic perfection seeks to express. But what is important here is to indicate that for Hartshorne the changing content of divine knowledge entails only growth and increase, never loss or decay (ibid., 118–19; NTOT, 127; MVG, 130–31). According to Hartshorne, creaturely knowledge is never pure gain; what is known is known only inadequately. It always entails forgetting and loss as well as new knowledge, and the creaturely knower is doomed to cease knowing altogether, that is, to die. In contrast, the divine knower, as necessarily existent, will never die. And further, omniscience entails the perfect adequacy of knowledge to its object and finally, as we shall presently see, the perfect retention and preservation of all values in the divine memory. Change, in terms of God, "consists in the sheer addition of

---

[20] Hartshorne, "Foreknowledge," *An Encyclopedia of Religion,* 284; LP, 171–73.

states, without any loss or subtraction, without the lamented temporal 'destructiveness' and 'separation.' The new is always together with what is not new."[21] God's receptive power is an ability to grow and to be continually enriched by an ever-changing world.

For Hartshorne, therefore, omniscience does not include knowledge of the future except as the determinable and open realm of possibilities. It is only insofar as possibilities become determinate and fixed that they become objects for the divine knower. There is, however, another implication of this correspondence of divine and the metaphysical status of its objects that causes confusion in the present context and will subsequently be seen to cause conflict concerning several of Hartshorne's fundamental assertions. This concerns the status of contemporaries. For many years Hartshorne maintained, contrary to fellow process philosopher Alfred North Whitehead, that divine knowledge included knowledge of God's contemporaries (WP, 3; CSPM, 115). In recent years, however, he has abandoned this claim and now asserts, in conformity with present-day physics as well as Whitehead, that contemporaries do not influence one another and that therefore God does not at any given moment know present, becoming actuality. In his words, "On the most concrete level, that of states, there is action, not interaction" (CSPM, 115). The conclusion is that God knows the past as actual and determinate, and the future as possible and indeterminate. The difficulty lies in that it is not clear what status the present, as nascent actuality, has in relation to this divine receptive power. If knowledge is to be equated with being influenced and contemporaries cannot influence one another, then God cannot know the present. Yet it is real in a way that is not true for the future. Hartshorne, unfortunately, is not precise concerning how this unique status of nascent actuality is to be interpreted in terms of divine knowledge. Perhaps God knows that there is a contemporary world but not its content. Yet if this is so, then it is difficult to maintain that God conforms to reality precisely as it is. In any case, Hartshorne's interpretation of knowledge as receptivity and reflection can be seen to create a dilemma or, at least, confusion concerning the relation of God to the contemporary world.

Hartshorne has thus argued that God's capacity to be influenced can be interpreted in terms of divine knowledge whereby God perfectly receives and corresponds to the multiple experience of worldly reality. But there is more to be said concerning this conformal character of divine knowledge, and it brings us close to the heart of the Hartshornian vision concerning this form of divine power. For Hartshorne, divine knowledge corresponds to its objects because it is perfect receptivity, perfect sensitivity to that which it knows. It is wholly adequate to its objects because it is the sympathetic

---

[21] Hartshorne, "Tillich's Doctrine of God," in Charles W. Kegley and Robert W. Bretall, eds., *The Theology of Paul Tillich* (New York: Macmillan, 1964) 173.

appropriation of and participation in them. Divine knowledge is perfect because it is love (BH, 19–20, 24, 195–96; NTOT, 13). Hartshorne declares, "I personally see no difference between knowledge or awareness in the ideal form and love in the ideal form" (CSPM, 262–63). It is necessary to explicate further this assertion, indeed identification, of knowledge as a form of power and love.

First, with this identification of knowledge and love Hartshorne is, as has been implicit all along, rejecting any idea of the knower as spectator (ibid., 263). There is no such thing as spectator knowledge whereby the knower is aware of its objects and is unaffected by them. All knowledge is participatory and therefore indifference is impossible (NTOT, 13). But second, Hartshorne also rejects any notion that knowledge and hatred could be correlated. Hatred is a function of ignorance and blindness, not sympathetic receptivity to others. Hatred is exclusive, while knowledge and love are inclusive. Humans can indeed divorce knowledge and love but this is not a sign either of strength or higher truth but of weakness and the degree to which they are dissociated is the measure of ignorance (BH, 25–26).

It can be further seen that with this union of love and responsive knowledge there is emerging an interpretation of divine love which is quite distinct from the Barthian conception. Barth, for his part, conceives of divine love just as divine knowledge, as God's gracious activity, and he emphasizes the causative, outgoing, and purely gratuitous character of such love. Although God's love is expressed most fully on the cross, this passion is to be interpreted for Barth within the context of God's free and active decision. Hartshorne, however, suggests a somewhat different understanding of divine love. Love, in this form, is social awareness (MVG, xvii; DR, 36). It is the power to see and know the other's perspective, to make the experience of others one's own. This means that divine love, just as God's knowledge, has at least in part a receptive and passive nature and lacks the purely gratuitous character emphasized by Barth. God's love just as God's knowledge does not choose its exact objects but receives them. The world presents itself, so to speak, to God, and God could not know it without loving it. There is a sense, therefore, in which the question of the world's worthiness of divine love is as meaningless for Hartshorne as it is for Barth. In the Barthian schema, nothing is worthy of divine love, so that love is wholly unconditional and utterly free. For Hartshorne, however, everything by virtue of existing is equally deserving of God's attention. "'Worthy of love' is a rather silly phrase, if love means adequate awareness of the value of others, whatever that happens to be. Everything is completely worthy of love, that is, of having its interests fully appreciated" (MVG, 165). God, therefore, extends God's sympathetic awareness equally to all. Divine love, identified with God's perfect knowledge, is universal in scope leaving nothing out but sympathetically including all.[22]

Such sympathetic receptivity does not entail for Hartshorne that God approve of everything God knows and loves. Sympathetic awareness and unqualified approval are not the same. God's knowledge is also a valuation process. While God is receptive of all things, even that which is evil, God does not thereby unconditionally accept all things. But the point in the present context is that such negative valuation does not involve less-sympathetic receptivity. God is, in all circumstances, equally receptive of the world.[23]

Thus far, we have seen that Hartshorne interprets God's capacity or power to be influenced in terms of God's perfect knowledge and further that such knowledge is supreme because it conforms to and is shaped by reality, reflecting its objects in the most thorough and adequate manner. And we have seen that such perfect reflection is possible because divine knowledge is also divine love through which God sympathetically receives the world into Godself. Such receptivity is not, for Hartshorne, a lesser form of power, but in its divine form an excellence beyond all others. In Hartshorne's words,

> We worship that second-best form of power which puts influences in
> balance by deficient, lukewarm response and does not readily recognize
> the superior power which, more humbly than the humblest of men, even
> perhaps than the one born in a manger, yields with exact adequacy to
> every pressure of creaturely activity.[24]

B. *Divine Knowledge as Inclusive*

This recognition that divine knowledge perfectly reflects its objects because it sympathetically participates in them and lovingly receives them brings us to the second way of expressing what Hartshorne means by the perfection of divine knowledge: divine knowledge is perfect because it is inclusive. God's loving awareness of the world entails the literal inclusion of that world within God's life. Indeed such inclusion is God's concrete life. It is necessary to explicate what Hartshorne means by this claim.

---

[22] Critics argue, contra Hartshorne, that social relation, through knowledge, does not always insure love, and that while love and receptivity to the other may go together, there can be receptivity that is not loving. For criticisms along these lines, see Joe Earl Elmore, "The Theme of the Suffering of God in the Thought of Nicholas Berdyaev, Charles Hartshorne, and Reinhold Niebuhr" (Ph.D. diss., Columbia University, 1963) 102; and Gunton, *Becoming and Being,* 78–80.

[23] Hartshorne, "A Philosopher's Assessment of Christianity," in Walter Leibrecht, ed., *Religion and Culture: Essays in Honor of Paul Tillich* (New York: Harper & Brothers, 1959) 168.

[24] MVG, 297; see also, Eugene H. Peters (*The Creative Advance* [St. Louis: Bethany, 1966] 97–98) for a discussion of Hartshorne's argument that receptivity is an aspect of omnipotence, not a weakness or defect.

It was argued in the preceding chapter that prehension, the activity whereby present experiences appropriate and synthesize the past into new actualities, entails that the prehending present is internally related to the past. And, for Hartshorne, knowledge as a high-level form or complexification of this prehending process involves, on both the divine and nondivine levels, the same internal relatedness of knower to known. What is of importance in Hartshorne's claim is that such internal relatedness or relativity of knower to known involves that the knower contains or includes its objects within itself (PSG, 18). This means that the world as the object of God's receptive awareness is literally within God's concrete life.

Hartshorne, with this claim, is emphatically rejecting the idea that the object known must be outside the knower. He acknowledges that in its creaturely form knowledge normally does not contain its objects. However, he denies that such exclusion is because of the nature of knowledge itself but contends that it is rather the result of the imperfection and inadequacy of creaturely knowledge (CSPM, 105). Human knowledge is mostly ignorance; it is vague, partial and fragmentary and that is why its data are excluded or lost (NTOT, 12). To identify the inadequacy of creaturely knowledge with the nature of knowledge itself and then project that onto divine knowledge is an "unconscious piece of anthropomorphism" (PSG, 19). Instead, perfect knowledge as direct, infallible, concrete, and conscious apprehension, takes into itself all that is known. As the failure to know, so too is the degree of exclusion equal to the degree of ignorance. And, in turn, true knowledge and internal inclusion are one.

It perhaps seems strange that the relation between knower and known should be spoken of in the spatial imagery of literal inclusion. But this terminology is not merely a poetic or metaphoric means of expression for Hartshorne. He means it in the most literal and exact way; God's receptive power is the power to include all reality within Godself. This claim will presently be seen to entail grave difficulties, but it is his conviction, indeed perhaps his most fundamental conviction, that "knowledge is deficient unless it fully and literally contains its objects" (ibid., 18). He states:

> Granted that we do not "include" mountains when we "know" them, unless in some very attenuated sense of include, equally we do not know mountains, except in a very attenuated sense of "know," by comparison with what the word means when we say that God knows mountains. (Ibid., 19)

> Strange that men should think to exalt God by putting everything outside him as knower. Almost everything is outside us and our knowledge and that is why we are not God! But nothing can be outside God, in his total reality. (NTOT, 12)

This claim that as the perfect knower God literally experiences and therefore includes all reality within Godself leads Hartshorne to assert that God must be understood as the Inclusive or Cosmic Whole. That is, God is the whole of reality or the cosmos as a unified and integrated individual. God is not other than or over against the world, but is the multiplicity of worldly experiences synthesized into one divine reality. This radical contention must be further unpacked.

First, Hartshorne's claim emerges out of the principles he has argued all along: individuals are the synthesizers of the multiplicity of past experiences into new and novel realities. God, as the perfect knower whose experience has all realities from the most minute to the greatest as its objects or data, is this process on a cosmic scale. Hartshorne therefore argues that not only does the concept of universe have concrete content and is not merely a limiting notion without literal reference but further that this notion be identified with God as sentient, indeed conscious, willing, active individual.[25] Hartshorne identifies this cosmic synthesizing or integration process with God as universal and inclusive knower, for the simple reason that according to him, if they are not identified, then there is a greater reality that consists of God-and-the-world (DR, 79; LP, 267). In his view,

> anything whatever, divine or otherwise, is either a constituent of the total reality or is itself the all-inclusive reality. Since the inclusive reality cannot be less than what it includes, though it can be more, God is either inclusive or he has a rival or superior. (CSPM, 265)

Thus, Hartshorne's interpretation of God as the cosmic knower, coupled with his understanding of knowledge as inclusive, leads him to the radical assertion that God is the totality of reality, or stated in another equally controversial way, the cosmos as unified and integrated is a sentient, experiencing, knowing individual—that is, God. "God is the 'world' understood, the world is 'God' understood" (MVG, 339).

But, in the second place, Hartshorne argues that he is not, through this identification of God and the cosmos as unified, suggesting any simple form of pantheism that merely collapses divine and nondivine reality or is an unsubtle apotheosis of the world.[26] Rather, Hartshorne distinguishes his

---

[25] Many critics would reject the notion of the universe as having any literal reference at all, while others would resist the identification of God and world. A form of the first type of criticism has been articulated by Bertrand Russell, among many others. In his words, "I think the word 'universe' is a handy word in some connections, but I don't think it stands for anything that has a meaning" ("A Debate on the Existence of God: Bertrand Russell and F. C. Copleston," in John Hick, ed., *The Existence of God* [New York: Macmillan, 1964] 174). The Barthian position stands as a good example of the latter kind of criticism rejecting the identification of God and world.

[26] Hartshorne's early work, esp. BH, has a much more pantheistic sound than his later work. In that early book (pp. 19, 23, 40, 55–57) God is often referred to as nature without all the qualifiers Hartshorne articulates in later materials.

position from any simple pantheism in several significant ways.

First, as has been repeatedly emphasized, Hartshorne argues that God is independent of any particular worldly realities in relation to God's existence and essence.[27] That is, God or the cosmos as a whole will always be, no matter the quality or quantity of its parts or constituents. The concrete content of God's life will change, but that there is such cosmic life will not. Second, and of great importance, Hartshorne contends that his vision is not to be equated with a simple pantheism; God or the Inclusive Whole is not merely the name for the sum or total of the world's parts. Rather, God as the cosmic whole is, as indeed is every moment of experience, more than the sum of its data or constituents.[28] This point is of extreme importance, for all that has been stated up to this juncture has emphasized the receptive and passive side of God's power as knowledge and little has been noted of the creative dimension of this process. Indeed, there has been no mention of the divine will at all. God has so far been most often spoken of as constituted by others. This emphasis upon the receptive side has corresponded to the central thrust of Hartshorne's position.[29] However, for Hartshorne, God is also creatively self-constituting, and it is to this constructive-as-willing dimension that attention must now be turned.

At the outset it must be stated one final time that God, as inclusive knower, is literally shaped and conditioned by the nondivine world and the world as the object of divine knowledge is co-creator of God's concrete life. In Hartshorne's words, "To know what the creatures decide to do is to be Himself in his cognitive state decided by these decisions" (NTOT, 123). However, divine knowledge is not merely the experience of these multiple stimuli or data, which are creaturely realities, in a diverse or disunified manner. Rather, the perfection of divine receptive power is the integration

---

[27] Hartshorne, "Interrogation," 344; NTOT, 27.

[28] Hartshorne, "Interrogation," 331; PSG, 32. Philosopher John Wild (Review of DR in *Review of Metaphysics* 2 [1948] 71) takes great exception to Hartshorne's claim concerning this transcendence of the world parts by the divine whole and insists instead that "while every whole is *constituted by* relational parts, it is not something over and above them which can be related *to* them. Rather it is *all* its parts. Wild, however, fails to to take adequate note of how Hartshorne makes this claim of transcendence on the part of God; the uniqueness of the whole in relation to its parts lies not in being "apart or above" the parts but in how the parts are integrated into a whole which is not a mere collection of unconnected items. While Wild recognizes but rejects Hartshorne's attempt to distinguish whole and parts, Edward Farley (*The Transcendence of God* [Philadelphia: Westminster, 1958] 130–32) fails to acknowledge sufficiently the kind of transcendence Hartshorne is arguing for, and hence his treatment of the problem if not incorrect nonetheless is insufficient.

[29] Hartshorne (PSG, 23–24) readily admits that his position places its major emphasis upon consciousness rather than volition, upon cognition rather than willing. He justifies this emphasis, on the one hand, in the name of balancing a traditional tendency in the other direction and, on the other hand, by incorporating a creative and constructive aspect into his conception of divine knowing.

of these disparate and even conflicting nondivine experiences into the creative unity of the one divine experience. Through knowing the world, God synthesizes the multiplicity of fragmented and noninclusive realities into one inclusive cosmic reality. In this sense, divine knowing is not merely a reflective process whereby God mirrors worldly reality but a creative process of evaluation and finally self-harmonization.[30]

This conception of divine knowledge as creative integration entails several things. On the one hand, it means that while God as responsive and receptive knower is indeed passive, that passivity must be understood as a dimension of divine creative action. That is, while God does not cause the objects of divine knowledge, God does actively and creatively appropriate them: synthesis or integration is always a decision, an act that moves beyond its data. It entails not only reflection of its objects but evaluation of them.[31] It is a positive act of willing. And, on the other hand, this divine unification is not only creative but, in that creativity, is also free. That is, while the multiplicity of nondivine experiences provide the data for God's unified experience and hence are determining of that experience, precisely how God will integrate them cannot be determined by them but is always a matter of divine free decision. God, perfect in receptive power, is the synthesis of the world, but the exact configuration of that synthesis cannot be deduced from or determined by its constituents. There are, for Hartshorne, infinite ways of unifying the past world in each successive divine experience and the precise "how" of the unification is God's creative self-determination. According to Hartshorne, "Since an object always influences but cannot dictate, the awareness of itself, we influence God by our experiences but do not thereby deprive him of freedom in his response to us" (DR, 141). With this notion of God's creative appropriation and unification of the nondivine world, there can be discerned a conception of freedom that contrasts sharply with the Barthian position. First, freedom understood as the power of creative self-determination or self-willing is a universal category; individuality, whether on a divine or nondivine level, involves the creative transformation of past data into new experience. Such transformation is not the prerogative merely of God but of the least of all creatures. Barth appeared to offer two different understandings of freedom in relation to God and worldly realities, while for Hartshorne the character of freedom is always the same, only its scope and degree vary. Second, freedom, for Hartshorne, does not entail the absence of influence but rather it is the capacity to receive influence in a creative

[30] MVG, 293.

[31] Howard L. Parsons ("Religious Naturalism and the Philosophy of Hartshorne," in William L. Reese and Eugene Freeman, eds., *Process and Divinity* [LaSalle, Illinois: Open Court, 1964] 555) raises questions concerning whether such creative evaluation, as movement beyond the data, does not cause a change in the data itself; that is, is it possible to maintain that divine knowledge is both conformal and creative?

and transforming manner. Divine freedom does not consist in the alternative of having a world or not having a world but in the alternative ways of experiencing the world God has. In that sense freedom and purely gratuitous action cannot be equated. Rather, divine freedom consists in how God wills or chooses to interact with the world, not whether God will interact. If divine freedom means, as it does for Barth, the choice to love or not love any world, then for Hartshorne God is not free in this sense. However, it is just this equation of freedom and non-necessity that Hartshorne rejects, and he suggests instead that freedom lies in the creative character of interaction. But finally, if for Hartshorne God must have, know, and love some world, how God experiences that world will contribute to how all future worlds will in turn experience God. That is, God's self-determination is God's means of determining and influencing subsequent nondivine realities. As each creature's self-determination decides how it will contribute to the divine life, so, too, does God's self-determination lay the foundation, on a vastly larger scale, for how God will shape the world. Creative self-determination is the only means of determining others.

Thus, Hartshorne develops a notion of divine willing by arguing that God's reception of the world is a creative and self-determining activity. God's knowledge is not only reflection but willing response; it is the decision through which God constitutes Godself.

There is a final way in which Hartshorne distinguishes his position from any simple form of pantheism. This consists in what Hartshorne takes to be the independence of the nondivine constituents of the cosmic whole in relation to that whole. God's own independence has already been stressed first through the claims of the absolute character of God's existence and essence and secondly through the claims of God's creative freedom to unify the world in a unique manner. And the creatures have been also seen to be self-determining, and therefore their action cannot simply be equated with or reduced to God's activity. But Hartshorne wants to claim as well that while God as cosmic knower is internally related to God's worldly objects, such nondivine entities are externally related to God (ibid., 92). That is, while God is affected by what God knows, the objects known are not altered or conditioned in any way by the experience (WP, 72). This claim is simply the outgrowth of Hartshorne's realistic epistemology and his interpretation of that epistemology in asymmetrical, temporal terms. That is, within Hartshorne's schema, the relation between knower and known is the relation between a becoming and undetermined present and a fixed and settled past. The objects known, as past, are completed and cannot be altered or changed by the present, though, for Hartshorne, they can be included in it. What is important to stress in this claim is that, for Hartshorne, the inclusive knowing experience is one that, even on a cosmic scale, maintains the independence and integrity of its constituents.[32]

Therefore, nondivine realities, though parts of the cosmic whole, are first individuals who have achieved unity and integrity on their own. The world, as plural, is in God, not simply identified with God. This inclusion without identity is what Hartshorne labels panentheism, and it is, in his view, as far from traditional pantheism as it is from classical theism.

There is a further and all-important implication of this Hartshornian idea of God as the inclusive whole that must be stated. God as the perfect and inclusive knower is finally "reality itself," or alternatively the "measure of all reality." In the last analysis, with Hartshorne's vision, to be real is to be real for God and to be actual or possible is to be so for divine experience. God as perfect knower is coextensive with reality, and therefore God's perfect knowledge defines the very meaning of reality itself (LP, 154; CSPM, 170). According to Hartshorne, "He is 'being itself' in the sense that what things are for him necessarily coincides with what they really are. Thus, to be is to be for God, to fail to be is to fail to be for God. He is the definitive reality, the measure of all truth."[33]

C. *Knowledge as Preservative*

One way of focusing this Hartshornian claim that the meaning of reality is to be equated with the content of divine knowledge is to state that God's knowledge is not only conforming and inclusive but it is also preservative; God not only perfectly corresponds to and includes the past but also perfectly remembers it for all time. Hartshorne speaks so often of divine knowledge as memory for the simple reason that, within his temporally defined schema, all knowledge is retrospective in character, and therefore all knowledge which is not merely anticipatory of the future is remembering. But Hartshorne also speaks of divine memory in order to emphasize the retentive and preservative character of God's receptive power whereby God's knowledge stands as an immortal record and standard of truth.

Hartshorne argues that the notion of a perfect knower, recording and preserving all reality forevermore, is implicit in our very idea of truth and indeed is logically required by it.[34] The notion of truth involves an appeal to an ideal standard of knowledge against which all inferior or fallible forms of experience can be judged. It points to a "public" and "permanent," not merely a private, sollipsistic, or passing measure of the content and significance of reality (MVG, 90). In Hartshorne's words, "To refer to

---

[32] Hartshorne, "Divine Relativity and Absoluteness," 52–53. Wild (Review of DR, 65–77) argues that inclusion of parts in a whole that is more than its constituents threatens the integrity and independence of those constituents despite Hartshorne's claims to the contrary.

[33] Hartshorne, "Could There Have Been Nothing? A Reply," *Process Studies* 1 (1971) 25.

[34] Hartshorne, "Development of Process Philosophy," 59.

'existence' as a public meaning is to refer to a register on which, with infinite exactitude, everything is recorded just as it 'really is' on pain of its not being really anything" (WP, 81).

For Hartshorne, the appeal to this standard is not the appeal to a merely hypothetical or an imaginative notion that does not really exist itself. Truth and its perfect knower are not merely limiting ideas which act as critical principles calling into question fallible human knowledge. Truth is not a formal, contentless principle but a content filled standard that makes it possible to say that once an experience has occurred it will be true that it has taken place forevermore. As such, truth entails the literal preservation of all that has occurred. In Hartshorne's words, "It is also a logical demand that after events have happened, it should always be true that they have. . . . Truth must be true of reality. If reality keeps fading out, so must truth."[35]

It is such literal preservation of past reality that human or creaturely knowers cannot provide. For, as has been argued throughout the analysis, nondivine knowledge is always fragmentary, partial, dim, leaving out as much or more than it includes (WP, 81, 137–38, 164; PSG, 93). "All our memories are adulterated with forgetting" (WP, 138). It is only the perfect knower, who literally includes and preserves all within God's life, that can fulfill the demands of truth.[36] It is only a memory which is sheer memory, that remembers but does not forget, that fulfills the logical necessities of knowledge.

The perfect knower and preserver of reality fulfills, indeed is the only individual who can fulfill, not only these logical demands but also the equally fundamental existential or practical demand that the value of experience not be lost. Faced with the inadequacy of the human preservation of past experience in both the individuals' and societal memories and with the inevitability of death for individuals and the probable destruction of the human species, Hartshorne asks what value experience and life can have if its meaning must be found only in these fallible and perishable forms. He queries, "If death is sheer destruction of an individual and all human individuals face this destruction, what in the long run do they accomplish by their endeavors?"[37] Hartshorne responds that it is only the divine knower who can provide an answer to this question in a manner which is neither the mere confirmation of the meaninglessness of life not the

---

[35] Ibid.

[36] P. H. Phenix (Review of DR, *Journal of Philosophy* 46 [1949] 596) rejects Hartshorne's claim that to know must mean to include, and he suggests that while cognitive apprehension alters the knower, the objects need not be understood as thereby incorporated into that knower. Cognition would mean only awareness not inclusion. However, Hartshorne argues that only inclusion and preservation make sense of the ideas of "truth" and "reality."

[37] Hartshorne, "The God of Religion and the God of Philosophy," in *Talk of God, Royal Institute of Philosophy Lectures, vol. 2, 1967–68* (London: Macmillan, 1969) 156.

denial of the reality of individual and corporate death. For the final value of life lies not in a precarious social memory or a questionable prolongation of individual experience but in the preservation of value within the divine life which knows and cherishes each experience through all time. What is loss, from the creaturely perspective, as death or forgetting, is permanent gain from the divine perspective. The immortality of every experience lies in its contribution to the memory of God (RSP, 143–44; WP, 110; LP, 243). It is alone such a perfect memory that can meet the need of experience to have permanent and nontransitory value.

Thus, Hartshorne argues that God as the perfect knower of all that is can be understood as both the measure of reality and the preserver of value and as such answers both the logical demands of truth and the existential demands of meaning. Truth and value coincide with the content of divine knowledge. Hartshorne, however, makes a further and highly controversial claim. He argues that not only does the assumption of an ideal knower respond to the demands intrinsic to our notion of value and truth and correspond as well to the premises of his creationist philosophy, but also that all humans, indeed all creatures, experience this inclusive knower. That is, Hartshorne claims that God, conceived as the inclusive totality of all that is, is a datum of every experience. More will be said presently concerning such nondivine experience of God and the difficulties this claim raises, but it is important at this juncture to stress that Hartshorne believes his assertion of the literal actuality of this perfect knower and valuer to be not only a necessity of thought but an assertion confirmed as well by experience. He claims, "Implicitly everyone knows (or at least feels) the divine existence" (LP, 110). It is this awareness, dim though it may be, that gives our ideas of truth and meaning more than a hypothetical and imaginative function. It is because we somehow, though inadequately, know truth, that even we can recognize error. And it is because we experience reality as appreciated and cherished that our own lives have secure value. In his words, "We know we are (or will be) known and our being entirely known is itself known by us" (DR, 141). To those who deny such experience Hartshorne replies that the experience is there; what is missing is an adequate recognition and interpretation of its meaning.[38]

Such Hartshornian claims clearly raise profound questions from a variety of directions. All this will look extremely suspicious to those who reject his understanding of truth as the retrospectively attained content of divine knowledge or deny his not easily or perhaps even possibly proven claim that the totality of this knowledge, that is, reality itself, is ever experienced, dimly or otherwise. And it will be unacceptable to those who repudiate his

---

[38] LP, 11. Schubert Ogden (*The Reality of God* [New York: Harper & Row, 1963]), a follower of the Hartshornian philosophy, articulates this claim of divine presence with creaturely experience as a central motif in his own constructive theology.

assertion that this totality is a sentient, conscious, and willing individual. Whether one is a Barthian, a Kantian, or a Positivist, the Hartshornian premises will be unacceptable and from those competing perspectives will appear very vulnerable indeed. But Hartshorne's claim that God is the measure of reality and value because God is the includer and preserver of all experience raises difficulties as well from within his own perspective and indicates internal conflicts concerning several of his basic assertions. While acknowledging the challenges that naturally arise from outside the Hartshornian perspective, it is important as well to examine some of these internal problems that challenge Hartshorne's position from within.

Dilemmas Confronting the Hartshornian Position

One of the central areas of confusion and criticism that emerges in relation to Hartshorne's position revolves around the question of just what is entailed in his assertion that God includes and preserves all reality in God-self. Hartshorne has argued that every individual entity experiences, indeed is, the immediacy of its own becoming or synthesis. That is, each entity experiences its past world in a unique, definite, and particular way peculiar to itself and no other entity. Such unique subjective immediacy is the very meaning of coming to be actuality.[39] Now it must be asked whether a distinct individual, even God as perfect in power, can experience another entity's immediacy or unique particularity in the same manner that it experiences it itself. That is, does not subjective experience entail some form of privacy, and does it not have a personal and particular character that is its alone and no one else's? In short, if the value of an experience lies in its immediacy, is this value not something that intrinsically escapes appropriation and preservation by another?

Hartshorne replies that, to the contrary, there is no "mere privacy" of experience, but rather all experience, including its immediacy and unique particularity, is expressible in terms of God's participation in it (LP, 154). What we perceive as the failure to appropriate another's perspective wholly is the result of inadequate knowledge and is not an intrinsic aspect of receptive power or knowledge itself. The "apparent nonimmediacy of the given actualities is exactly what distinguishes ordinary from eminent or divine prehensions."[40] But Hartshorne also claims that such apprehension of the other's immediate experience does not entail the collapse of the distinction between knower and known. He states, "I feel *how* the other felt, I do not feel *as* the other felt."[41] This distinction holds true on the divine level as well. But it does not seem to me, nor to a number of other Hartshornian

---

[39] See above, 4.3.

[40] Hartshorne, "The Dipolar Conception of Deity," *Review of Metaphysics* 21 (1967) 287.

[41] Hartshorne, "The Structure of Givenness," *The Philosophical Forum* 18 (1960/61) 33.

commentators, that Hartshorne can maintain both the claim that God knows and experiences the immediacy of creaturely realities and his claim that the perspective of the known is distinct from that of the knower. One's knowledge can be qualified by the recognition of another's experience but only the other can have that experience. If to "feel how" is different than to "feel as," then something is lost in the transition. If, however, how and as coincide in God, then the distinction between perspectives is collapsed, and with it the independence and integrity of the known object is destroyed. Hartshorne wants to affirm both claims and failure to do so is a serious challenge to his system. On the one hand, to deny the distinction of knower and known jeopardizes the integrity of the world that Hartshorne has sought so assiduously to defend. But, on the other hand, the rejection of the full appropriation and preservation of immediacy would entail the collapse of Hartshorne's claim that God is the measure and preserver of reality. However, it does not appear to me that these Hartshornian claims can indeed be reconciled. As with so many Barthian claims, they are held together by assertion and insistence rather than by any true reconciliation.

Another way to state this dilemma is to put it in temporal terms: if the known is past, as it always is within the Hartshornian schema, does not that temporal status entail intrinsically the loss or cessation of immediacy and therefore whatever is preserved in the divine life it is not that? That is, is there not a profound difference between "has been" and "is" that Hartshorne's claim of the inclusion of immediacy fails to respect? Hartshorne rejects this criticism just as the above one and asserts, to the contrary, that pastness does not entail intrinsic loss of immediacy.[42] Entities become but do not change or "un-become."[43] Pastness means not the loss of something positive or vital but the availability of that experience for the future. With this assertion, Hartshorne is denying, on the one hand that in order for immediacy not to be lost, an event or experience must recur or continue to occur indefinitely and hence not really be past. To the contrary, he states:

> To become past or to persist is not to alter; . . . it only means a new entity becomes which feels the previous entity. For a unit of becoming to be thus felt by a new unit, there is no need for the previous becoming to become over again. Its "decision" has once and for all been made and it is available in *its* entirety as material for a new decision about a new experiential synthesis.[44]

---

[42] Because of his claim that God includes all reality in Godself, Hartshorne (WP, 2; "Dipolar Conception of Deity," 287) rejects Alfred North Whitehead's suggestion that pastness entails "perishing" and labels this terminology as a "misleading and dangerous metaphor."

[43] Hartshorne, "Dipolar Conception of Deity," preceding note.

[44] Hartshorne, "The Immortality of the Past," *Review of Metaphysics* 7 (1953) 109.

And, on the other hand, Hartshorne is contending that while an entity as past is fixed and settled, such facticity does not entail a lack of the vividness, indeed life, that characterized its present actuality.[45] The transition from "is" to "has been" is not a diminution or loss of anything that was "true" about the experience (CSPM, 16). In Hartshorne's words,

> If the experience is now intense in just a certain degree and manner, it must always thereafter be true that there was this degree and manner. Thus the characters of the experience all survive, only with the label "has been" or "no longer." Nothing positive truly assertible of the present can be obliterated by this translation into the has been. . . . I hold that the status "has been" is not a subtraction from an event's character. (Ibid., 16)

Once more the challenge to Hartshorne's system is clear: if events recur or continue to occur then the temporal and progressive character of experience as Hartshorne has interpreted it becomes problematic, while if the immediacy and vividness is lost, then God fails to be the true measure of reality and loss becomes an intrinsic dimension of all divine experience. But, as above, Hartshorne's response is not convincing and, more seriously, appears to be made at the expense of calling into question his own radical differentiation between past and present. Against Hartshorne, and in agreement with his critics, I would assert that vividness which is no longer being experienced is not the same as immediate aliveness; "has been" is not "is" and the difference is the loss of subjective immediacy. If temporal progression entails the gain of new experience, it involves as well, in every moment, the loss of immediacy that marks the transition of present to past. I would maintain therefore that while there is no sheer subtraction neither is there sheer construction, and if Hartshorne is to maintain his categorical distinction between past and present, it appears that it will be necessary to maintain as well a distinction between immediacy as lived and as remembered and that such a distinction will need to entail the recognition of some sort of loss in the translation from one to the other and therefore within God's life itself.[46]

---

[45] Hartshorne, "Dipolar Conception of Deity," above n. 42.

[46] A number of Hartshornian commentators have dealt with this issue and have concluded as well that God cannot include that subjective immediacy, and therefore it cannot be understood to be preserved by God in the same manner that it is experienced by the nondivine realities. For further discussion of this matter, see Peters, *Hartshorne and Neoclassical Metaphysics*, 118–21; idem, *Creative Advance*, 125–28; Ford, "Whitehead's Difference from Hartshorne," 72–74; Parsons, "Religious Naturalism and the Philosophy of Charles Hartshorne," 554–55; Henry Nelson Wieman, Review of DR, *Philosophical Review* 58 (1949) 79; Robertson, "Concept of Person," 150–51. For a more sympathetic but still critical analysis, see Griffin, "Hartshorne's Differences from Whitehead," 52–55.

Another area of concern emerges in relation to the earlier-cited claim that God's knowledge is both conformal and creative and that it both perfectly mirrors the world and is creatively unified into one experience. It must be asked if the creative integration and synthesis and the divine evaluation that goes along with it must not be understood as somehow altering its objects. Hartshorne rejects this notion and seems to indicate that while the creative appropriation is novel to God, it does not entail any newness in the entities received. However, it is not altogether clear on what grounds Hartshorne can make this assertion. If God's creative receptivity entails novel movement beyond the data received, then those data are no longer precisely what they were in themselves. However, if no such creative transformation occurs, then God is indeed merely the sum of the world constituents and nothing more. Either claim is damaging to Hartshorne's position, and the relationship between conformity and creativity remains, therefore, problematic.[47]

There is a further serious dilemma arising from the Hartshornian position that reflects the conflicting character of several of his central assumptions and claims. Hartshorne has been seen to argue that God, as perfect knower, is the all-inclusive reality, the totality of all that is. And as we also stated earlier, Hartshorne held for many years that God knew God's contemporaries in any given moment of divine experience. Such a claim corresponded to and supported his conviction that God was this inclusive totality. However, Hartshorne has repudiated the position that contemporaries can influence each other, and with that alteration in position has come a serious undermining of his assertion that God is Inclusive Whole. For the rejection of relations between contemporaries entails the corresponding rejection of the idea that God, as a perfect power, is coextensive with reality. If God does not know and include contemporaries, then at any given moment there is God including the past world plus the nascent world of contemporaries. If such a contemporary world is not fully actual, neither is it merely possible. It is real in a unique way that Hartshorne's temporally defined epistemology cannot account for without denying that God is inclusive of all reality. Hartshorne's God can neither include it nor be its measure; God and reality thereby are no longer strictly correlative. The result, according to Hartshornian commentator Gene Reeves, is that "'God and the world' is a more inclusive term than 'the world in God.'"[48]

Hartshorne himself is fully aware of the difficulty and the challenges it

---

[47] Parsons ("Religious Naturalism and the Philosophy of Charles Hartshorne," 554–55) discusses this issue in terms of love and the question of whether love does not by nature involve a "selective principle," an evaluative aspect, that would alter its objects.

[48] Reeves, "Whitehead and Hartshorne," 136.

presents but professes to be puzzled as to any possible solution.[49] But without such a solution the basis of the Hartshornian claim that God includes and is the measure of all reality cannot be upheld: to be as nascent actuality is not to be for God. And when this difficulty is combined with the above suggestion that the relation between knower—even the divine knower—and known is one in which subjectivity is not preserved, then Hartshorne's fundamental conception of God as the all-inclusive Cosmic Whole must be acknowledged to have serious problems which arise from its own premises. The Inclusive Whole turns out to be less than all-embracing, and the divine knower and reality no longer perfectly coincide.

Another difficulty which arises from this repudiation of interaction between contemporaries is that God no longer can be understood to perform one of the most important functions Hartshorne assigned the divine knower: the unification of the world. Hartshorne has placed considerable emphasis upon the claim that God, through God's receptive power, unifies and integrates the world through God's prehensive experience. However, if God does not include contemporaries at a given moment, there is a multiplicity of unconnected individuals existing, so to speak, side by side but with no unity. The world as nascent, coming to be actuality, has no coherence or interconnectedness. Either no such unifying structure is required and then Hartshorne's God is, at least in terms of this problem, superfluous or such unity is necessary and Hartshorne's position cannot provide it.[50]

A final criticism emerges from the field of science and relativity theory. Hartshorne in his work has been particularly concerned to take account of the claims of science, but there is one point especially where this has been difficult. This concerns the fact that according to Einstein's theory of relativity there is no simultaneous present whereby a clear and absolute distinction can be made between past and present. If this rejection of an absolute cosmic simultaneity is accepted, then it is difficult to uphold at the same time the Hartshornian assertion that at any given moment God surveys the whole past up to that moment for there is no vantage point from which God could do this. Hartshorne has long recognized the conflict between his own position and that of the science with which he wishes to agree (LP, xi, 204; WP, 86–87). However, even after he abandoned the notion of contemporaries' influencing each other, he still argued for what he termed a "cosmic front." He asserted, "I suppose God to have this cosmic now as his psychological simultaneity."[51] It is only in very recent years that Hartshorne has begun to alter his position to reflect the claims of relativity theory and

---

[49] Hartshorne, "Interrogation," 326; CSPM, 115.

[50] For a discussion of this concern, see Robert Neville, "Neoclassical Theology and Christology: A Critical Study of Ogden's *Reality of God*," *International Philosophical Quarterly* 9 (1969) 604–24.

[51] Hartshorne, "Interrogation," 324.

has begun to refer, not to God-now but to "God here-now" (CSPM, 123). But such an alteration, while closer to relativity physics, raises problems within Hartshorne's own schema. On the one hand, if there is a God here-now and a God somewhere-else-now and they are not the same, then the idea of God as a cosmic individual constituted by a linear succession of states is broken down or at least does not make much sense in analogy to nondivine localized individuals.[52] And, on the other hand, it raises a question of whether there is indeed one divine individual at all or rather somehow a plurality of cosmic knowers. That is, does Hartshorne's recognition of God here-now and God there-now entail a move toward some form of polytheism?[53] At any rate, Hartshorne's reconciliation of this position with relativity theory can be seen to open up problems in relation to other basic assertions that he wants to maintain. And once more it is not clear if Hartshorne can balance all his often-conflicting and sometimes-contradictory claims.

This section has examined Hartshorne's claim that divine power, in its receptive form, is the capacity to be influenced and it has further explicated Hartshorne's interpretation of this power in terms of the perfection of divine knowledge. Such interpretation of power as knowledge was seen to entail a conception of that divine knowledge as conformal, inclusive, and preservative and to involve the conclusions that God and reality coincide, and that God as the perfection of receptive power is the measure of all truth and meaning. Thus, from the initial claim that power has a receptive form, radical and far-reaching repercussions have been seen to flow, and with the analysis of that receptive form of power we have come to the very heart of Hartshorne's understanding of God. This understanding of divine reality as the Cosmic Whole, including the unifying all nondivine reality, presents a clear contrast to what Barth was understood to mean by God; indeed, it is not certain that the two thinkers are speaking of the same reality but rather they appear to stand as challengers to one another's positions, each calling into question the legitimacy of the other's interpretation.

This section also raised questions concerning tensions within the Hartshornian schema itself that seriously call into question whether Hartshorne can maintain his philosophical vision in its current form. Thus, while Hartshorne has argued persuasively that receptive power or the capacity to be influenced is not a lesser form of power or a weakness unsuited to deity, as it seems to be for Barth, his particular interpretation of receptivity

---

[52] For discussion of this issue, see Frederic F. Fost, "Relativity Theory and Hartshorne's Dipolar Theism," in *Two Process Philosophers,* 89–91; John Wilcox, "A Question from Physics for Certain Theists," *JR* 40 (1961) 293–300; Lewis S. Ford, "Is Process Theism Compatible with Relativity Theory?," *JR* 48 (1968) 124–35; and Gunton, *Becoming and Being,* 62–64.

[53] Hartshorne mentioned this possibility in passing in conversation. See also Griffin, "Hartshorne's Differences from Whitehead," 36.

and social relation along the lines of literal inclusion has been seen to entail such internal contradictions and inconsistencies that his definition of God as Inclusive Whole seems in danger of being reduced to incoherency and with it his conception of perfect power as the divine capacity to receive the world into Godself. Keeping in mind both the challenge of the Barthian position and the difficulties that arise in terms of Hartshorne's own premises, we may now turn to the second form of divine power and to explicate the Hartshornian claims concerning God's capacity to influence the world.

5.3 *Divine Power as Power to Influence*

The preceding analysis has explored at length the Hartshornian assertion that divine power must be conceived, in one of its basic expressions, to be creative receptivity or responsive knowing. Hartshorne argues as well that the seemingly more traditional conception of power as the capacity to influence is, in its preeminent form, an equally fundamental prerogative of the divine capacity, reflecting the principles of his social philosophy, as unique as its receptive counterpart and offers, even in this "agential" form, a sharply defined alternative to the Barthian position. It is the purpose of this section to delineate this alternative conception of how God acts upon the world.

It must be stated at the outset that Hartshorne's position concerning divine power as the capacity to influence is far less developed and clearly articulated than is his conception of receptive power. In comparison to his richly textured and thoroughly worked out interpretation of God as effect, his understanding of God as cause seems developed in only the most rudimentary manner. The fact that this dimension of Hartshorne's position lacks the wealth of detail obvious in the foregoing analysis has less, I would suggest, to do with the intrinsic possibilities of his vision than with his polemical way of doing philosophy. That is, much of his intellectual effort has consisted in correcting or balancing what he has taken to be a misguided interpretation of God as unaffected and unconditioned by creaturely realities. As a result, most of his work has been concerned with the development of a conception of a preeminently receptive and responsive deity. However, in principle Hartshorne's philosophy calls for an equally preeminent form of divine influence upon a receptive world. And if he has failed to offer a fully constructed position, he has nonetheless given enough details to suggest its shape and features and has set down the principles according to which any future construction will need to be developed.

Divine Action as World Maintenance

Hartshorne suggests that God's power to influence the creaturely world can be conceived, in broad terms, to be the capacity to maintain the existence of some world as the divine individual's "field of social relations" (DR, 134). If God's power of self-sufficiency consisted in the divine ability to assimilate all nondivine influences and maintain Godself as a social being in each successive moment, then the alternative expression of divine power lies in God's capacity to insure that there will be a world to whom God can in turn contribute (WP, 76–77). In Hartshorne's words,

> God is not viewed as a being that could exist in solitary independence, but as the being uniquely able to maintain the society of which it is member, the *only* social being unconditionally able to guarantee the survival, the minimal integrity, of its society and of itself as member of that society. This is a new definition of omnipotence. It means power adequate to preserve the society no matter what other members may do. (RSP, 40–41)

This power to maintain the world as God's social partner is not the ability to determine precisely what that world will be nor to decide in advance how the nondivine individuals will react to God's action upon them. This form of power, just as the previous one, is thoroughly social in nature and thereby entails God's action toward a world that is itself composed of self-active and creative powers. Hartshorne suggests, therefore, that God's power to act upon the world is best understood as the capacity to set conditions within which the nondivine powers make their own decisions or alternatively stated, to encourage a direction of world development without determining the exact outcome of decisions by localized agents (DR, 135). This is not the power of absolute fiat or a capacity to create ex nihilo. Rather, it is the ability to influence on a cosmic scale all subsequent events in a manner which insures that there will be some such events, that the world will neither collapse into utter chaos nor devolve into nothingness but will continue to produce localized self-creative powers who in turn will contribute to and influence the divine life (WP, 76–77). Hartshorne rejects the suggestion that this form of power is inferior to or a limitation of the more often-cited conception of divine power as the capacity to make or cause in an absolute manner. It is in no sense for him a "mediocre" power. Rather, he states:

> Just the contrary, "making" in the normal sense is a restriction upon what power in general is. Mere making is power so far as the thing upon which the power is exercised or in which it issues is negligibly endowed with self-activity (as in the famous "potter's clay"). This means that the result of the power is in itself trivial (mere "stuff" or "matter") or to us appears so. This is not the ideal of power but merely power manifested in inferior kinds of effect! God's power is actually greater than sheer "omnipotence," sheer making by fiat, whose products could only be lifeless and without individuality. The divine power is the fostering of other wills, other powers, other self-creative agents,

endowed with a measure of self-creativity. The ability to foster the
becoming and growth of such agents is incomparably greater than this
matter of sheer fiat of which we have heard so much. (PSG, 444)

God's Action as Divine Self-Determination

For Hartshorne, this power to foster wills is profoundly connected with
God's capacity to receive influences. Indeed, it is the divine process of
creative synthesis as it issues forth in a unified decision which subsequent
nondivine realities must take into account. It is God's creative self-
determination viewed from the perspective of creaturely entities for whom it
has become a datum to be appropriated in their own creative self-
determination. It is important to explicate this Hartshornian claim.

As has become clear in the preceding analysis, creaturely entities
influence and contribute to God's life by means of being experiences or
objects of knowledge that God appropriates and makes God's own. God's
power over the world consists in a divine version of this way of influencing.
Just as, for Hartshorne, divine knowledge or receptivity did not entail the
reversal of the cognitive processes found on the creaturely level, neither does
God's ability to condition the world involve a reversal or deviation from the
ordinary means of influencing but rather is its preeminent form (BH,
284–85). That is, God influences and acts upon the world by becoming the
one datum of experience or object of knowledge that every subsequent nondivine entity must appropriate as a factor in its own self-creation; God acts
upon the world by being a stimulus to which each new moment of nondivine
reality must react. As God was seen to be the one cosmic subject receiving
into Godself every nondivine influence, now, in turn, God can be understood to be as well the one cosmic object whose influence is absolutely
universal in scope and whose effect is felt by every other reality.

That God acts upon the world in this fashion means, therefore, that it is
in the first instance God's self-determination that decides the content and
shape of God's determination of the world. It is God's creative self-willing
that in turn sets the limits and defines the possibilities of the world that will
come to appropriate this cosmic object. God's constitution of the world is
first self-constitution. Now, for Barth as well, it is true that God's self-
creative decision is the foundation for any divine decision concerning the
world. However, the radical difference between the Hartshornian and
Barthian interpretation of this divine self-constitution lies in that this divine
decision occurs for Barth in independence from any relation with the world
and such relation is solely the result of God's own decision, while for
Hartshorne God's self-determination is the product of God's relation with
the nondivine world. In an endless process of give and take, how God, in
each new moment, reacts to the multiplicity of past worldly realities determines the divine life to which in each subsequent moment a new world will
have to react. In Hartshorne's words, "The mode of influence is the

dialogue. I speak, you listen and then you speak and I listen."[54]

According to Hartshorne, it is precisely because God's self-determination entails perfect receptivity of all nondivine influences that God's determination of the world is always perfect in adequacy as well. God's action upon the world is always commensurate to the needs and possibilities of the cosmos because God's life is a literal response to worldly realities which leaves nothing out but takes account of everything in its turn. For Hartshorne, perfect action can only be the other dimension of perfect reaction. In his words, "He influences us supremely because he is supremely open to our influence . . . He contributes to our lives in a superior fashion because, in equally superior fashion, he receives contributions from us" (CSPM, 12).

Divine Action as Love of World and Self-Love

This fact that God's action upon the world entails perfect awareness of the world means, for Hartshorne, that God's power is never arbitrary, irresponsible, or irrelevant. It can never take the form of blind force or insensitive autocratic rule. On the one hand, this is so for reasons similar to the ones articulated in the previous section concerning why knowledge and hatred never coincide: an awareness that takes into account the most subtle nuance of creaturely reality cannot result in a form of influence that is destructive, or even one-sided, or inappropriate. Action which is fully informed must, as well, be balanced and measured in relation to all who feel its effect. It is this awareness of and sensitivity to the multiplicity of interests that is at the heart of what is meant by virtuous or ethical action.[55] Only influence over others which is first sensitivity to others can be understood as virtuous behavior (DR, 124–25). But in all nondivine realities these two are never fully coincident, and as a result all creaturely action is always imperfect influence, marred by ignorance and its lack of adequate sensitivity. Divine action, however, presupposing complete awareness, is the perfect union of power and virtue. In Hartshorne's words,

> There can be no ethical appeal beyond the decision of the one who in his decision takes account of all actuality and possibility. . . . There could not be a wrong decision which thus took account of the situation; for a right decision can be defined as one adequately informed as to its context. Omniscience in action is by definition right action.[56]

---

[54] Hartshorne, "Divine Absoluteness and Divine Relativity," 166.

[55] MVG, 192–93. According to Hartshorne, ethical rules are substitutes for adequate awareness whose purpose is to balance interests.

[56] Ibid.

There is another reason as well why divine influence upon the world can always be assumed to be perfect in its adequacy and appropriateness. This reason lies in what Hartshorne understands to be the coincidence of divine self-interest and the interests of the world. [57] Stated more fully, within this temporally defined schema, what God does for the world now, God is also doing for a future state of God's own self for which that world will become the data of divine experience. Hartshorne concludes from this that what is good or creative for God and what is best for the world are one and the same. There is no way that God could harm the world without also diminishing Godself or benefit the world without benefitting Godself. There are several interesting and important implications of this claim that must be explicated.

First, Hartshorne's assertion that divine and worldly interests or needs coincide entails the rejection of the claim that God's action toward the world is self-sacrificial in nature. As has been argued throughout the analysis, the Hartshornian deity is not the possessor of all possible value, enjoying sheer bliss, incapable of growth in knowledge or joy. If God were such a being, then relations with the world would indeed be purely gratuitous in character and God would gain no benefit from such relations but would have to be understood as either freely giving of Godself out of an abundance of divine love, as in the Barthian schema, or freely sacrificing God's own well-being for that of the creatures. But the Hartshornian God is not this self-complete being but rather is a deity that in every successive state enjoys new value and growth through the creative appropriation of the changing world. Therefore, each benefit that God bestows upon the world is a benefit whose value God will come to enjoy in the future. What God does for the world is indeed for the sake of the world, but it is also for the sake of the divine life itself.

Hartshorne argues that without this recognition that God literally receives value from the world's existence any notion of divine creation of nondivine reality or creative activity in relation to that reality is essentially nonsensical. [58] He contends that the only conceivable purpose of creation is the achievement of new value and value which is not value for God is, in essence, nothing. Referring to the multiplicity of creaturely reality, he states:

> If, however, variety is said not to be a value for God, then one asks,
> Why a creation at all? Why should he add to his own perfection the

---

[57] MVG, 161. Bernard Loomer ("Two Conceptions of Power," *Process Studies* 6 [1976] 15–16) suggests that love interpreted only as outgoing and self-giving, only concerned for the other, with no concern for the self, may well be an attempt to compensate for a one-sided linear notion of power and suggests that as power needs to be reinterpreted, so, too, does love.

[58] Hartshorne, "Cause," *An Encyclopedia of Religion,* 134.

contrast of the purely inferior creatures, unless contrast as such is valu-
able? ... It is no use to say that God creates the creatures out of generosity or love; for if he loves the valueless, so much the worse for his
love, and what but the value of contrast can the creatures add to
existence? (MVG, 39)

Hence, God and the world are not in opposition; their goals coincide. In
relation to divine action and purpose toward the world, altruism and egoism
are the same (MVG, 161; CSPM, 309–10). In Hartshorne's words, "In
God there is indeed a perfect agreement of altruism and egoism. For whatever good God may do to any being anywhere, he himself, through his
omniscient sympathy, will inevitably enjoy" (MVG, 161). Therefore, God's
action toward the world is always a loving influence that has as its aim the
fulfillment of creaturely needs and the actualization of new nondivine
values. But such loving action is not self-renouncing; it instead entails
God's own drive toward divine satisfaction.

To this conception of the nongratuitous character of divine love and
action and the claim of coincidence between egoism and altruism in God, a
chorus of objections immediately arises. The first is that it introduces need
into God's relation with the world. Hartshorne's position does indeed entail
need upon the part of God (ibid., 164). However, as has been stated on a
number of occasions, such need does not concern the question of divine
existence. No matter what world exists, God will exist as knowing it.
Rather, divine need concerns how rich and full of value the content of God's
concrete life will be, and that content depends upon the worldly realities
that are its raw material or data.

But with the admission that God depends upon the world the question
arises of whether God's action is not also self-interest, but only self-concern.
That is, if God benefits from the world, is divine action only for that self-
benefit and not for the good of the world? Does not need entail selfishness?
Hartshorne replies to this objection with an emphatic "No." On the
creaturely level, need does indeed most often involve the conflict of
interests, and proper action always calls for the balancing of one's own right-
ful needs in relation to the rights and needs of others. But for God,
Hartshorne reiterates, this is not so, for God requires precisely a world as
full of value and satisfaction as is possible. It is not need per se that causes
selfishness but the inability to fulfill one's needs through knowledge and
love of others. Hartshorne, in rejecting the notion that God's love of the
world must be separated from the divine need for the world, states:

An objection that some will certainly make is the following: on the view
I have been taking, God's love is really self-interest. Instead, one
should say that while we creatures cannot help aiming at our own good,
God is superior because he has his good once for all simply in himself.
If he aims at our good, that is a sheer gratuitous addition, pure

generosity. This, however, is the pseudo-conception of perfection that we have rejected. The idea of doing good to others, without hope that this good will necessarily turn out to be in its entirety also one's own, is appropriate only to partly ignorant, mortal, and not unsurpassably loving beings, such as are we. . . . But God does not die and cannot fail to apprehend every achievement in its full concrete value. The issue of selfishness vs. unselfishness is not an issue for God, just because he is God; but it is an issue for us, just because we are not God. God has no nonloving self, we do; he has no ignorant, mortal self, we do. We are but fragments of life and value. God is the inclusive life and value. What could it mean for him to promote a good simply outside his own? [59]

Thus, as Hartshorne closely linked divine power in its receptive mode to divine love, so too does he associate power and love in their more active forms. Divine influence upon the world is always for Hartshorne, as for Barth, gracious activity. However, contra to all Barthian claims, Hartshorne argues that the gracious character of divine action flows not from the fact that it is purely gratuitous and reflects no need or desire upon God's part. Rather, it is gracious because God's own needs and desires are finally the same as the world's .[60] The Hartshornian God is no self-renouncing deity, but one who with greatest receptivity receives the values the world offers.

And finally, Hartshorne suggests that a love that can only give to others but never receive value from others, that is only outgoing without being also receptive, is a love that does not answer what is to him one of the most central needs of all entities: the need to contribute to the lives of others. That is, Hartshorne suggests the need to love is just as primary for creatures as the need to be loved, and it is just this fundamental need that purely gratuitous action, however gracious or even self-sacrificial in character, can never answer. In his words,

> If God permits us every privilege but not that of enriching his life by contributing the unique quality of our own experience to the more inclusive quality of his, by virtue of his sympathetic interest in us, then he does less for us than the poorest of human creatures. (DR, 55)

Divine Action as the Aim at Aesthetic Value

Thus, divine purpose and the true aim of the world are one. And, this divine purpose, toward which all God's decisions and activity are oriented,

---

[59] Hartshorne, "Process and the Nature of God," 138–39.

[60] Hartshorne recognizes that in their egoistic moments humans fail to see this commonality of interests but nonetheless he argues that what is best for God and the world coincide and therefore although God's actions may contradict certain perceived interests of creatures, such divine influence is, in reality, for the true interests of the creatures.

is the actualization of the greatest possible good. Further, in this schema, this one primary good is that the "creatures should enjoy rich harmonies of living and pour this richness into the one ultimate receptacle of all achievements, the life of God" (ibid., 127–28). Hartshorne's interpretation of such "rich harmonies of living" closely corresponds to his fellow process thinker, Alfred North Whitehead's conception of the good: the fundamental good consists in the balance or interweaving of harmony and intensity of experience or, according to Whitehead, in beauty. It consists in the equilibrium of vitality and concord.[61] God's action upon the world, with the actualization of this richness of experience as its goal, seeks to set optimal conditions that encourage vitality and zest while preventing the lapse of creaturely experience either into chaos or monotony (PSG, 436–37). It seeks, in other words, to encourage the achievement of maximal aesthetic value.

It is therefore value defined aesthetically rather than morally or ethically that is the fundamental universal good. "The concrete values," Hartshorne states, "are aesthetic, not ethical, as Kant clearly saw and we all should never forget."[62] And it is toward the realization of this intensity and harmony of experience that the divine purpose is oriented. However, it must be asked, what happens to the moral good in all this? If God's purpose is aesthetic, can it be stated that God has any sort of moral will or intention? The relation of aesthetic and moral good will be explored more thoroughly in the following chapter, but a few remarks must be made at this juncture. Although, as will be made clear, Hartshorne rejects the idea that aesthetic and moral value ultimately conflict or are in opposition, there is a sense in which God's will or purpose is more than or transcends the ethical will of creatures which needs to balance benefit to self with benefit to others (CSPM, 309). Because God's future as cosmic recipient of all values is assured, there is no sense in which God's aim for God's own good needs to be weighed against the good of the world. It is precisely because of this coincidence that God's aesthetic purpose is also a moral purpose, seeking the most value for all creatures whatsoever. There is, for Hartshorne, no tension between God's aesthetic and moral aim; altruism and egoism in God are one. "The aesthetic value of good will, of aiming at the general aesthetic good, is in God ideally complete, and is the same as his righteousness" (ibid., 310). The divine moral will or purpose consists therefore in aiming at the intensity and harmony of experience for all worldly entities and thereby at the achievement of aesthetic value on a universal scale, both for creatures and through them for Godself.

God's encouragement of this aesthetic development has several forms. In

---

[61] Hartshorne, "Beyond Enlightened Self-Interest," in Harry James Cargas and Bernard Lee, eds., *Religious Experience and Process Theology* (New York: Paulist, 1976) 318–19; Hartshorne, "Divine Absoluteness and Divine Relativity," 167.

[62] Hartshorne, "Divine Absoluteness and Divine Relativity," preceding note.

the first place, God's purpose in relation to the world has an abstract and absolute form (PSG, 189, 502; NTOT, 60). That is, God's general purpose toward the world is always fixed and unmoved; God in all circumstances seeks the greatest possible actualization of value and is thereby the cosmic ground of the actualization of any value whatsoever. In Hartshorne's words, "This purpose, in its most general and primordial aspect, is literally unchanged, an unmoved mover of all things."[63]

Divine Determination of Cosmic Order

However, for Hartshorne God's abstract, general purpose is always expressed through the divine life and decision. That is, in every moment the general divine ideal is given specific expression through particular, concrete decisions as to how God will influence the world. And this particularization and specification of God's purpose consists in the divine self-determination through which God unifies and integrates all worldly experience into one divine experience which all subsequent worlds in turn must take into account. Hartshorne is not always clear concerning the exact forms of this world determination. As will be argued momentarily, he sometimes indicates that God's self-determination includes specific ideals and aims for future nondivine experiences. However, most often he suggests that this specification of the divine aim for aesthetic value can best be expressed by stating that by ordering Godself, God sets the limits to and determines the order of the creaturely realm (PSG, 493). God's action upon the world consists in a primary way in the cosmic order God imposes upon that world through which God governs the direction of world development and creaturely actualization of value. This interpretation of divine influence as cosmic ordering must be explicated further.

First, and for the most part, Hartshorne suggests that God's ordering of the world consists in the setting of cosmic laws or the laws of nature. These laws do not entail the divine determination of each creaturely activity. Rather, they involve the "setting of limits" within which individual creaturely entities determine themselves. In Hartshorne's words, "God decides upon the basic outlines of creaturely actions, the guaranteed limits within which freedom is to operate."[64] God's power to influence is therefore a structuring power. And such a capacity to determine order on the cosmic scale is of absolute necessity (NTOT, 59, 120; WP, 133; RSP, 39). For if complete chaos and mutual destruction are to be avoided, there must be a means by which the multiplicity of localized worldly powers are coordinated into some form of harmonious interaction. Hartshorne suggests that it is only through a common, universal power or influence that such mutual

[63] Hartshorne, "Efficient Causality in Aristotle and St. Thomas," *JR* 25 (1945) 29.

[64] Hartshorne, "A New Look at the Problem of Evil," in Frederick C. Dommeyer, ed., *Current Philosophical Issues: Essays in Honor of Curt John Ducasse* (Springfield, Illinois: Charles Thomas, 1966) 206.

adjustment can take place. The myriad of creatures harmonize at least to the extent that they "constitute a viable cosmos" only because there is a universal ordering influence to which all are alike subjected.[65]

God therefore, by ordering Godself, gives to the world a common structure that permits the adjustment and coordination of the plurality of worldly powers. And by so doing God performs an action that only a cosmic agent, universal in the scope of its influence, could carry out. "Only God can decide natural or cosmic laws."[66] But while Hartshorne is insistent that such cosmic order is always required in some form, he is also adamant that just what order does occur is the result of God's free and creative self-determination. That is, cosmic laws are neither eternal nor unchangeable but are the result of the temporal decision of a self-changing deity and they represent a choice among a plurality of alternatives. Several factors are involved in this assertion.

First, this claim entails the rejection of the notion that there is one "best possible course of action" (DR, 137; WP, 158). God's decision for the world, as fully informed and gracious in character, can never be an inferior choice, but it is still a decision among equally possible alternative courses of action. The statement that God "'could not have done better' does not imply that he could have done equally well though differently" (PSG, 140). That there is an order of some sort is not a decision left open to God, for God must always integrate and unify the divine experience, but just what order will prevail is a matter for the divine self-willing and free choice.

Further, this claim that the cosmic order is a result of God's free self-determination entails as well the recognition that these universal laws are not, by any necessity, permanent but are subject to change. That is, it is within the divine prerogative to alter the direction of the cosmos. The only requirement incumbent upon this divine choice is that, informed by perfect knowledge of the past world, it set limits upon the world which will insure that optimal conditions will pertain for the actualization of aesthetic value. Such "optimal conditions" mean for Hartshorne that the opportunities for the realization of value be as great or greater than the risks involved. He equates optimal conditions with the balance of risk and opportunities, rather than merely opportunities, for he is convinced that the level of aesthetic value is correlative to the amount of free creativity present in each experience. That is, freedom and value are proportionate to one another, and if there is to be great actualization of value, then there must also be great freedom and creativity. And such freedom inevitably entails the risk of failure and destruction. Thus, God's decision must balance the possibilities of achievement of value with those risks of failure (LP, 203–4).

There are several further factors concerning Hartshorne's conception of

---

[65] Hartshorne, "Development of Process Philosophy," 60.
[66] Hartshorne, "New Look at the Problem of Evil," 209.

divine power as the capacity to determine the cosmic order that must be discussed. The first is that this position clearly entails the rejection of any
notion that God creates this or any world out of nothing in a single act of
divine decision.[67] God's action is indeed supremely creative, but as has been
contended throughout, such divine action always presupposes creaturely
experiences that God's decision transforms into God's own. There is therefore no first moment of creation. Divine creativity is instead a moment-by-
moment affair that entails response to and transformation of other realities.
According to Hartshorne,

> To imagine God before *all* creation deciding upon the whole once and
> for all is to slide into the eternalistic dream in which nothing really
> makes sense. Creation is not a one-step process. Merely possible worlds
> set no soluble problem, even to the All-wise; for where no conditions are
> fixed, there is no definite problem to solve. Only a world already in
> being gives God anything to decide about. (AD, 187–88)

Thus, God creates not once and for all but continually through the
transformation of each successive phase of worldly experience (DR, 30).
That God, in each moment, always deals with an already existent world,
does not mean, however, that there ever could be a world that somehow preceded or escaped divine influence. Rather, every momentary world that precedes God was first preceded by God in an earlier state of the divine life.
God never relates to a world whose "coming to be antedates his own entire
existence" (ibid.). According to Hartshorne, "There is no presupposed
'stuff' alien to God's creative work; but rather that everything that
influences God has already been influenced by him" (ibid.).

A second implication that emerges from this interpretation of divine
activity is the assertion that creation, preservation, providence, and indeed
salvation are all one. These terms do not refer, as they do within the
Barthian schema, to distinct phases or aspects of divine decision and activity
but to different ways of looking at the one divine self-determination. They
are the one step-by-step process that occurs continually throughout time.
God's creativity is always providential, and the divine providence always
seeks further creative realization.

A final and inclusive implication of this interpretation of God's action as
constituting the cosmic laws is that such laws must be clearly distinguished
from the metaphysical categories discussed both here and in the preceding

---

[67] MVG, 231–33; AD, 187–88. Philosopher Robert Neville (*God the Creator* [Chicago:
University of Chicago Press, 1968] 108–9) has difficulty with the Hartshornian position concerning this matter and suggests that while the neoclassical position may explain coming to be
within the created order, it does not explain the world itself. Hartshorne, for his part, rejects
all moves to get beyond the temporally defined creative process to some point at which that
process came into being. It has always been and always will be.

chapter. Cosmic laws are the result of God's decision; they are not necessary, and they can be altered. Metaphysical categories are necessary and universal and will pertain no matter what cosmic or natural laws are in effect in any particular cosmic epoch. The cosmic order is contingent; that there is some order is metaphysical and necessary. [68]

Determination of Individual Aims

Thus, Hartshorne can be understood to argue that God influences the world by determining the cosmic order within which creatures will determine their own and each other's destinies. But is this structuring activity the only way in which God influences the world? Barth's God influenced, indeed determined in an absolute manner, the least detail of creaturely reality. Does Hartshorne's God in some parallel manner, contribute anything more specific than a general structure and order? Unfortunately, Hartshorne has not developed this dimension of his position in any detail or with much clarity. Indeed, except for some brief remarks, he has had little to say directly concerning this question. As a result, some commentators have concluded that according to the Hartshornian principles, God can know and preserve the world and can set cosmic limits but cannot offer specific ideals or aims to individual realities. That is, God's purposes are general, not specific. Lewis S. Ford, working out of a more Whiteheadian perspective, argues this interpretation and concludes that as a result Hartshorne's God leaves much to be desired from an existential or religious perspective. He states:

> The imposition of the laws of nature, however, seems deficient in religious inspiration, even if it is God's primary mode of acting. While we may be comforted and reassured that God thereby protects us from chaos, this is primarily a matter for physics rather than for ethics and religion. [69]

However, other commentators assert that Hartshorne, if he fails to develop this side of his position, nonetheless presupposes a more specific form of divine activity. [70] There seem to be several reasons to assume that

---

[68] Edgar A. Towne ("Metaphysics as Method in Charles Hartshorne's Thought," *The Southern Journal of Philosophy* 6 [1968] 130) suggests that Hartshorne is making too large and ambitious claims concerning the distinction between metaphysical and cosmological ideas and suggests that he should perhaps understand the metaphysical claims, not as necessary traits of all reality in every epoch, but as cosmological characteristics applicable to this cosmic epoch and therefore as contingent and relative as are the cosmic laws.

[69] Ford, "Whitehead's Differences from Hartshorne," 79.

[70] Reeves ("Whitehead and Hartshorne," 134) argues against Lewis Ford on this point among others. Parsons ("Religious Naturalism and the Philosophy of Charles Hartshorne,"

the logic of Hartshorne's position entails a more specific mode of action. First, Hartshorne argues extensively that God's causal influence upon the world is so preeminent by virtue of God's sensitivity toward and receptivity of the world's experience. It is reasonable to conclude that this sensitivity does not merely issue forth in general cosmic laws but rather that God's apprehension of the creaturely world entails a purposive and evaluative dimension that subsequent individuals experience as God's aim or ideal for those individuals. Hartshorne commentator Gene Reeves states: "God limits our freedom by creating order in the world to be sure, but he also limits our freedom by providing aims and ideals."[71] Second, there are occasions when Hartshorne refers directly to God's particular purposes for the world.[72] And third, Hartshorne often speaks of the creaturely capacity to deviate from the divinely proposed norms, and while often this is in reference to freedom within the limits set by God, there are times as well when Hartshorne is certainly presupposing more specific divinely decreed ideals. This creaturely capacity for disobedience lends support to the interpretation of Hartshorne that argues for both divine action at the level of cosmic laws and on the more particular level of specific divine ideals for creaturely action.

It can be concluded that Hartshorne argues for divine influence both in terms of instituting a cosmic order and of providing specific aims that shape and condition the development of individuals and lure them toward new heights of actualization. While I concur with such commentators as Gene Reeves rather than Lewis Ford on this issue, I must also state that Hartshorne's failure to develop this dimension of his thought leaves a large gap in his work and with it the suspicion that God's action upon the world is of only negligible import and is basically irrelevant to the personal and individual concerns of the creatures. Cosmic laws are of such a basic and pervasive nature and change in them is, if it comes at all, so imperceptible to ordinary individuals that, in the end, it seems irrelevant whether they are the result of a blind cosmic force or a benevolent deity. And further notions of creaturely response, love, or worship all seem inappropriate if the only experience of deity is through cosmic order. If Hartshorne is to maintain the connection which he so consistently has sought between his metaphysically defined fact and the religiously defined God of love, he will need to develop this dimension of his thought more fully.

In summary, it can be stated that Hartshorne develops his understanding of the divine power to influence the world, for the most part, in terms of

---

556–57) seems to conclude that Hartshorne assumes a more specific mode of activity but raises doubts concerning how he would know this divine aim or ideal.

[71] Reeves, "Whitehead and Hartshorne," 134.

[72] WP, 92. In this context Hartshorne is speaking of Whitehead's idea of God but is apparently in agreement on this point.

God's capacity to order the world through God's own self-ordering. By this action, God does not determine creaturely decisions but rather sets the limits within which creatures decide for themselves. Hartshorne further suggests, though with less clarity, that God offers creaturely realities more specific aims or ideals as a means of influencing the direction of worldly development. By way of bringing this analysis to a close, it must be asked finally how Hartshorne conceives of the mechanics of this influence. That is, how indeed does God's power act upon the world?

The Means of Divine Influence

As was stated at the beginning of this section, the mode of God's influence upon the world is not the reversal of the manner of influence exhibited by creatures in relation to God but the preeminent exemplification of this form of power. This means that God conditions and determines nondivine realities by being an object of their knowledge, a datum of their experience which must be taken into account to which they must respond. For Hartshorne, the "power of God over us consists in his being the supreme object of our awareness."[73] There are several components of this claim that must be examined.

It is clear that Hartshorne has been espousing a very particular and circumscribed form of influential power or mode of causality. That is, for him, because all experience of actual realities is retrospective in character, then causal influence can be seen always to be a function of memory, of knowledge of that which has already happened. According to the Hartshornian principles, the "only experienced causality is memory."[74] God has power over the world because the divine experience forms the content of worldly memory. And second, Hartshorne further argues, because God is the inclusive whole who incorporates all nondivine reality into Godself, it follows necessarily that the experience or memory of anything is the experience of God.[75] To be aware of any reality whatsoever is to be aware, though dimly, of the totality of which it is a part.[76] Thus, God is an immediate datum of experience, present at all times. However, in the third place, Hartshorne acknowledges that while God is an ever-present datum of experience, the creaturely awareness of the deity is mostly unconscious and

[73] Hartshorne, "Divine Absoluteness and Divine Relativity," 166.

[74] Hartshorne, "Contingency and the New Era in Metaphysics," *The Journal of Philosophy* 29 (1932) 446.

[75] Hartshorne, "God's Existence: A Conceptual Problem," in Sidney Hook, ed., *Religious Experience and Truth* (New York: New York University Press, 1961) 211; AD, 219.

[76] Hartshorne, "The Formal Validity and Real Significance of the Ontological Argument," *The Philosophical Review* 53 (1944) 235.

not readily accessible to fully cognitive scrutiny. [77] On the one hand, this is so because immediate memory or experience on the part of creatures is simply not conscious by nature.[78] And, on the other hand, creatures, precisely because they are creatures, experience God and all else in a deficient manner that responds to their objects without full understanding of that to which they react.[79] Thus, creatures directly but vaguely feel God, rather than consciously know God. However, it must be reiterated that although such experience is unconscious and for the most part vague, nonetheless God is always experienced in some manner, and hence Hartshorne can conclude that the "difference between believer and unbeliever is one of levels of awareness."[80] For Barth, too, the difference between believer and unbeliever is knowledge or awareness of God. However, Barth aserts that God chooses those who will be aware of the divine reality, while Hartshorne argues that God is present for all to apprehend and recognition, and acknowledgement of deity is therefore entirely dependent upon the human capacity to understand correctly its experience rather than upon God's special decision or election.

If, however, in Hartshorne's view creatures are not always fully conscious of God's power, he nonetheless asserts that God influences and shapes creatures to God's own intentions in a most comprehensive and pervasive manner. All creatures, though most often unconsciously, respond to and are conditioned by divine reality, and Hartshorne suggests that this divine influence is so pervasive and indeed often irresistable because God is the supremely lovable and beautiful object of experience (LP, 275; PSG, 274; WP, 134; CSPM, 12). That is, Hartshorne argues that God's influence is efficacious not because God imposes, by coercive force, God's will and purposive vision upon the world but because God, as supremely sensitive to all needs and desires, offers the world the most perfect vision of what it might be. God moves the world not by force or imposition but by persuasion, by the lure of value and the vision of hope; God's influence is supreme because God's love is perfect, offering to the world precisely what it requires for the richness and beauty of experience. In Hartshorne's words,

> We now ask ourselves, why is the divine fiat universally and incomparably influential? I answer with an old doctrine (perhaps first stated by Aristotle), somewhat transformed: God is uniquely influential because he is uniquely good or beautiful. As Whitehead puts it, "the power of God is the worship he inspires." Not, the power inspires worship, but

---

[77] Hartshorne, "God's Existence: A Conceptual Problem," 211.

[78] Hartshorne, "Religion in Process Philosophy," 257.

[79] Hartshorne, "Process as Inclusive Category: A Reply," *The Journal of Philosophy* 50 (1955) 99–100.

[80] Hartshorne, "Is God's Existence a State of Affairs?," in John Hick, ed., *Faith and the Philosophers* (London: Macmillan, 1964) 31.

the worshipfulness is the power. The creatures admire or worship God, they directly feel his worshipful excellence and beauty, and this inspires and influences them, which inspiring beauty is power. The principle here is: no creature can respond to anything except value, goodness, or beauty in some form. All power is of the nature of appeal, attractiveness, or "charm," acting either directly or indirectly. A tyrant need not charm all his subjects, it is true, but he "charms" at least the members of his own physical body, or they would not act in accordance with his thoughts and purposes, and the movements of his body "charm" the surrounding molecules, voice, and so on. The tyrant may also—to some extent must—charm his personal followers. Each link in this chain is either inexplicable, a mere mystery, or a case of the appeal of value to some creature. [81]

Thus, in the final analysis divine power in its form of casual influence is persuasive power that moves the world by offering itself as the supreme vision of purpose and possibility. "Power is influence, perfect power is perfect influence" (MVG, xvi). In all this, Hartshorne definitely appears to presuppose that individuals experience this purpose and possibility, not only as cosmic laws but also as ideals of individual development. And further, Hartshorne's interpretation of this form of power presupposes as well, just as did its receptive counterpart, a multiplicity of agents whose own power consists in their capacity creatively to receive and respond to the divine influence. Hence, while such divine influence is supreme and efficacious beyond all others, this does not and cannot mean that it is fully determining. Influence, even divine influence, cannot be equated with a monopoly of decision-making capacity. It can only be an element, though perhaps the dominant element, in a decision that can finally only be each individual's. It is to the exploration of this creaturely capacity for self-determination and its implication for the problems of evil and sin that the following chapter is devoted, but at this juncture, let it suffice to say that the Hartshornian conclusion is that "God cannot simply 'coerce' anything: he can only inspire it to act in a certain sort of way." [82]

Questions Concerning Divine Action

Before turning to the implications of this Hartshornian claim of persuasive and inspiring power, it is necessary to examine several questions that

---

[81] Hartshorne, "Religion in Process Philosophy," 258. He acknowledges (p. 261) that there is coercive power or even "brute force" but suggests that this is only "indirect power whose direct links are left unexplained," and that it is only persuasive power that is direct.

[82] Hartshorne, "Religion in Process Philosophy," 262. Numerous commentators and critics find the notion of power as persuasion inadequate as a conception of divine activity and willing. See Robertson, "Concept of Person," 166; and Gunton, *Becoming and Being*, 45.

such a position suggests. One such concern revolves around the experience of God and what Hartshorne could possibly mean by this. Hartshorne has argued that experience of God is a universal phenomenon, an implication of every experience whatsoever. However, he has also acknowledged that such experience is vague and only dimly given. Once more it is difficult to understand what import or consequence this vague, for the most part unconscious, experience could have. The question remains whether the Hartshornian deity makes any difference whatsoever to the lives and actions of individuals who "feel" but do not "know" God. In the words of Howard L. Parsons,

> But exactly how men know God empirically is not made plain—because God is known "vaguely." Such an account will perhaps satisfy the man with a strongly esthetic response to the world; but men of action demand that they come to grips with a tangible deity that makes a difference to perception and conduct.[83]

Another question that arises concerns the Hartshornian claim that every experience of the world is also an experience of God. It must be asked whether there is any difference between experiencing God and a nondivine entity. Parsons expresses difficulty concerning this point as well, stating that "it becomes difficult experientially to distinguish God's love from man's love" (ibid., 557). Hartshorne speaks of the fact that somehow, though dimly, creatures experience God as the totality of all past reality in and through experiencing nondivine entities as part of that totality. Thus, the nondivine element experienced as part of the divine totality might provide for the contrast Parsons seeks. However, what it could possibly mean to experience the totality of all past actuality Hartshorne never makes adequately clear, and such an experience appears almost impossible to conceive. It must be very, very vague indeed!

Other critics of the Hartshornian schema claim that divine action understood as persuasion forecloses the possibility of God's acting in history and only allows God to be an object for history. And, for those who work out of traditions that stress the historical agency of the divine being, the "mighty acts of God," this presents a profound difficulty.[84] The conclusion to be drawn, though not all Hartshornian followers draw it, is that all events in history are influenced by God in the same manner and the result is that no event any more than another can be argued to have, in principle, a special

---

[83] Parsons, "Religious Naturalism and the Philosophy of Charles Hartshorne," 556.

[84] Gunton (*Becoming and Being*, 49) is particularly critical of this point and argues that it is difficult within this schema to claim that certain historical events are "more appropriately described in theological language than others. What about Jesus?"

relation to deity.[85] The difference between secular and religious experience is only a difference in levels of awareness and forms of expression concerning that experience. God is equally present in both. Thus the, in principle, distinct quality of religious experience is denied.[86] Another repercussion of this universal experience of the divine is that not only is the difference between secular and religious experience rejected, but so too are the differences among various forms of religious experience. That is, Hartshorne conludes that the various historical religions are really referring to similar experiences. The historical expressions may be different but not the content of the experience. Once more, those who seek a distinctive and unique form of divine action, as Barth most certainly presupposed, will find no support here. Nor will those who have a sociologically and anthropologically informed sense of the role historically defined symbols and language play in determining the content of any experience whatsoever. Hartshorne, in the most unhistorical manner, seems to be suggesting a new version of the old idea of perennial philosophy and thereby leaves himself open to all the criticisms that this historically unsophisticated notion invited.

I shall return to some of these reflections in the Conclusion of this dissertation, but at this juncture I would suggest that the difficulties Hartshorne's position entails highlight the general problem of identifying any experience as experience of God. Those critics who worry that every experience is of God have an equally difficult time justifying their own claims for distinctive and unique experiences of the deity. How one identifies an "experience of the divine" has been an age-old problem which in the modern era has increasingly raised questions whether this is the most appropriate way to conceive of the idea of God at all. Whether it is the Barthian God available only to faith or Hartshorne's metaphysical deity available to every individual, the question remains whether the idea of the experience of such an entity has any cognitive reference whatsoever. And as the analysis of this thesis has shown, neither Barth nor Hartshorne is finally clear about what that reference might explicitly be. In both instances, it remains more of an assertion than a clearly and intelligibly explicated position.

5.4 Summary Remarks

The foregoing analysis has revealed that Hartshorne offers a twofold interpretation of divine power: divine power is, in one of its expressions, the

---

[85] Ogden (*The Reality of God* [New York: Harper & Row, 1963]) has attempted more than any other Hartshornian follower to be faithful to Hartshorne's claims of universal experience of the divine while also arguing for a distinctive understanding of Jesus.

[86] A number of Hartshornian commentators criticize Hartshorne on this point, arguing that the "mysterious" element of religious experience is lost. See Neville, *God the Creator*, 266, 331–32.

capacity to receive all nondivine realities into God's own experience in a creative and transforming manner, and it is, in its alternative dimension, the capacity to influence creaturely experience to an unsurpassed degree. This Hartshornian position can be seen to have significant points of common concern with the Barthian schema. Both Barth and Hartshorne consistently tie power to knowledge and love, and seek, at all times, to differentiate divine power from all forms of brute or evil force. Divine power moves always and everywhere in love and knowledge and its character is ever gracious. But each thinker develops radically different and finally contradictory interpretations of that power, knowledge, and love. Barth suggests an interpretation of all three in primarily active terms, while Hartshorne develops a receptive and responsive understanding of all of them and a very different conception of their active dimensions as well.

The analysis has revealed not only differences with Barth's conceptions of divine power but also several profound tensions within the Hartshornian schema itself. These internal conflicts were further seen to be of such a fundamental nature that, just as with Barth before him, it is not certain whether Hartshorne can resolve these problems in a manner that keeps his basic assumptions intact. Thus, while Hartshorne offers a clear-cut alternative to Barth, it is evident that this alternative has, just as its Barthian counterposition, problems which call into question its ultimate acceptability. It is now time to analyze how the differences between Barth and Hartshorne manifest themselves in relation to the question of creaturely freedom and power and the problem of evil, and to ascertain what light such differences might shed upon our final evaluation of these twentieth-century theological alternatives.

6

DIVINE POWER AND WORLDLY REALITY
ACCORDING TO HARTSHORNE

The foregoing analysis has revealed that not only do Karl Barth and Charles Hartshorne espouse different and conflicting methodological principles and procedures but further that the conceptions of divine power that emerge within their respective conceptual frameworks diverge from one another in equally fundamental ways. Their differences are not merely matters of emphasis or nuance but rather reflect fundamentally conflicting claims concerning how this power is to be conceived. This opposition of basic assumptions is clearly apparent in that Hartshorne argues for a receptive as well as causative form of divine power, while Barth consistently emphasizes the agential dimension. The opposition is equally apparent, however, in that while each asserts that God's power does have a causal mode, they reach radically different conclusions as to how that influencing power and its relation to and implications for the nondivine realm must be indeterminism, while Barth posits a deterministic view of divine action.

Barth, for his part, develops his deterministic position by arguing that the scope and efficacy of divine action is such that it controls the fact, content, and character of all worldly occurrence in the most absolute manner. Nothing, according to Barth, happens outside God's causative awareness and all-determinative rule. God's action is the ground and cause of all creaturely activity, not as a general precondition or a source of multiple possibilities, but as the one omnipotent action that decides the precise outcome and the exact details of nondivine action and decision.

Charles Hartshorne, in contrast, offers a view of divine influence that differs significantly from this Barthian vision; it suggests a fundamentally different understanding of the relation between divine and creaturely activity. Hartshorne, for the most part, develops a notion of causal power as the divine capacity to set the optimal conditions for the actualization of good within the creaturely realm. The setting of such optimal conditions involves not the determination of specific concrete happenings but rather divine decision concerning the range of possibilities that will be open for creaturely realization. Divine causal influence consists in the establishment of those parameters within which creatures will make their own decisions. And, Hartshorne suggests, such divinely set limits can be equated with the laws of nature. Hartshorne also occasionally alludes to and often seems to presuppose that God also offers to creatures more specific aims that influence the direction of the universe's development. However, these more particularized ideals cannot be assumed, according to the tenets of the Hartshornian philosophy, to be any more strictly determining than the cosmic laws but must be understood as well as a range of opportunities in relation to which creatures must make their own decisions.

Hartshorne argues as well that God's causal influence is efficacious to the degree that a certain order and harmony persists in the world, but he rejects all suggestions that this efficacy is to be equated with any form of strict determinism. Rather, the relation between God's causal influence and creaturely activity is one of a relative conditioning that presupposes indeterminism on all levels of reality. Hartshorne argues that divine action only limits or relatively conditions creaturely experience for a variety of reasons, and as a means of explicating the relation between divine and nondivine action, it is necessary to examine some of these Hartshornian arguments for an undetermined universe. For the most part, Hartshorne develops these arguments with specific reference to the cosmic laws rather than in relation to particular divine ideals for individuals. The treatment set forth here therefore follows this line of argumentation. However, if the divine aims toward realization of particular value are also conceived in terms of ranges of possibility, as I think they should be, then the following arguments will hold for them as well.

6.1 Divine Influence as Indeterministic

In the first place, Hartshorne contends, causal influence and indeterminism go together. For this divine power, expressed in the cosmic laws, does not involve the manipulation of concrete happenings but the determination of broad and general kinds or classes of possibilities.[1] From the decision concerning the kinds of alternatives available to creatures, the precise choice of specific alternatives is not deducible. Cosmic laws, according to Hartshorne, presuppose freedom of choice within the limits set by such laws.

In the second place, Hartshorne suggests that even the broad limits set by the cosmic laws are not inflexible. That is, he argues that not only does there exist freedom within the parameters of cosmic limits but that there is even freedom in terms of the laws themselves. Hartshorne is not always clear concerning this matter and sometimes appears to vacillate concerning his claim. On the one hand, he speaks of the "irresistibility" of God's causal

---

[1] Hartshorne, "New Look at the Evil Problem," 208.

influence and suggests that distinction should be made between what God prefers and what God permits to occur. In his words, "God has two intentions in mind, what He *prefers*, should the creatures freely cooperate to produce it, and what He will infallibly bring to pass by setting limits, if necessary, to such freedom, in order to guarantee a world, even if not the best possible."[2] Statements of this kind appear to indicate that while some divine initiatives (perhaps those elusive divine lures toward maximization of value) might be disregarded or inadequately conformed to, other divine decisions, such as the cosmic laws, cannot be deviated from and are thus irresistible.[3] That is, while God has preferences for how creaturely freedom should be actualized within the limits of the cosmic order and these preferences might indeed be thwarted, nonetheless the cosmic order itself is not open to rejection or alteration concerning its basic features. (An example of this might be that to defy or not defy gravity is not an option for creatures.) In this case, the cosmic laws would be completely deterministic with indeterminism or freedom taking place within the context of an absolute order. The order would have built into it a flexible range of possibilities, but its own outer limits could not be transgressed by creatures but only by the cosmic agent who could alter them through the divine self-ordering. It is possible to see why Hartshorne sometimes appears to move in this direction. Without being able to impose some order, even if minimal, God could not maintain the world as God's social partner and hence Godself as a social being, and Hartshorne has further argued that it is not because God is coercive but rather incomparably persuasive that this order is irresistible. However, problems immediately arise with this claim. On the one hand, it is difficult to discern any difference between Hartshorne's irresistible persuasion and Barth's gracious determinism at this point. In both cases, the divine purpose and will is completely efficacious. The difference lies in the fact that for Hartshorne there is freedom of choice within the divine decision, that is, the details are left open, while for Barth the divine efficacy is extended to the details as well. On the other hand, if God can be so completely persuasive on the level of cosmic laws, then it must be asked why that persuasion is less efficacious in terms of the divine preferences concerning particular developments within that cosmic order. If God is irresistible on one level why not the other? Hartshorne does not directly resolve these dilemmas, and as long as the notion of absolute irresistibility is associated with the cosmic laws, then suspicions will remain concerning whether Hartshorne is offering a disguised determinism or merely an ill-conceived indeterminism.

[2] Hartshorne, "Santayana's Doctrine of Essence," in Paul A. Schilpp, ed., *The Philosophy of George Santayana* (Evanston: Northwestern University Press, 1941) 180.

[3] Gene Reeves ("Whitehead and Hartshorne," 134) argues this position, suggesting that while cosmic laws are irresistible and cannot be defied, more particular aims and ideals can be disregarded.

Hartshorne, however, perhaps recognizing the problems inherent in any suggestion of inevitable conformity to divine purposes, speaks more often of a certain, if small, flexibility in terms of the laws of nature. He asserts that the laws refer to statistical regularities, not any absolute conformity. That is, while most creatures do indeed conform to God's overwhelming influence (and even those creatures who deviate from the divine purpose must nonetheless take it into account), still there is the possibility that such non-conformity can occur.[4] The cosmic laws do indeed hold, for the most part, but such coincidence between God's purposive order and creaturely conformity to that order is not absolutely necessary. Hartshorne states:

> If you ask, must not the laws and the antecedent conditions entirely determine the detailed phenomena, the answer is, not if law is conceived as physicists now incline to conceive it, as essentially statistical, a matter of averages in large groups of similar cases. The new outlook in physics thus fits our doctrine of pervasive freedom, as the Newtonian outlook did not.[5]

Hartshorne further argues that such indeterminism is necessary even in relation to the cosmic laws for if it were absolutely missing, then basic notions like "possibility" are contentless and contradictory (BH, 129). In his words, "If laws are absolute regularities rendering the outcome of situations in principle uniquely derivable, then only for ignorance of the situation is the outcome a matter of 'possibility,' rather than sheer inevitability."[6] It is possible, I think, to interpret this sense of flexibility not as freedom in relation to the laws but as freedom within the cosmic laws. But then the problems of determinism and levels of persuasiveness emerge. Therefore, I think it can be argued that Hartshorne favors an indeterminist view concerning the cosmic laws themselves and that such a view would be compatible with the understanding of divine influence as persuasion and with the notion that God offers more specific ideals which also may be accepted or rejected.

However, it must be asked if deviance from the cosmic laws and thereby the divinely instituted world order is possible in any slight degree, then Is it not also possible, if not probable, on a massive scale? That is, is it not possible, at least logically, that cosmic rebellion could take place resulting in absolute chaos rather than a world and destroying the social fabric of the divine-world relation? (Thus, it could be argued that while the world might

---

[4] In this interpretation I am differing from Ford ("Whitehead's Differences from Hartshorne," 79) who states: "But there is no way to respond to a law of nature, particularly imposed by God; it must simply be obeyed willy nilly, for we have no choice in the matter." I am also disagreeing with Reeves ("Whitehead and Hartshorne," 134) who argues that the laws of nature are irresistible but more specific aims are not.

[5] Hartshorne, "Modern World and a Modern View of God," 476.

[6] Hartshorne, "Real Possibility," *Journal of Philosophy* 60 (1963) 600.

always have existed there is no logical reason to assume it always will exist.)
If this is possible, then Hartshorne's claim that God, necessarily and without
possibility of failure, maintains both Godself and the world is open to question. I think, however, Hartshorne's reply to this is that while indeterminism denies any strict or absolute causality, it does not deny causality per se.
That is, every creature must take account of the divine order and is thereby
conditioned by it in some manner with the result being that while absolute
conformity is ruled out, so too is absolute deviance from the norm. In
Hartshorne's view, "To disobey is not the same as to disregard. The diso-
bedient is not uninfluenced by the command he refuses to accept; for it puts
him in a state of rebellion or resistance to suggestion which is not the same
as the state of simple unawareness of the suggestion."[7] Thus, Hartshorne's
position can be interpreted as arguing for an indeterminism that recognizes,
indeed depends upon, a relative determinism; causality and freedom are not
opposed or contradictory, but each in its relative form complements the
other (BH, 150). There is no absolute determinism as opposed to absolute
freedom but relative forms of each that allow, on the one hand, novel and
nondetermined creaturely experiences to occur but, on the other hand,
insure that some such worldly happenings will continue to take place.
Thus, while on occasion Hartshorne sounds a deterministic note, the concerns for the maintenance of minimal order that can be seen to prompt such
statements can be answered within his frequently argued position that calls
for a relative indeterminism or, alternatively stated, a relative determinism.

A third reason Hartshorne argues for an indeterministic interpretation of
divine influence is that all purposes are, by nature, less determinate and
definite than their final actualization (PSG, 70). According to him, purposes, whether in terms of cosmic structures or specific aims, are general in
character, while realizations are concrete and specific. Concrete events are
always more determinate than the purposes that condition and guide them.
Without such differentiation between purpose and realization, Hartshorne
argues, the latter would be a mere repetition or reenactment of the former
and there would be, in the end, no difference between the past and the
future. In Hartshorne's words,

> A purpose is a determinable, for which any realization of the purpose is
> determinate. ... A person who gets what he wanted cannot have
> wanted precisely what he got, but only something less completely
> defined. There can be no such thing as a final cause coincident with its
> fulfillment. ... Neither man nor God can intend the concrete course of
> events, for "intention" in the purposive sense contradicts such coin-
> cidence of aim and achievement. It would make the achievement
> merely the intention over again. (CSPM, 66)

---

[7] Hartshorne, "Religion in Process Philosophy," 258.

Thus, while Hartshorne argues that God indeed envisages aims and goals for the world and that these divine purposes, usually understood as exemplified in the cosmic order, condition and influence the direction of creaturely development, they do not by their very nature as aims entail any specific realization of those aims. Divine purposes may indeed be final causes, but in the end only an event can fully determine itself.

A fourth and related reason Hartshorne argues for an indeterministic relation between divine decision and influence and creaturely activity lies in the mode of that influence itself. All influence, divine and nondivine alike, takes place by virtue of the influence's being an object of awareness or experience for those who are influenced. This means, however, that the efficacy of the influence always depends upon the degree and quality of response upon the part of the recipient. Such response can never be dictated but always entails some element of self-decision. Thus, the final outcome of any event is the result of the conditions and possibilities determined by others, including both God and creatures, and the decision made by the event itself. "Decision," for Hartshorne, "is always *shared,* so far as effects upon others are concerned."[8] Hartshorne, commenting upon Whitehead but concurring, states:

> This influence, like any influence in this philosophy, can only operate by the influencer getting himself prehended by the things influenced; and therefore by the asymmetry of prehensive relatedness, there can be no strict entailment of the result. No matter what God decides for the world, the result, the world's prehensive response, involves an element of self-determination or creature freedom. (WP, 158)

Hence, the shared quality of all decision rules out any strict determinism. God's action can decide the realm of possibility, whether on a cosmic or individual level, within which the creatures must move. The responses of the creatures alone decide the exact conditions and content of realized experience. In Hartshorne's words,

> God determines what creatures can do, but only they determine what they do. . . . Enslavement, even to the divine, cannot be absolute—not only because the divine is generous, but because power means influence of one free act upon another free act. (Or else we do not know wherein power consists.)[9]

The structure of all creaturely experience is the structure of decision, that is, influenced and conditioned by its antecedents, but it is self-determinative in its final expressions. In the final analysis, the logic of experience,

---

[8] Hartshorne, "Modern World and a Modern View of God," 474.
[9] Hartshorne, "Religion in Process Philosophy," 261–62.

understood as decision, dictates that "not a single act of a single creature has been or could have been simply decided by divine action" (CSPM, 239).

Hartshorne offers another rationale for his indeterministic or relatively deterministic interpretation of God's causal influence. He suggests that while God does not determine absolutely any creaturely experience, nonetheless all creatures bear marks, so to speak, of this preeminent influence, and he suggests that creaturely creativity and freedom is just such a mark of divine presence. That is, though a cause cannot dictate its precise effect, nonetheless that "effect must in some way express the nature of its cause" (ibid., 11). And God, as the preeminently creative and free being, could therefore not produce absolutely noncreative creatures. Rather, divine causal influence issues forth in beings that are expressions, on their own creaturely level, of creativity and freedom (ibid., 10–11). More traditionally put, Hartshorne argues, creatures are made in God's image.

Thus, Hartshorne can be seen to argue that while God's influence upon the world is preeminent and universal, it does not deny creaturely self-determination. Rather, it is a free decision that sets limits to other free decisions but never denies them. And in turn those creaturely free decisions will come to influence and condition God in their own turn. Every causal influence, divine and creaturely alike, was first itself a self-determining response to prior causal influence.[10] Thus, Hartshorne claims freedom and causality are, in truth, complementary modes of ongoing experience. They do not contradict each other but are experience viewed from two temporally different perspectives, and together they embody the structure of all reality. In Hartshorne's words, "That the freedom of one agent is limited by the freedom of others is the social structure of existence. That one's freedom now is limited by the freedom already exercised in the past is the temporal structure of existence."[11] Causality is crystalized freedom, freedom is causality in the making (LP, 233).

And finally, Hartshorne can be seen to argue that the divine purpose or aim for creaturely reality is not one of servitude or abject obedience in which creatures merely conform to prior divine decisions. Rather, God's purpose is to foster and encourage self-creativity and freedom upon the part of creatures. The limits that are set by divine decision are not to hamper this creaturely creativity, but to determine the conditions that are most conducive to it. God demands not blind obedience and subjugation of creaturely wills, but rather God seeks to inspire the highest level of creative response. God seeks social partners, not slaves.

> The higher forms of power are not those which inhibit freedom of others, but rather those which inspire appropriate degrees and kinds of

[10] Hartshorne, "Development of Process Philosophy," 55.
[11] Hartshorne, "New Look at the Problem of Evil," 211.

freedom in them, the power of artists, prophets, men of genius of all freedom, not the all-determining coercive tyrant, or (if possible) even worse, the irresistible hypnotist who dictates specific actions while hiding his operations from the hypnotized. The worship of power in any such sense is idolatry in a rather brutal form. The admirable rulers are not those who try to make all decisions themselves, but those who put others in a position to make fruitful decisions of their own. As Berdyaev says, the divine imperative to us is not mechanical obedience to ready-made or eternal divine decisions, but creative response to the divine creativity: be creative and foster creativity in them.[12]

6.2 Divine Influence and Creaturely Freedom

As the preceding analysis reveals, divine causal influence and creaturely freedom do not stand in opposition within the Hartshornian social schema. Rather, all entities whatsoever, by virtue of being actual, are free to some extent. "Existence and freedom are two aspects of the same thing" (CSPM, 312). Freedom indeed is the core of all individuality (RSP, 190). And God's purpose is not to destroy or subordinate this freedom but to enhance it on every level of reality. It is important at this juncture to set forth in more precise terms what has been implicitly assumed in the foregoing discussion concerning the Hartshornian understanding of the nature and content of this creaturely freedom and to explore how his interpretation of this matter contrasts with the Barthian conception of nondivine freedom.

The Nature of Creaturely Freedom

Barth, we have suggested, argues that God's action and decision are all-determining in relation to the creaturely sphere. However, he does not conclude from this assertion that creaturely freedom is not real. To the contrary, he contends that it is only through and because of divine activity that creatures can attain freedom at all. In order to make sense of this double claim of absolute divine determination and creaturely freedom, Barth posits a very particular conception of creaturely freedom: he suggests that freedom, on the nondivine level, consists not in a neutral capacity to choose among alternative possibilities of good or evil, but rather it is the purely positive capacity to be for God. This ability is not innate in creatures but it is the free gift of God. As such its ultimate expression is acknowledgement of and subordination to the divine purpose. That is, according to Barth, creaturely freedom consists finally in obedience to God.

Hartshorne, for his part, develops a very different understanding of

---

[12] Hartshorne, "Divine Absoluteness and Divine Relativity," 169.

creaturely freedom than this Barthian conception. In the first instance, he argues that freedom entails the presence of real alternatives (LP, 138). Every individual or event is a decision for Hartshorne, and all decisions, on whatever level they occur, require a range of possibilities to choose among. The range may indeed be small, on some levels of reality infinitesimal, but some such range there must be. Hartshorne states: "I deny categorically that a genuine act of choice is ever the only possible act." [13] Further, the degree of flexibility in terms of choice corresponds to the level of existence a creature has reached; the more advanced the being, the greater flexibility of choice and thereby freedom of action. According to Hartshorne, "the higher the being, the greater the range of possibilities which it is able to appreciate and choose from; hence the wider the scope of its free action" (BH, 215).

One of the reasons for the difference between Hartshorne and Barth concerning this matter of choices is that Barth appears to conceive of only two broad alternatives: God's good decision and an evil decision. Hartshorne, on the other hand, interprets alternatives to include certainly some good or evil choices but also some equally good ones. That is, choice does not always entail choosing between good and evil but is most often decision among comparable goods. There is in this sense no one decision that is correct or best. Freedom consists in actualizing one alternative while others might have been equally as fruitful in terms of realizing value. Hartshorne might agree with Barth that the evil utilization is not true freedom, or at least is an inferior use of freedom, but such a recognition does not mean for him, as it appears to for Barth, that alternative choice must be denied if freedom is to be understood as positive capacity. The good has multiple forms within the Hartshornian schema, and it is the task of freedom to choose which expressions of value will be realized.

A second point where Hartshorne clearly departs from the Barthian conception of creaturely freedom concerns what Barth took to be the coincidence of divine and human action. [14] That is, one of the conclusions of Barth's deterministic schema was that God's own activity takes place in, with, and over the activity of the creatures: the two actions are not collapsed, but there is nonetheless a sense, mysterious though it was seen to be, in which they are one decision. This coincidence is impossible for Hartshorne. Agents make his or her own decisions, and while others can contribute to those decisions, none can make another's act their own. [15]

[13] Hartshorne, "Interrogation," 341.

[14] See above 3.3.

[15] This raises the question, examined in Chapter 5, of whether God can ever really appropriate another's action fully. If an action is always one individual's alone, then even perfect knowledge could not include it completely. If God cannot prospectively determine another's decision, it is also not clear that God can retrospectively possess that decision as God's own; see above 5.3.

Agents, while social, are also individual and singular. In Hartshorne's words,

> To be such an individual is to make one's own place, in a certain measure, and put oneself in it. No other individual can do this for one, even if the other individual be God. It is not that God is weak, but that my act is mine, and it is senseless to say that God simply makes this act; for if this were so, it would be His act and not mine at all. (LP, 313)

Hartshorne, with his conception of creaturely freedom, disputes, in the third place, the claim that the idea of all-determining divine decision has any meaning whatsoever. He argues that if God fully determines all creaturely activity, then it is absurd to speak of decision, choice, or action on the nondivine level.[16] If divine decision and freedom entail, as they do for Barth, the alternative of acting or not acting, choosing this possibility or that, while on the creaturely level free decision implies only conformity to divine decision, then the use of the notions of decision and freedom in terms of both God and creatures is pure equivocation. The only acceptable rationale for utilizing these ideas in reference to God and worldly reality is that while there are differences there are also basic similarities of meaning that are assumed on both levels of use. The scope of the decision or the degree of freedom may vary, but the fundamental structure of decision and freedom is the same for both God and creatures. Hartshorne states:

> The theistic version of strict determinism is the most glaringly inconsistent of all. For it splits decision into two forms which differ absolutely: the divine deciding, back of which is nothing whatever (neither any necessity of the agent's nature, nor any influence of other agents), contrasted to our deciding, which is wholly determined by antecedent influence. So we have agents with no individuality of decision making on the one hand, and an agent whose decisions are absolutely individual, totally uninfluenced or without social character, on the other. It is playing with words to speak of "decision" or "individuality" on both sides of this absolute contrast.[17]

Hartshorne's interpretation of worldly freedom suggests a further way in which his position can be differentiated from the Barthian conception in that he argues that freedom entails more than the mere absence of

---

[16] Hartshorne, "Process Philosophy as a Resource for Christian Thought," in Perry LeFevre, ed., *Philosophical Resources for Christian Thought* (New York: Abingdon, 1968) 54.

[17] Hartshorne, "New Look at the Problem of Evil," 204.

coercion.[18] Barth, for his part, while maintaining the deterministic character of divine action, also argues that creaturely action is not coerced or constrained but rather is voluntarily chosen. Though no alternatives for different decisions exist, the creaturely actions are not done under duress or threat, nor because of external compulsion. Rather, they conform to the divine decisions by virtue of the internal workings of the Spirit through which creatures come to will what God has already chosen for them. Hartshorne, however, argues contra positions such as this that freedom is more than merely voluntary or noncoerced action. It indeed entails voluntary action, but freedom involves as well the possibility of creative movement beyond all causal determinants. Freedom entails, for Hartshorne, the possibility of actualizing new and novel values:

> Only a self which is partially free, not only to do as it wishes, but to wish in partial independence of all the world, and of all past history, is really a self. Otherwise it would be meaningless to ask what "it" wished; for the determination of the wish being fully provided by antecedent causes, localization of the agency in the present self would be arbitrary. The deeper meaning of the open future now becomes clear. The (partial) independence of each moment of time from all its predecessors is one with the possibility of distinct agents, real selves, acting in that moment. Unless each self is partially distinct and hence free, each self is causally indistinguishable not only from its past states but from those of its ancestors, and thus all distinctness of self vanishes in one cosmic Activity be this god, devil or machine. (BH, 156)

Stated succinctly, Hartshorne argues that freedom entails creativity (LP, 181). Freedom always involves deciding the previously undecided. If causal influences must be taken into account, then freedom consists of the transformation of those influences into a new and unique experience. Every action, insofar as it is free, is creation de novo. There are always open alternatives, real ambiguities that need to be resolved or determined, and freedom as creativity brings about this resolution. Creaturely freedom, no less than divine, is the capacity to create the new. It is not merely the capacity to conform to God's creative decisions. Hartshorne declares, "Freedom in the full sense means more than just voluntariness, and no voluntary animal is free in that sense only. Freedom in the full sense means creativity, resolving antecedent, though most slight, indeterminacies."[19]

Thus, creaturely freedom entails not only the presence of real alternatives and the absence of coercion, but finally it consists in the capacity to be self-creative and thereby world-creating. This element of self-creativity is missing from the Barthian conception of freedom, and its absence is indicative of

---

[18] Hartshorne, "Beyond Enlightened Self-Interest," 313; and LP, 19.

[19] Hartshorne, "Beyond Enlightened Self-Interest," 314.

how the relation of divine action and creaturely action is finally construed. God within this schema is the only real creator, freely (i.e., with open alternatives) bringing the new into being. Creaturely freedom does not consist in a lesser or inferior form of this capacity to be creative but only in the ability to conform, to be obedient. God, in the end, creates both Godself and the world, while creatures enact decisions that have already been made for them. Hartshorne argues contra Barthian type visions by insisting that freedom entails true creativity, that creatures finally create themselves; they are their own *causa sui*. Reality has not been decided by any one decision maker, even the cosmic one. Rather, reality is in the making (LP, 233). Hartshorne states:

> In creationist metaphysics, all concrete reality is in principle creative. But then what happens, is never, as it stands, simply attributable to "the" Creator, but only to deity *and* the creatures together. Reality is always in part self-created, *causa sui,* creativity being, in this philosophy, the supreme transcendental. All creatures have creativity above zero, all are creators. (NTOT, 82)

Hartshorne argues further that freedom conceived as creativity is not merely an attribute of human existence but is universally exhibited by all reality. "Creativity is not, taken generically," according to Hartshorne, "unique to man, or indeed to animals."[20] With this claim Hartshorne is rejecting any assumption that while indeterminism or freedom of action holds within the human realm, the nonhuman world operates according to strict determinism, with nonhuman entities, be they atoms or animals, moving according to a rigidly set causality. Hartshorne contends, rather, that no such dualism between humans and the nonhuman world exists and that the character of existence is everywhere self-creative. Thus, in principle, though certainly not in degree or quality, the same freedom that characterizes human experience is also found in the experience of electrons and cells, to say nothing of animals (AD, 206–7). Freedom is inherent to individuality as such, whether that be on the atomic, human, or divine level.[21]

The Nature of Moral Freedom

Thus, creative freedom is a universal category for Hartshorne. It is a metaphysical category intrinsic to all actuality whatsoever. This Hartshornian assumption has been present throughout all the preceding analysis, but at this juncture its human variation must be examined more closely, both in terms of its commonalities with such freedom in its nonhuman forms and in

---

[20] Ibid.
[21] Hartshorne, "New Look at the Problem of Evil," 204–5.

relation to its distinctive human expression. On the one hand, Hartshorne argues that the assumption that freedom is a universal category allows the universe to be understood as exhibiting one common character with humans as a natural part of their environment, rather than an utterly unique exception to it. The assumption of universal freedom (along with the other metaphysical principles articulated in Chapter 4) entails the rejection of any radical dualism between humans and nature, as well as between the world and God. Humans do not exist over against a natural world which is lacking in intrinsic freedom and value existing purely for human use or abuse. Rather, human beings and all other worldly entities form a continuum of existence that manifests on every level the capacity for creative self-decision. Thus, "we need not make man an arbitrary exception to the general principles of nature" (LP, 164).

Nature and humanity are in a very real sense, therefore, one reality. And the acknowledgement of this unity will have far-reaching implications for Hartshorne for a new vision of the relation between the two. When humanity is no longer the grand exception to the natural order, then perhaps a new vision of respect for and care of the nonhuman realm will come to replace the policies of abuse and exploitation that grew out of the dualistic vision. However, while adhering to this vision of one reality, Hartshorne also acknowledges that creative freedom on the human level is a distinct and unique expression of this universally exhibited capacity.

For Hartshorne, the uniqueness of human freedom lies in the fact that it is not just creative response to antecedent events but that it entails the capacity for conscious moral choice. That is, human freedom is not just aesthetic freedom but is moral freedom as well. It is not merely unconscious transformation of causal influences but conscious decision as to the direction and content of that transformation. It is necessary to explicate this moral interpretation of freedom more fully.

First, to reiterate an already obvious point, moral freedom is not, in principle, utterly different from nonmoral freedom. It is a particularly developed form of the creative transformation found on lower levels of existence. Moral freedom is a "special, high-level case of the creative leap inherent in all process" (ibid., 169).

Second, while lower levels of freedom often consist primarily of a spontaneity of action, human freedom in its most advanced form entails rational reflection and deliberate decision making. It is not merely spontaneous adjustment to causal determinants but is the conscious choice of a course of action based upon deliberation concerning alternative ways of proceeding and the repercussions involved in those choices.

Hartshorne, in the third place, wants to argue that this rational reflection does not involve decision among choices already determined in detail but as a form of creativity always indicates a movement beyond all causal influences or determining factors. Moral freedom, just as its lesser forms, is a creative leap beyond "anything made inevitable or predictable by the causal conditions" (ibid., 164). And on the conscious level, Hartshorne suggests, this leap is made possible to such a great extent because of the unique human capacity to generalize. It is through this capacity to reflect in general terms, to formulate principles and ideals, that human action and decision are moved beyond their immediate and more narrowly circumscribed context. They are placed, by rational reflection, in a wider context that brings with it different possibilities for action and broader criteria for the assessment of those alternatives. Moral freedom, grounded in rational reflection, consists in the capacity to evaluate one's choices in a universal perspective according to consciously formulated, or at least appropriated, ethical ideals.

> Ethics is the *generalization of instinctive concern,* which in principle transcends the immediate state of the self and even the long-run career of the self, and embraces the ongoing communal process of life as such. The privilege of thought carries with it the sense of a goal that is universal and everlasting, not merely individual and temporary. It makes the individual trustee for nature at large, in the sense in which nature includes humanity. Anything short of this is not quite ethics in the clear-headed sense but mere expediency, or failure to think the ethical business through. [22]

It is this capacity to formulate general conceptions that is the ground for humans to move creatively beyond any causal conditions, whether they be "irresistible impulse, habit, or antecedent character" (LP, 170). It must be asked, however, whether this capacity of generalization, unique to humans and other rational beings if they exist, is not so different from the creative spontaneity found on lower levels of existence that to term both freedom is a questionable practice. That is, while one might acknowledge spontaneity on all levels of reality, one might reject the identification of that spontaneity with free decision. Theologian Julian Hartt states: "Hartshorne has not convinced me that subatomic particles can be said to be free in anything like the way we say a person is free." [23] Rather, freedom entails conscious decision for Hartt, not unconscious spontaneity. Hartshorne, however, rejects reasoning of this sort. The question concerning freedom is not whether an act is conscious decision but rather whether causal influences are open to creative transformation. In this sense the structure of subatomic spontaneity and human conscious decision is the same: both entail the appropriation of

---

[22] Hartshorne, "Beyond Enlightened Self-Interest," 318.

[23] Julian Hartt, Review of LP, *Review of Metaphysics* 16 (1962/63) 761. Gunton (*Becoming and Being,* 69) voices the same concern and raises questions concerning the legitimacy of using the notion of freedom to cover both moral choice and the "element of randomness in the behaviour of subatomic particles."

past causal determinants in a creative manner. The difference lies in that human action, informed by imaginative generalization, has a far greater flexibility in terms of its antecedents and therefore an infinitely wider range of alternative options for behavior than does any atom. Such great difference does not mean that the human is free while the atom is not but only that the scope and degree of that freedom varies with the level of existence. To argue otherwise entails either the assertion of an absolute determinism on nonhuman levels of reality (a claim even contemporary physics disputes) or the assumption that creativity takes place on all levels with the nonhuman and human forms of such creativity having nothing in common. Both of these options Hartshorne consistently and thoroughly rejects, and he maintains throughout his work that freedom is indeed creativity and everywhere manifest.

If moral freedom entails the capacity to widen one's horizons, to assume a universal perspective rather than a narrowly circumscribed view, then we must ask what is the goal or intention of such morally free action, what is the aim of this inclusive vision? Hartshorne replies that the aim or purpose of morally free decision is the "inclusive good." And with this claim we are brought again to Hartshorne's vision of the relation between moral and aesthetic good examined in the preceding chapter. For, according to Hartshorne, the fundamental good or value is aesthetic, not moral or ethical, in nature. The basic value that all action seeks is the actualization of beauty, the realization of intensity and harmony in experience. In Hartshorne's words, "What indeed is 'good,' whether mine or someone elses? Here ethics must lean upon aesthetics. For the only good that is intrinsically good, good in itself, is good experience, and the criteria for this are aesthetic."[24]

The aim or intention of moral action is not, therefore, something that denies this aesthetic good or subordinates it to some higher ethical good but rather, according to Hartshorne, seeks the realization of aesthetic value on increasingly wider scales. That is, the goal of moral action is aesthetic enjoyment for the greatest possible number of beings. Ethical and aesthetic value are not antithetical but rather ethical good consists in broad—indeed the aim should be for universal—aesthetic value. In Hartshorne's words, "*To be ethical is to seek aesthetic optimization for the community.*"[25]

Thus, being ethical entails the willing of aesthetic good for all reality. Hartshorne, however, is concerned that this understanding of moral goodness in terms of aesthetic value not appear facile or as denying the significance and necessity of ethical behavior. According to Hartshorne, the aesthetic and the moral are intimately connected in that all aesthetic value is social value; it is not self-enclosed and indifferenct to experience other than

---

[24] Hartshorne, "Beyond Enlightened Self-Interest," 318.
[25] Ibid., 319.

its own but receives or fails to receive its richness from its social world. Aesthetic value, social in character, is that to which the joy or sorrow, the happiness or pain of others always makes a difference; it is not uninvolved or disinterested value but a good that depends upon the well-being of all others for its own actualization. The role of rational reflection and consciousness lie in the fact that they raise this social dimension of aesthetic experience to universal proportions. Thus, the ethical and the aesthetic, interpreted socially, do not conflict but entail motivation toward a common goal. "The ethical side comes in through the social character of being, which makes the aim at beauty an aim not just for self, and also makes it include, as a supreme form of beauty, the beauty of companionship and generosity" (WP, 107).

While Hartshorne argues that the aesthetic and the ethical are not to be seen in opposition, he also recognizes that humans, limited in vision and knowledge, often disconnect the two and understand the aesthetic as the drive toward self-centered value, while the ethical is the orientation toward social value. It is precisely this disjunction which the above analysis shows Hartshorne seeks to deny. For, according to Hartshorne, the aesthetic, properly understood, is the social and nothing else.

And further, this connection between the moral and the aesthetic entails the implication that moral action involves obligation and responsibility to not only the human community but all reality, both in its subhuman and suprahuman form. That is, the experience of nonhuman animals and entities must be acknowledged to have some moral importance and some claim to intrinsic value that cannot simply be disregarded as ethically irrelevant. The human condition is finally, for Hartshorne, a cosmic community, and the ethical ideals that have as their goal the maximalization of the good must come to reflect, in a manner hitherto absent, those nonhuman claims to value. Hartshorne's position entails the further recognition that moral obligation must be extended to deity as well. When value is aesthetic, always capable of increase for everyone, including God, then moral responsibility does not mean merely obedience to divine decrees but creative contribution of value to the divine life. The divine imperative demands not mere obedience but free creativity. And for Hartshorne such creative action is the highest and indeed only moral behavior possible.

In summary, it can be stated that the understanding of the relation of divine action to creaturely activity in the Hartshornian schema is far different than the conception of that relation articulated by Barth. For Barth the relation is one of divine determinism in which creaturely freedom is equated with obedience, while for Hartshorne divine influence is only relatively determining and creaturely freedom entails the presence of genuine choices and consists, finally, in self-creation. Strict determinism cannot, for Hartshorne, be made compatible with a freedom that is essentially creative in nature. Barth attempts to bring freedom and determinism together by emphasizing the gracious and loving character of God's all-powerful influence and by arguing that the creatures' deepest purposes and natures are fulfilled not by creaturely self-creation but rather by conformity to the divine creative action. Hartshorne, in contrast, argues that the gracious character of absolute power in no way mitigates its tyrannical nature but only makes it benevolently dictatorial, and, finally, he asserts that where there is no possibility for creation, there is no freedom. In sum he contends that "no benevolence will suffice unless it includes respect for the freedom of others to make their own decisions, to be creators, each in his own proper sphere."[26] It is now time to examine what repercussions follow from this Hartshornian claim of indeterministic influence and self-creative freedom. That is, we must ask what this position entails for the questions of evil and sin.

6.3 The Problem of Evil and Sin

The foregoing analysis has revealed that within the Hartshornian schema the relation between divine and creaturely activity is one of relative indeterminism or, what amounts to the same thing, relative determinism. By insisting upon the creative freedom of all experience, Hartshorne did not, thereby, deny causal conditioning but only that such influence, whether divine or creaturely in form, is ever causative of its effects in a strict and absolute manner. Hartshorne's conclusion is that exact events or experiences, while always conditioned, in the end are self-created, not caused by others.

The result of this universal self-creation is that both the course of history as a whole and the experience of individuals are finally the outcome of multiple freedoms, not the deterministic purpose of one divine being. While God has a vision for the development of the universe, embodied most clearly in the cosmic laws, that vision is enacted or instantiated by self-creating entities whose exact configuration and interrelationships are beyond any purpose. In short, Hartshorne claims that the relation between causal influence and self-creativity in the universe means that what ultimately does occur is a matter of chance.

Chance Character of Existence

Chance refers to the "unintentioned character" of the details of the world (LP, 206). It points to the fact event or experience just occurs; there is no absolute reason or explanatory cause for why it is precisely what it is (BH, 131).

---

[26] Hartshorne, "Process Philosophy as a Resource for Christian Thought," in Perry LeFevre, ed., *Philosophical Resources for Christian Thought* (New York: Abingdon, 1968) 64.

To ask why events occur exactly as they do, or who is responsible in a world of multiple freedom, is a misguided and finally pseudoquestion. Influences are multiple and so too is responsibility. In the end, individual facts and their interconnection (i.e., history) are accidents, arbitrary in nature, not the inevitable unfolding of a divinely conceived and executed plan. In Hartshorne's words,

> I decide my act, you decide yours, but how my act and yours flow together to constitute a new total situation of potential absolute relata for subsequent acts of self-relating neither I nor you nor anyone, and not God, decides. Nor does any necessity bring it about. It simply happens. In other words, if "by chance" is equivalent to "neither by necessity nor by intention," then literally all things, in their concrete details, happen by chance. How much bitterness has been due to the notion that whatever happens, someone must have been "responsible"![27]

There are several further claims that Hartshorne makes concerning this chance character of the cosmos. First, by arguing for the ultimately unintentioned character of all experience, he is not denying providential guidance by God. That is, chance is not to be equated with lawlessness. God's influence does not, as we have argued, determine events but sets the limits within which events take place. Chance is, therefore, real but the preeminent divine influence channels it in the direction of optimal maximization of value. Divine providential and creative activity go together with chance within the Hartshornian vision. Hartshorne, referring to his metaphysical vision, states: "It views providence and chance, not as alternatives, but as complementaries, both applying universally to events, which in details must always be unintended" (LP, 44).

Second, Hartshorne is not, by advocating the notion that ultimately events occur by chance, abandoning his above stated position concerning moral freedom and responsibility. Chance does not mean the lack or absence of responsibility or free choice but indicates that free decision alone cannot determine the outcome of an event. If every experience is self-creative, it is not only that but other factors contribute as well, none—including freedom—fully determining the end result. In Hartshorne's words, "Moral freedom is chance plus something and no one (except a man of straw) identifies the two" (LP, 169).

Another conclusion Hartshorne draws from his conviction that events are not fully determined but are the unintended product of the interaction of multiple freedoms is that no matter what the divine intention toward the good may be, the final outcome often falls short of that purpose. That is, multiple freedom results not only in good but also issues forth in evil. It is

---

[27] Hartshorne, "Religion in Process Philosophy," 266.

important to examine Hartshorne's understanding of both the how and why of evil and its contents as well as its rather substantial differences from the Barthian position concerning this matter.

Aesthetic Form of Evil

Just as the basic form of the good is aesthetic, so too is the fundamental form of evil. The good consists, within the Hartshornian schema, in the actualization of value or intensity and harmony of experience. Evil therefore lies either in a lack of harmony or an absence of vitality. That is, evil, interpreted aesthetically, is either discord or tedium.

Hartshorne turns most of his attention toward the experience of discord, conflict, and suffering; and, for the most part, he equates this lack of harmony with aesthetic evil while recognizing that the evil of "deadly monotony and insipidity" is also a danger.[28] This aesthetic evil, given expression in conflict and suffering, is not the product of evil or immoral intention or decision. Therefore, it is not the direct result or even indirect by-product of a moral form of evil, that is, sin.[29] Rather, it is the outcome of the interaction of multiple freedoms; it is the result of the fact that plural freedoms simply cannot be absolutely ordered. "Evil, in the sense of conflict and suffering," according to the Hartshornian tenets, "is explained by the existence of many free beings."[30]

Hartshorne suggests that there are several reasons why conflict and suffering emerge in a world of free beings. First, aesthetic evil arises because of the fact that values, while good in themselves, often clash with one another. Free beings often pursue, not out of malice or evil intent, values that are incompatible, and realization of value for one being thereby results in the loss of value for another. "A's success means B's failure" (WP, 186). Hartshorne finds support for his position concerning this matter in the thought of Berdyaev and Whitehead, and referring to them he states: "Berdyaev says that true tragedy is not a clash of good with evil, but of good with good, of two equally noble ideals; Whitehead means the same thing when he says that evil is good out of season or in conflict with some other good" (ibid.). In this sense, aesthetic evil points not to any Barthian wholly evil *das Nichtige* dramatically menacing a completely good creation but to the more ordinary and mundane fact that the realization of value often brings with it unwelcome suffering and pain as it conflicts with other values.

A second reason aesthetic evil occurs is that creatures, by virtue of their creaturely status, make decisions and choose values to a significant extent in ignorance of each other. That is, discord arises because creatures lack the

---

[28] Hartshorne, "Modern World and a Modern View of God," 474–75.

[29] Hartshorne, "New Look at the Problem of Evil," 205.

[30] Ibid., 211.

wisdom and comprehensive vision that God has by virtue of being omniscient. Creaturely decisions are choices made on partial and inadequate
knowledge, and such blindness, apart from any ill intent, is enough to insure
the possibility of conflict and suffering. In Hartshorne's words, "A multi-
tude of partly free individuals are bound sometimes to clash, for their
choices are made in comparative ignorance of each other, and are thus leaps
in the dark, so far as effects upon others are concerned" (RSP, 148).

A third reason discord and suffering are possible lies in what we earlier
referred to as the chance character of experience. Even if every creature
and God had as its explicit purpose social harmony and acted solely out of
that aim, there could be no guarantee that such harmonious interaction
would result. Such intention toward harmony will surely help the chances
of its occurrence, but no one can inevitably produce concord, not even God.
Hartshorne states:

> If what x decided harmonizes with what y decides, that is good luck
> and if it doesn't, that is bad luck. It really is luck, for neither x nor y,
> nor yet z, even if z is God, can simply decide that harmony shall reign.
> All can aim at harmony, but none can guarantee it, not because some-
> one, say God, is weak, but because it is the very meaning of the social
> situation in which all value and all sentient existence consists that each
> must decide in some measure for himself, and that the decisions of
> another cannot be foreseen in their concreteness.[31]

Thus, the possibility of aesthetic evil arises out of the nature of individual
existence itself. Conflict, and with it pain and suffering, are always possible,
if not necessary, because individuals are both social beings, influencing and
being influenced by one another, and free beings, making decisions which
will affect others. Multiple freedom in a social universe makes the possibility of discord inevitable. As long as there are free creatures there will be
aesthetic evil as well, and no action upon the part of God will change this
situation. In Hartshorne's words, "Within a multiplicity of creative agents,
some risk of conflict and suffering is inevitable. The source of evil is precisely this multiplicity" (CSPM, 238).

Several interesting contrasts with the Barthian conception of evil can be
drawn at this juncture. Barth takes great pains to emphasize the wholly
good nature of creation.[32] And, within the Barthian schema, this insistence
is necessary, for creation is wholly the product of God's causative knowledge
and will; to suggest that evil or even a propensity toward evil inheres in
creation leads irrevocably toward the conclusion that God is its cause and
raises, thereby, profound questions concerning the gracious and loving character of divine action. Barth attempts to resolve this dilemma by

---

[31] Hartshorne, "New Look at the Problem of Evil," 205–6.
[32] See above, 3.2.

maintaining the goodness of creation and interpreting evil as a negative force that menaces that good creation from without. Hartshorne, however, offers a fundamentally different interpretation of the relation of evil and the goodness of creation. Because the world is not a product solely of God's action (which, for Hartshorne no less than for Barth, intends only good) but is the outcome of multiple decisions, it is indeed not only good but a mixture of good and evil.

There are several ways of understanding this mixture of good and evil. On the one hand, it indicates that creation bears within itself the possibility of evil. The potentiality for conflict is intrinsic to reality. Hartshorne's world is not wholly good in the Barthian sense of a creation without inherent propensity toward evil. Thus, there is no mystery for Hartshorne as there is for Barth, as to why evil occurs; it is, in the Hartshornian schema, a phenomenon understood through natural categories.

On the other hand, the mixture of good and evil can be seen in that while creation consists always in the realization of value, the fact that it is produced by multiple decisions means that the end result in any moment might not be so good as it could have been (AD, 193). That is, multiple decision in a social universe can result in a world that is not the "best possible world." In a social universe great value is achieved, but great opportunities are lost as well. Hartshorne states: "At any stage of the cosmic process there may be possibilities of value for that stage greater than those actually achieved in it, because of the unlucky or even perverse actions of the creatures. All does not occur for the best" (WP, 70).

Within the Hartshornian vision, however, if all is not for the best, neither is anything wholly evil or lacking in intrinsic value and worth. Barth argues for a wholly good creation and a wholly evil power that, while it does not exist as God or the good creation exist, nonetheless is a potent and real force. *Das Nichtige* has no positive value according to Barth but is wholly and inherently evil. Hartshorne rejects the notion that anything that is actual can lack value. Actuality and the realization of some value are one. Only nonentity is wholly lacking in any intrinsic worth. Thus, Hartshorne concludes that "any evil has some value from some perspective, for even to know it exists is to make it contributory to a good, knowledge itself being a good."[33]

But this recognition of the intrinsic value of all experience does not mean that Hartshorne thinks that aesthetic evil is not genuine evil or that conflict

---

[33] NTOT, 80. Hartshorne ("New Look at the Problem of Evil," 210) also notes that entities can achieve value in themselves, and thus be good, but can cause discord or suffering in relation to others. An example he offers of this is cancer cells which are not in themselves evil but in relation to their wider organism are the cause of evil.

and pain can be approved or justified.[34] For, the acknowledgment of the value found even in evil entails as well the recognition that a far greater value would have been achieved through harmony than through conflict. To salvage whatever value can possibly be saved from an evil situation is not to say that the situation was therefore not evil but good. Aesthetic evil is genuine evil and insofar as it occurs, reality is less than it might have been. Some value may be saved but in itself conflict and pain serve no good end and are therefore not to be accepted but resisted on every level. Hartshorne states:

> But any evil is also in some degree a misfortune, and in my opinion the theological "problem of evil" is quite misconceived if it is seen as that of justifying particular evils. Evils are to be avoided where possible; where not, to be mitigated or utilized for good in whatever way possible—but never, for heaven's sake, to be metaphysically justified. (NTOT, 80–81)

Thus, genuine evil is not to be equated with utter lack of value for all actuality entails some, if meager, worth. Rather, genuine evil refers to an inferior and minimal value where there might have been greater value. Hartshorne steadfastly insists that such a position does not transform evil into a hidden good; it is neither a disguised blessing nor an instrumental good serving some subtle purpose (CSPM, 317). It is just what it is—less than it could have been—and in so being it thwarts the divine purpose that everywhere seeks maximum value.

If, however, Hartshorne's aesthetic evil is not to be identified with Barth's *das Nichtige,* is it perhaps what Barth meant by the shadowside of existence? There are, indeed, points where the two conceptions sound quite similar; Barth's shadowside of existence consists in the inherent dialectic within creation itself while Hartshorne's aesthetic evil appears at times to be the inevitable outcome of the creative process. Both refer to failure and loss. However, despite some similarities and overlap between the two conceptions, I do not think that an exact equation can be made between them. One difference between them is that for Barth the shadowside of existence is not intrinsically evil; it is a dimension of God's good creation and only appears as evil from the perspective of a consciousness distorted by sin. Death, decay, and loss are, in reality, natural and good aspects of God's plan. Thus, for Barth, *das Nichtige* and its concrete and dynamic form of sin or moral evil are the only form of genuine evil; the shadowside of existence

---

[34] Process theologian David R. Griffin (*God, Power and Evil,* 324), working out a position closely aligned with Hartshorne, states that "genuine evil only occurs when the actualization of a lesser possibility eliminates one that would have been better, all things considered." Hartshorne appears to assume a similar conception of genuine evil.

is merely perceived as evil. Hartshorne agrees with the Barthian assessment of death and decay as natural and, indeed, asserts that endless continuation of life on the creaturely level would be itself an evil (PSG, 480). He is one with Barth in arguing that the "finiteness of our life-span is thus aesthetically appropriate" (ibid.). In this sense, they are both in opposition to those who take the very fact of death to be the worst evil. Though they deplore how it sometimes comes, the fact that it comes is finally for both thinkers a natural and good close to creaturely existence. However, what Hartshorne takes to be aesthetic evil in terms of conflict and the pain and suffering that arise from it are not simply mistaken for evil. They are genuinely evil, and this is not the result of a distorted vision but of what they truly are. Their assessment as evil is not a matter of perspective but of fact. And, further, while Barth's God positively chooses and wills the shadowside of existence, aesthetic evil is not part of the divine plan as Hartshorne interprets it. For him, the "evils are not fulfillments of any cosmic purpose" (CSPM, 317).

What the above analysis suggests is that where Barth posits two categories for considering these matters, Hartshorne develops three. Barth sets forth the categories of (1) *das Nichtige*, in terms of which he interprets genuine and, therefore, moral evil, and (2) the shadowside of existence which is merely perceived evil. Hartshorne, in his turn, develops the categories of (1) aesthetic evil, (2) moral evil, to which we shall presently turn, and (3) the natural processes of creative advance that involve death and decay as well as growth and new value. The discrepancy between the Hartshornian and Barthian positions lies, I would suggest, in the inability of the Barthian view to admit any true evil as part of creation. As long as the world is fully the product of an all-determining will, whatever possibilities are intrinsic to it must be purely positive. For Hartshorne, however, creation, as a product of multiple decisions, can be interpreted as intrinsically involving the possibility of evil without calling into question the goodness and benevolence of God's purpose in relation to this creation or suggesting divine responsibility for such evil.

However, if the possibility of evil does not, within the Hartshornian schema, call into question divine benevolence, it must be asked whether the amount or degree of evil jeopardizes God's status as loving and wise. That is, if God, as preeminently influential, sets the limits within which creatures make their own decision, does the amount of conflict and disharmony in the world suggest that the divine decisions are not the best? Is there some way in which the possibility for good could be maximized, while the potentiality for evil is minimized? Hartshorne replies in the negative to these questions and he suggests, on the contrary, that the possibility for good and evil are correlative to one another; as the opportunity for good increases, so, too, does the risk of evil.

This correlation of good and evil possibilities arises because, in the end, both good and evil have the same source: the freedom of social beings (LP,

231). Without such freedom no value would exist; indeed, nothing actual would occur, but with freedom inevitably comes the potentiality for conflict. For Barth, true freedom, as obedience, and the possibility of evil are inversely related. For Hartshorne, however, this inverse relationship does not hold, but rather freedom, as creativity, and the potentiality for evil as well as the opportunites for good decrease or increase together. In Hartshorne's words,

> Harmony and discord, as values, have the very same source, freedom. Harmony in freedom is good, conflict in freedom is evil, and the greater the freedom the greater the chances both of good and of evil. [35]
>
> The risks of freedom are inseparable from freedom and the price of its opportunities. [36]

Thus, the conditions that make great value a possibility also lay the foundation for potential evil. The outcome of this intimate connection is that the reduction of the risk of evil involves a corresponding reduction in the opportunity for good. The divine order could, Hartshorne argues, limit the risks of conflict more radically by narrowing the parameters within which free creaturely decision occurs. But such limitation would entail inevitably the loss of possible value and would relegate the amount of good achieved in the world to an inferior level. It is with this recognition that Hartshorne returns to his argument that aesthetic evil has two forms: conflict and tedium or lack of vitality. If high levels of freedom open the way to the first form of evil, low levels of freedom entail the second, equally unfortunate, result. Negligible value, just as conflict and pain, is an evil to be avoided. Both are failures to achieve rich and vital harmonious experience. And Hartshorne believes that the basic affirmation of life and vitality found in all living things indicates a deep and instinctual recognition that while pain and conflict are evil and to be avoided, so too are monotony and trivial existence, and he holds that the thrust toward life and value thereby judges the risks worth incurring. "If merely avoiding pain and ennui were the aim, we should only have to die" (PSG, 446).

Hartshorne concludes therefore that the aim of divine action cannot be merely the elimination of the possibility of evil. Rather, God's purpose, embodied in the cosmic order and individual aims, must be to insure that the risks of evil and the opportunites for good are balanced in the most optimal way (RSP, 190). The aim is toward the achievement of creative value and with it the avoidance of not only great and destructive conflict but also that deadly monotony and boredom which is little more than nothingness itself. Hartshorne is intent, however, that the recognition that risk and

---

[35] Hartshorne, "Modern World and a Modern View of God," 474–75.
[36] Hartshorne, "New Look at the Problem of Evil," 208.

opportunity go hand in hand not be interpreted as a justification of evil or a transfiguration of evil into good. It is the creative freedom that is good, never the evil that may result from it. If that freedom in some way justifies the potentiality for evil, it does so only because of the opportunities for good that are its primary aim. According to Hartshorne,

> The justification of evil is not that it is really good or partly good or necessary to good, but that the creaturely freedom from which evils spring, with probability in particular cases and inevitably in the general case, is also an essential aspect of all goods, so that the price of a guaranteed absence of evil would be the equally guaranteed absence of good. (NTOT, 81)

Hence, Hartshorne concludes that the benevolent and wise deity has, by determining the cosmic order, set propitious limits within which creatures seek to realize the good. There are, however, several questions that arise at this juncture (though they are equally applicable to the problem of moral evil). The first concerns the benevolence of divine action. This question or criticism was originally voiced by Stephen Lee Ely in relation to Whitehead [37] and has been raised anew by Edward H. Madden and Peter H. Hare. [38] If the primary good is aesthetic, that is, intensity and harmony of experience, does not the suspicion arise that God might seek or encourage creaturely conflict or suffering as a means of increasing the contrast within God's own experience thereby enhancing its aesthetic value at a cost to the nondivine individuals? That is, might God, seeking intensity of experience, sacrifice the experience of God's creatures for God's own ends? Or stated otherwise, can what is aesthetically good for God be evil for creatures? Ely argues for this conclusion in the following way:

> All values are then fundamentally aesthetic. ... God ... is not concerned with our finite sufferings, difficulties, and triumphs—except as material for aesthetic delight. God, we must say definitely, is not primarily good. He does not will the good. He wills the beautiful. [39]

And Madden and Hare offer a similar evaluation: "Certainly a God who is

[37] Ely, *The Religious Availability of Whitehead's God: A Critical Analysis* (Madison: University of Wisconsin Press, 1942) 52.

[38] Madden and Peter Hare, "Evil and Unlimited Power," *Review of Metaphysics* 20 (1966) 286–88; idem, "Evil and Persuasive Power," *Process Studies* 2 (1972) 44–48; and idem, *Evil and the Concept of God* (Springfield, Illinois: Thomas, 1968) 115–25.

[39] Ely, *Availability of Whitehead's God,* 52.

willing to pay any amount in moral and physical evil to gain aesthetic value is an unlovable being."[40]

Hartshorne, however, adamantly rejects such a proposal as a proper evaluation either of his own position or Whitehead's. He argues that for God altruism and egoism are the same; God's own individual interest is the general good. God as the recipient of all worldly values seeks, both for God's own sake and for the world's, the greatest value possible. In order to demonstrate that this was not so but that there was a disjunction between the divine good and creaturely good, one would need to prove that God, as experiencer of all things, could achieve more value from conflict or suffering than harmonious experience, that is, that God could gain more value from creatures' pain than from their happiness (WP, 104). Hartshorne insists that the very understanding of evil as a failure to achieve possible value indicates that this can never be so. Evil, whether interpreted as conflict or as lack of vitality, is always less in value than good, and hence God as the cosmic seeker of value could only have that greater value as the divine aim. And further, this God is no spectator deity, observing the world from a removed and safe position, but the most sympathetic participator in all experience who could not thereby but suffer as the creatures do. Hartshorne's conclusion is, therefore, that Ely and Madden and Hare are incorrect, and the benevolence and aesthetic experience do not conflict, but are, finally, the same.[41]

A second question that emerges also concerns divine benevolence or moral goodness. If God is not responsible for the general possibility of evil, since it is inherent in all experience, is not God, however, responsible for the level of the evil? That is, given the tremendous amount of evil, both aesthetic and moral, is it not possible to question the benevolence of a deity that would set limits or conditions that would permit such high and intense levels of these forms of evil? The question can be phrased, alternatively, in terms of divine wisdom instead of divine benevolence. Presupposing creaturely freedom and the risks it entails, is it possible that God could make a mistake or a miscalculation concerning the conditions for and direction of worldly development? Hartshorne's reply to both forms of the question is that God, as omniscient, sets conditions which could not be surpassed, though they could be equaled, by any other conceivable conditions. However, this does not quite answer the question. Omniscience may, as Hartshorne maintains, guarantee prospectively the best choice but could that choice be judged retrospectively, though perhaps only by God, to have been less judicious than expected? If indeed God's decision concerning limitations of freedom and order is, as it seems to be, the result both of God's

---

[40] Madden and Hare, "Evil and Unlimited Power," 287.

[41] For a more extended discussion of this issue from a process perspective, see Griffin, *God, Power and Evil*, 300–302.

past knowledge and of God's own imaginative projection of the future, could not that decision, given the uncertainty and undetermined quality of that future, be judged to be less propitious than intended. That is, if the world destroys itself, must we still assume that the balance of risk and opportunity was optimal? David Griffin, in his own process theodicy, raises a similar question asking, "Should God, for the sake of avoiding 'man's inhumanity to man' have avoided humanity (or some comparatively complex species) altogether?"[42] Griffin's conclusion is that God could indeed be held accountable (or in his words "indictable") for the levels of evil that occur but only if one were willing to argue that the good that had emerged really was not comparable to the evil—that the possibility of Hitler made the possibility of Jesus not worth the risk. He answers his own question by saying, "Only those who could sincerely answer this question affirmatively could indict the God of process theology on the basis of the evil in the world."[43] Hartshorne would, I believe, concur with Griffin and answer the question in the negative; the wise and loving deity sets the optimal conditions and while the risk of evil is always present and evil itself is to be rejected and opposed, nonetheless good outdistances that evil, and the value achieved makes the rest worth it. And, finally, as has been argued throughout, God as the one necessary being always will have the capacity to maintain Godself and some world so that while setbacks occur, nonetheless, absolute loss of value is not an option.

In sum, Hartshorne argues that aesthetic evil, in its two forms of discord and lack of vitality, is genuine evil and to be resisted wherever possible. But he further contends that this evil is the result neither of creaturely ill intention or divine malice, but is the unfortunate by-product of the social and free character of existence. As such it is a universal possibility inherent on every level of reality in a degree proportionate to the level of freedom present.[44] As such it can be resisted but its possibility will always remain. Freedom, risk, and opportunity are of one piece and to eradicate any one of the three destroys the other two as well. In Hartshorne's view, "We can compromise our conflicts, mitigate their destructiveness, and we should try to do this; but it is in vain to decide that there shall be no conflicts."[45]

Moral Form of Evil or Sin

But if aesthetic evil consists in conflict, suffering, and monotony interpreted as the unintended result of social interaction, what of moral evil? Of what does moral evil consist? Why does it exist? And what are its

---

[42] Ibid., 309.

[43] Ibid.

[44] Hartshorne, "New Look at the Problem of Evil," 207–8.

[45] Ibid., 210.

repercussions? Ethical or moral goodness, as stated above, consists in the Hartshornian schema in the promotion of the aesthetic good on the widest possible scale; it entails a broadening of one's concerns and inclusion of the needs and interests of others within one's aim at value. Moral evil consists in the deliberate repudiation of those broader concerns; it entails the exclusion of the interests of the community in favor of narrow and selfishly defined goals. It is necessary to unpack the various features of this claim.

First, Hartshorne defines moral evil or sin as a deliberate noninterest or lack of concern for others. It is the failure to take account of those persons or things outside the narrowly circumscribed circle of personal or group interest, be that family, country, or even humanity. It entails, in other words, the failure to universalize. By nature, it thereby excludes the interests of others while the aim toward moral goodness is always of such concerns. Hartshorne states: "Wickedness is essentially exclusion, exclusion of the interests of others from our purview and responsive appreciation" (PSG, 161).

Second, Hartshorne argues that what is so odious about moral evil is that, while aesthetic evil arises by chance and is unintended, moral insensitivity to others results in conflict and suffering that are not chance occurrences but are the outcome of deliberate choices that need not have been made. Moral evil, through the exclusion of broader interests, is the choice of a greater evil in the face of an opportunity for a greater good. It is not the innocent clash of equal values but the conflict between the unequal values of social and private good. In Hartshorne's words,

> The world is tragic, not only because conflict is inevitable between free and ignorant beings, but because there is an inner conflict in men between their will to serve a common good and their desire to promote a private or tribal goal. Some conflicts are chosen where a less destructive, more fruitful form of interaction is known. This is sin, the supreme tragedy. (RSP, 149)

Third, Hartshorne suggests that moral evil, interpreted as exclusion, is not a positive quality but is fundamentally negative in character; it is a non-quality. This negativity is in radical contrast to aesthetic evil understood as conflict and suffering. Discord and pain are for Hartshorne positive in character; they do not entail the absence or exclusion of qualities but the inclusion of unfortunate ones (PSG, 161; MVG, 196). Aesthetic evil is not, therefore, the "absence of things which harmonize but the presence of things which conflict" (MVG, 197). Nor is "pain the absence of pleasure."[46] Moral evil, in contrast, entails an essentially privative aspect; it indicates an absence or a void where the interests of others would be. In Hartshorne's

---

[46] Hartshorne, "Omniscience," 547.

words, "Whereas suffering is a positive quality, not the mere absence of one, moral evil, like ignorance, is a non-quality—namely a (willful) non-taking-account of the interests of others. It is non-interest in interests."[47]

Fourth, in the end, this exclusion of the wider interests of the social community is a form of ignorance, though a willful one. There is an ultimate connection between the lack of goodness and lack of awareness (MVG, 197). It is precisely God's perfect knowledge that insures the benevolence of God's action or, stated alternatively, God's perfect love, inclusive of all values, bears the fruit of perfect knowledge. On the human level it is the failure to know that bears the fruit of evil action. Moral evil is a form of blindness; sin is ignorance, willfully chosen. Speaking of moral evil, Hartshorne states: "It is the willful failure to give adequate place in one's awareness (at the moment of choosing a course of action) to the interests of others. It is a kind of ignorance, though a voluntary and perhaps momentary one."[48]

Thus, moral evil and cognitive failure are inseparable. But if ignorance and sin go together, Hartshorne takes pains to insist that this ignorance is not necessary. Sinful ignorance is the failure to be aware when knowledge is equally possible. It is blindness where there could have been sight. It is this deliberate character of ignorance that indicates the responsibility of the human agent in these situations. However, while Hartshorne acknowledges this deliberate aspect of moral evil, his emphasis is upon the negative character of what is chosen—that is, ignorance. He does this because deliberateness is positive in character and he wants to maintain the essentially negative quality of moral evil. Therefore, while he acknowledges that morally evil choice involves deliberateness, he argues as well that the real evil resides in the choice of noninterest, not in the deliberate character of that choice. "True, it is deliberate, but the evil is not in the deliberateness, but in the deliberate non-interest."[49]

And finally, it must be stated that moral evil is the property of humans or at least rational animals alone. As deliberately chosen ignorance it is not a universal phenomenon in the same way that aesthetic evil is. Its effects can be felt throughout the cosmos, and indeed its ramifications are found within God's life as well. But only conscious, rational beings who have the capacity for ignorance as well as knowledge can choose moral evil. For the perfect knower for whom ignorance is an impossibility and for creatures who lack all power of thought moral evil is equally ruled out. They can suffer its effects; neither can deliberately choose it.

In sum, it can be stated that Hartshorne has presented a conception of sin as willful ignorance that chooses private or narrow interests over social

---

[47] Hartshorne, "Perfect, Perfection," *An Encyclopedia of Religion*, 573.

[48] Hartshorne, "Omniscience," above n. 46. (p.547)

[49] Hartshorne, "Perfect, Perfection," above n. 47.

goals. In so doing the sinner undermines the social fabric of existence itself
and in the end always achieves a lesser value than was possible. Because the
good is always social in nature, the failure to include the interests of the
community means that not only does the community achieve lesser value
but so too does the individual sinner. The acknowledgment of the social
nature of existence brings with it the recognition that the interest of the
individual and community are not opposed but are, finally, the same. It is
in the end, for Hartshorne, a lack of awareness that causes altruism and
egoism to appear to be in such great conflict.

This Hartshornian conception of moral evil as the willful exclusion of
others' interests raises some of the same questions as did Barth's understanding of sin. According to Barth, sin is the concrete and dynamic form of
opposition to God. It is disobedience to the divine decision. But in a
schema in which God's knowledge and will are interpreted as causative and
all-determining in nature and in which creation is wholly good, lacking all
propensity toward evil, questions inevitably arise concerning how and why
sin could occur in such circumstances. Barth's answers to these queries are
not fully satisfactory, and his own final conclusion is that sin is an absurdity
lacking all ground and rationale and is beyond all attempts to comprehend
it. In Hartshorne's view moral evil as exclusion can also be seen as a form
of rebellion against the divine imperative; by excluding the interests of others, sin inevitably leads to lower levels of the creative activity which is the
purpose God envisages for the world. However, while within the Hartshornian schema the how of moral evil is clearer than it is within the Barthian
framework, I am not sure if the why makes any more sense. It is clear that
just as with aesthetic evil, creaturely freedom explains how sin could take
place; creatures make their own decisions and no influence, divine or otherwise, can determine those choices in their exact detail. But why creatures,
whose nature is oriented toward the realization of value, would deliberately
choose less value than is possible is not obvious. Hartshorne's reply is that
choice is made through ignorance, but if that ignorance itself is chosen, then
it must be asked why anyone would, in a deliberate and free manner, decide
for that. In an interesting manner, knowledge seems to function for
Hartshorne the way freedom does for Barth. In Barth, true freedom cannot
issue forth in sin; it is the capacity for and only for God and the good. For
Hartshorne, it is true or adequate knowledge that rules out sinful activity;
really to know is to act for the good. And for both the problem remains:
how to understand why humans would refuse either freedom or knowledge?
Hartshorne, with his indeterministic position, avoids the problem of full
divine responsibility that remains a central difficulty within the Barthian
deterministic schema, but he does not illuminate the question of deliberate
decision for lesser value by beings whose nature is oriented toward the
achievement of value. In the end, the perversity of moral evil remains for
Hartshorne, as for Barth, a mystery, an absurd denial of creaturely

fulfillment.[50] This difficulty of the why of moral evil can be posed another way. If God is so preeminently persuasive, why do creatures fail to be moved by the beauty of the vision God offers?[51] Once more the question arises concerning the nature of this vision. If God's purposive activity is confined to the setting of general cosmic parameters, then it is understandable how sin (as well as aesthetic evil) could occur. God would indeed be preeminently influential on this general level while the sphere in which human moral decision takes place would not be directly influenced by specific divine purposes. However, to limit God's action to this general ordering activity seems to deny God any substantial initiative and to define too narrow a role for God, even within the confines of the Hartshornian view, in the creation of new and novel value. Alternately, to assert that God not only has a general purpose for the universe, exhibited in the cosmic laws, but also offers to every experience a vision of possibility and a lure toward new value, raises the question of why God is so persuasive on one level and appears to be so unpersuasive on another level. Why does God compel agreement concerning the cosmic laws but not concerning the moral vision? I do not think Hartshorne answers this question, and his failure to do so indicates once more confusion concerning the precise nature and mode of divine action toward the world. And until this ambiguity is resolved the suspicion will remain that either divine activity is of small import or it is lacking in the efficacy Hartshorne attributes to it; either it is merely general or it is far from preeminently efficacious.

Repercussions of Evil

The repercussions in relation to the creaturely sphere are easily imagined and quite obvious: to the extent that evil occurs the world is less than it might have been. Creative value is achieved, but richer and more harmonious experience was a possibility that was missed or foregone. But if the occurrence of evil means that the world is less than it might have been, it means, as well, that God as inclusive of all reality is also less than God might have been. It is necessary to unpack the implications of this Hartshornian claim.

First, Hartshorne argues that the divine concrete life, just as all life,

---

[50] Hartshorne ("Comment by Professor Hartshorne," in Peters, *Creative Advance*, 141–42) acknowledges the mysteriousness of human motivation in terms of sin. He states: "It is rather something like the old Socratic mystery, how can one know the good and not want to actualize it? Or, if one does not know the good which one fails to act upon, the failure must be innocent."

[51] Madden and Hare ("Evil and Persuasive Power," 46) raise this question, and while I do not think their position overall offers a very clear understanding of Hartshorne's position and the process perspective as a whole, I do think this is a legitimate query.

consists in the creative appropriation and transformation of the past world. The content, richness, and quality of the divine experience, therefore, depend upon the world as God's social partner. If the cosmic process, at any stage, is less rich than it could have been, then "this means that God's concrete being is not all that it might have been as 'inheriting' that stage" (WP, 70). The profound implications of sin become clear at this juncture. Through moral evil, human beings choose not only to injure themselves and each other but to hurt God as well. The repercussions of every act resound not only in the worldly sphere, but in the divine life as well; sin is not just rebellion against God but the direct diminishing of God's very life. In Hartshorne's words, "Thus God has a destiny, things happen to him—not indeed from without but from within. He is tortured, not by himself, but by the creatures who, in injuring each other, in some degree and manner crucify deity itself" (PSG, 210). Second, Hartshorne contends that God's perfect knowledge of all reality entails that God literally includes and experiences evil. Omniscience, as conformative, inclusive, and preservative, leaves nothing out but brings all into the divine life. "It is to be noted that omniscience must in some fashion know evil. Now to know involves experience, hence God must experience the quality of evil" (MVG, 196). The ramifications of this inclusion of evil are several. To begin with, it means that God suffers the conflict and pain that is aesthetic evil. Divine knowledge, as perfect sympathy, entails the literal participation in the pain and discord of others. This knowledge of aesthetic evil is not a spectator knowledge, occurring at a distance and unaffected by the sufferings of its objects. Rather, it is the most perfect appropriation and appreciation of creaturely experiences in all their dimensions, discordant or sorrowful as well as joyful or harmonious. According to Hartshorne,

> God's knowledge is concrete and intimate. It therefore unites him with the suffering creatures much more fully than any sympathy of ours can unite us with those suffering individuals we care about. God does not simply know *that* we suffer, he knows our actual suffering in this concreteness. . . . It is logically impossible to know suffering in its concreteness and not in some sense suffer also. It follows that when we inflict sufferings upon one another, often innocently, we inflict them also upon God, who lovingly shares in them.[52]

God does not, therefore, escape suffering, pain, and conflict but possesses them in their fullness. For Hartshorne, this sympathetic participation in the sufferings of others is what the cross symbolizes. It has been obvious throughout this analysis that Hartshorne is not setting forth an intentionally Christian philosophy though many of his ideals and assumptions are clearly

---

[52] Hartshorne, "New Look at the Problem of Evil," 207.

tied to the Christian tradition. The christocentrically defined presuppositions articulated by Barth are nowhere present in the Hartshornian schema.
Nonetheless, Hartshorne believes his secular philosophy resonates on the
deepest level with the, for him, basic religious insight that God is love.
Love is social awareness and sympathetic sharing in the lives of others, and
it is just this companionship that Hartshorne finds in the cross.[53] The cross
is not, as it is for Barth, the sign of divine triumph over evil, but rather it
attests to the fact that God is the "fellow sufferer who understands" (Whitehead). The meaning of divine love is not absolute victory over evil but companionship in suffering. In Hartshorne's words, "Unlimited companionship
in the tragedies which freedom makes more or less inevitable is the theologi-
cally most neglected of divine prerogatives" (MVG, xvi).

But if God includes aesthetic evil in the divine life and suffers others'
pain and conflict as God's own, then it must be asked how God experiences
moral evil; that is, does God participate in moral wickedness in a manner
comparable to the divine experience or discord? Hartshorne's response is
an emphatic "No." God knows sin, but that knowing is not, in this unique
case, the same as being or possessing what is known. Hartshorne argues that
the reason this differentiation between the ways God experiences aesthetic
and moral evil can be made lies in the fundamentally different character of
the "two forms of evil; aesthetic evil is positive in character, while moral evil
is a negative quality" (ibid., 197; DR, 145; LP, 43–44; PSG, 161). It now
becomes clear why Hartshorne is insistent upon the privative nature of
moral evil; if moral evil were positive, God as the inclusive knower would be
qualified by it. It is only by maintaining its negative quality that
Hartshorne can resolve the dilemma that arises from his claim of God as all-
inclusive. For Barth, the interpretation of God's knowledge as causative
raises questions concerning the divine responsibility for evil, while for
Hartshorne the assertion of divine knowledge as all-inclusive suggests the
question of God's literal identification with evil. It is only because moral
evil is the absence of positive quality that Hartshorne claims that he can circumvent this problem of identification. Thus, he argues, "Though to be
acquainted with suffering is to suffer, to be acquainted with sin is not to sin,
for moral evil is not a quality but the absence of one."[54]

Thus, God includes wicked beings within Godself and knows their
wickedness for what it is, but it remains their evil and does not, as in the
case with aesthetic evil, become God's own (DR, 145). It is only insofar as
they entail positive value which they indeed necessarily entail to some
degree, for nothing is purely negative, that God is qualified by such beings.
Another way Hartshorne expresses this divine experience of moral evil is to
say that while human beings choose moral evil God only endures it. God is

[53] Hartshorne, "Divine Absoluteness and Divine Relativity," 166; PSG, 15.
[54] Hartshorne, "Omniscience," 547.

affected by evil choices but as a victim of them, not as a perpetuation of
such decisions. Hartshorne suggests that this endurance of evil choices on
God's part can be understood by stating that what is moral evil in humans
becomes aesthetic evil as God's:

> Moreover, the necessary being will not only have accidents, it will have
> *all* accidents, since all that happens will happen to it. (Even evils will
> qualify it, except moral evil as such, for moral evil as happening *to* one
> is not moral, but aesthetic, as one's friends' wickedness may make one
> suffer but not, *ipso facto*, make one wicked. . . . The necessary being can
> be exempt from no suffering, but evil choices in others it may merely
> endure, without itself making any.)[55]

If it is now possible to understand the reason for Hartshorne's insistence
upon the negative quality of moral evil, it is now possible as well to
comprehend his equally adamant insistence that moral evil is not a universal
quality but one confined to the realm of human experience. For if moral
evil were a universal category, then God would as the exemplification of all
ultimate contraries also have to exemplify evil. The contrast of moral good
and moral evil is, however, not applicable to reality as a whole but only nondivine rational beings. Thus, the assertion that God exemplifies all ultimate
contrasts can be maintained while at the same time the denial of moral evil
as a divine option can also be upheld (WP, 198). Suffering, on the other
hand, is universal in scope according to Hartshorne and therefore can be
interpreted as a category exhibited on every level of reality and can be
preeminently exemplified on the divine level (ibid.). Hartshorne states:

> Now evil, in the sense of wickedness, is not a universal category. For
> example, the animals are incapable of it, because of their unconscious-
> ness of principles and God is incapable of it. . . . Thus wickedness is not
> in the divine "character" at all. Evil, in the sense of suffering, however,
> is indeed, we believe, a category and, if so, the dipolar view must hold
> not only that God contains suffering but that he suffers and that it is in
> his character to suffer, in accordance with the suffering in the world.
> (PSG, 15)

Thus, Hartshorne argues that God, on the one hand, participates fully in
aesthetic evil as a faithful fellow sufferer and, on the other hand, knows
moral evil without participating in it. And he asserts that in all this God
remains the all-inclusive being, for moral evil is negative in character and
therefore does not exist to be included. However, I would suggest that
despite Hartshorne's claims to the contrary, moral evil presents difficulties

[55] Hartshorne, "Santayana's Doctrine of Essence," in Paul A. Schilpp, ed., *The Philosophy of
George Santayana* (Evanston: Northwestern University Press, 1941) 144.

concerning the Hartshornian assertion of divine all-inclusiveness. For, if God knows moral evil, let us say evil intention, but does not experience it as the human does, then something is missing from the divine experience as all-inclusive. While ignorance may result in hatred it is difficult to assume that the human experience of hatred is one of mere absence; it has its own intensity and dimension of feeling for which assertion of nonquality fails to take account. Another example of this might be despair. According to Hartshorne, God knows the creatures' despair but does not despair Godself. However, once more despair, while it is indeed a lack of hope, cannot be reduced to an absence of feeling or quality. And if this is so, then either God as all-inclusive is qualified by such feeling or, if God is not so qualified, I would suggest that God is no longer the sum of reality.[56] This is once more, merely in different guise, the same question that arose earlier concerning the inclusion of subjective experience within the divine life and the problem of contemporaries for divine knowledge. It, however, highlights the difficulty of understanding reality as a whole in terms of good and evil, especially moral good and evil, and it raises the question of whether it is indeed appropriate to speak of reality in such personal amd moral terms as benevolence, love, and conscious purposiveness. The only way Hartshorne can maintain both his conception of God as Reality itself and God as benevolent and loving is to assert that evil is sheer absence, and while this mode of arguing has a long tradition, it is one that to me seems to be question begging and ultimately unsatisfactory. Just as Hartshorne's assertion of divine all-inclusiveness is not easily reconciled with the questions of private experience and nonrelated contemporaries, neither is it easily accommodated to the presence of moral evil in the world. As such this claim of divine inclusion and the equation of God and Reality remains one of the most vulnerable and least satisfactory of all Hartshorne's assertions and repeatedly can be seen to call into question the Hartshornian schema as a whole.

The emphasis in the foregoing has been upon the divine experience of evil. It must be asked if God can only suffer that evil or whether God can somehow triumph over it as well. Hartshorne asserts that God can be interpreted to triumph in certain senses but not in the absolute sense of eliminating the possibility of future evil or of eradicating entirel;* the repercussions of past evils.[57] On the one hand, God always makes the best of evil. God

---

[56] Peters (*Hartshorne and Neoclassical Metaphysics*, 121) raises similar difficulties concerning the relation of moral evil and divine inclusion.

[57] My interpretation concerning this issue differs from two other, somewhat contrasting positions. Neville (*God the Creator*, 301) thinks that while God's purpose can be thwarted in terms of individuals, in the long run God is triumphant. He has problems concerning this for he feels that it calls into question "our freedom and integrity to oppose him; we cannot win. . . . There is . . . no possibility of really thwarting God; yet that possibility should follow if one is

takes whatever value is achieved and utilizes it in the most creative fashion possible. According to Hartshorne, "Granting that evil does arise, God does wring some good out of it" (WP, 94). On the other hand, God as the perfect knower is capable of receiving any value, however meager or tinged with conflict or pain. Hence, as has been argued throughout the analysis, no evil can threaten God's existence though evil does diminish the richness of the divine life. Hartshorne concludes, therefore, that the reality of evil cannot be seen as an argument against the divine existence, for that existence is compatible with any actuality no matter how relatively good or evil. Once more Hartshorne asserts that empirical facts cannot be taken as proof or disproof for the existence of a divine reality, but that this is solely a metaphysical question. [58]

And finally Hartshorne argues that while evil may be present, reality as a whole is always more positive than negative; the good always outweighs the evil (PSG, 160, 446). Actuality, for Hartshorne, primarily realizes the good, and only secondarily evil. [59] This is acknowledged even on the human level by the simple fact of continued life that attests that experience is basically a value rather than a disvalue. And it is infinitely truer on the divine level where God as the cosmic experiencer and preserver of all values harmonizes and transforms all creaturely experience into God's own. Thus, for Hartshorne, while God suffers, ultimately the divine experience is of joy in and enjoyment of the values offered to God by the world.

---

to have integrity. Nor is there the possibility of damning oneself; one can only play a less-than-capacity role in bringing about God's will in the end" (ibid.). While I agree with Neville that humans, no matter how evil, cannot destroy all value (hence, cannot damn themselves) I do not think his first claim is correct. God cannot be thwarted in the sense of being destroyed but in the long run, just as in the short term, value for God can be less than God desires. Madden and Hare ("Evil and Persuasive Power," 46; "Evil and Unlimited Power," 288) have the opposite problem and think that the difficulty lies in that the Hartshornian God cannot insure an ultimate triumph of good over evil. While it is true that Hartshorne's God cannot eliminate the possibility of evil, the reason lies not, as Madden and Hare assume, in the divine weakness, but in the nature of reality itself.

[58] Hartshorne, "New Look at the Problem of Evil," 201. Madden and Hare ("Evil and Persuasive Power," 47–48) also have problems with this claim and assert that if empirical facts of evil are irrelevant to questions of divine existence, then divine power loses coherency and meaning in terms of empirical reality. They state: "Does it make conceptual sense to speak of a sort of power whose nature and extent is in principle impossible to estimate experientially? In ordinary contexts power is always something that can be at least indirectly and roughly measured experientially. To speak of completely unmeasurable power appears to be as much a 'pseudo-idea' as to speak of weight that can never require force to lift (ibid.)."

[59] Madden and Hare ("Evil and Persuasive Power," 288) reject this claim as well: "That simple existence is a value seems doubtful. It runs counter to the ordinary notion that some things ought not to be." Hartshorne would argue that some things are less than they should be but, for him, something is always better than nothing; meager value is better than non-value.

But if God is not ultimately threatened by evil and if value always outbalances evil, God nonetheless does not triumph over evil in any absolute manner. The possibility of evil is inherent in freedom and therefore God cannot eliminate it. As new opportunities arise, so, too, will new risks of evil in both its moral and aesthetic forms. For, God's power is finally social power and entails necessarily the existence of other powers capable of their own decisions which shape and determine, in their own small way, the development of reality. As long as life is creation there can be no victory that eradicates the potentiality for evil. In Hartshorne's words,

> Good is not an army and evil another, with the desirable outcome the unconditional surrender or absolute disappearance of the second army. . . . Life is more than a battle, especially a battle between abstractions. It is an art of creation, with God the eminent but not the sole creator.[60]

Thus, finally reality is tragic; it is always the mixture of good and evil, joy and sorrow, gain and loss. This Hartshornian sense of the tragic quality of existence is, in the end, far removed from the Barthian cry of divine triumph. For Barth, the cross is a sign of victory, a triumphant declaration that evil is no more. God as powerful and all-loving has defeated the enemy. For Hartshorne, on the other hand, the cross is the symbol of shared sorrow. Hartshorne does not think that this tragic dimension of reality is reason for despair for it is never sheer tragedy; there is always reason for joy and hope and there always exists the capacity to mitigate, if not to eliminate, evil in its many expressions. But Hartshorne's final message is a sobering one; it is that God's love and power neither cause us evil nor can they prevent its possibility. We free creatures are its source, and our task is to fight it wherever possible and suffer it wherever necessary. For Hartshorne, ultimately "freedom is our opportunity and our tragic destiny" (LP, 14).

6.4 Summary Remarks

The foregoing analysis has revealed once more the profound differences between Hartshorne and Barth. As their methodological presuppositions and their conceptions of the nature and content of divine power differ, so too do their understandings of creaturely freedom and the nature of evil. Barth argues for a radical, if benevolent, determinism and a conception of creaturely freedom as obedience, while Hartshorne posits a relative indeterminism and a definition of creaturely freedom in terms of creativity and multiple alternatives for decisions. And finally, the two thinkers differ as to the ultimate character of existence itself, with Barth arguing for a joyful triumph

---

[60] Hartshorne, "The Dipolar Conception of Deity," *Review of Metaphysics* 21 (1967) 285.

by a loving and irresistible God and Hartshorne suggesting that finally reality is a tragic beauty full of conflict, pain, and evil but also joy, value, and ever new possibility both for God and the world.

Both of these positions have much to commend them, and each appeals on a variety of levels. But both have, as well, profound internal difficulties. Concerning Barth, the suspicion remains that either God is responsible for evil and sin or that such evil is really a disguised good, a subtle blessing contributing to a hidden divine purpose. In the end, the Barthian coincidence of an all-determining power and a gracious love seems a questionable claim in the face of radical evil. Hartshorne, by denying the all-determining character of divine power, avoids the difficulties evil and sin present to Barth, and his position has therefore a greater internal coherence. Moreover, because of his social vision of power, indeed of reality, Hartshorne also is able to develop a more subtly argued and richly textured understanding of creaturely freedom, and with this interpretation of freedom as creativity he is able to safeguard the integrity, partial independence, and responsibility of nondivine individuals in a manner that is not possible for Barth. Thus, I would suggest that Hartshorne's position offers a number of advantages that Barth's does not and that his social vision of power is very suggestive concerning how the notions of divine power and creaturely integrity might be reconciled in a creative manner. However, Hartshorne, just as Barth, fails to give an adequate explanation of the why of moral evil, and further, his insistence that knowledge is inclusion—and that perfect knowledge is radical and complete inclusion—raises the possibility either of the identification of God as a Cosmic Whole with moral evil or the loss of some form of experience to that Cosmic Whole. In the first instance God can no longer be considered only good and in the second God can no longer be equated with reality itself. In either case the Hartshornian claims are undermined in a serious fashion. Thus, while Hartshorne's social vision offers great promise, once more his particular interpretation of social relation as inclusion can be seen to introduce significant difficulties that cannot be ignored.

The analysis of the positions of these two forceful thinkers has followed a long and complicated path and has indicated the multidimensional nature of the question of divine power. It is now necessary to turn from this detailed analysis to some general comments and overarching observations. It is to this final evaluation that the Conclusion is devoted.

CONCLUSION

The purpose of this dissertation has been to set forth and critically examine two important twentieth-century conceptions of God: the revelationally based vision of Karl Barth and the metaphysically grounded position of Charles Hartshorne. This examination has been carried out, in reference to each thinker, in a threefold manner; first, through the articulation of the principles that guide the thought of each and the methodological approaches that embody these underlying assumptions; second, through the explicit and detailed analysis of the Barthian and Hartshornian conceptions of divine power; and finally, through the examination of the repercussions of Barth's and Hartshorne's understandings of God's power as they pertain to human freedom and the problems of evil and sin.

This threefold analysis has revealed a number of interesting and provocative similarities and dissimilarities between the positions developed by Barth and Hartshorne. The similarities are most clear in these thinkers' common effort to offer, in distinction from many static classical conceptions, an understanding of deity and power in dynamic and progressive terms that emphasize the centrality and importance of God's relationships with the world. Guided by this intention, both develop conceptions of divine power which seek to preserve and indeed embody this dynamic and social vision of deity. Hence, both Barth and Hartshorne seek to associate, in the most emphatic manner, divine power with God's knowledge, love, and freedom. And each conceives of that power as having as a primary aim the development, preservation, and fulfillment of a gracious and loving relationship between God and the world.

Despite these common concerns and insights, important though they are, Barth and Hartshorne offer positions that contrast profoundly with one another and finally, by implication at least, challenge the validity and adequacy of each other both in terms of methodological approach and material content. The examination of their thought revealed that they argue for conflicting sources of knowledge of God and norms for evaluating that knowledge, with Barth maintaining that such knowledge results only from a faith experience grounded in Christian revelation, and with Hartshorne asserting that such knowledge is available to all humans through their innate capacities to reflect metaphysically. The analysis revealed further that Barth and Hartshorne, though they agree on the association of power, love, knowledge, and freedom, develop very distinct ways of understanding these ideas and their interrelation. Barth, for his part emphasizes divine initiative, agency, and independence and accentuates the causative function and gratuitous character of all these attributes. Hartshorne, in contrast, stresses the social character of power, knowledge, love, and freedom and, as a result, develops a vision of reality which emphasizes the necessary interdependence and mutual conditioning of God and the world.

Much of the preceding analysis has been concerned to delineate and to explore these differences, and there is no need to rehearse these contrasting claims in the present context. Rather, having set forth the Barthian and Hartshornian positions, it is now important to draw some general conclusions and reach a final evaluation of these contrasting visions in relation to present-day theological concerns. That is, having detailed their positions, how do I finally assess these distinct viewpoints as alternatives for contemporary theology?

I would like to state my final conclusions by evaluating these positions on two levels or from two directions; the first consists in evaluating Barth and Hartshorne from their own perspectives. That is, I want to ask, given their premises, how well does each succeed in carrying out his theological or philosophical intention? To what extent do they present internally consistent and coherent visions?

The second level of evaluation concerns the question of how adequate these positions are to the insights and presuppositions of contemporary thought. That is, beyond the question of internal coherence lies the question of general adequacy and meaning and the availability of these positions for contemporary appropriation. As a way of focusing this latter concern, I want to ask how well or adequately these positions take account of the historical and social consciousness that has become almost axiomatic to twentieth-century thought. Through this twofold approach of internal and external evaluation I hope thereby to reach some final conclusions concerning the viability of these two theological perspectives.

Internal Conflicts

There is a sense in which the entire analysis set forth in the preceding chapters has had as its aim the evaluation of Barth's and Hartshorne's positions from within their respective visions and according to the criteria each thinker accepts as legitimate and appropriate in relation to his thought. While the comparative nature of this study has meant that Barth and Hartshorne have each stood as an external challenger and implicit critic of the other's perspective, a central concern of this examination has been to argue both these alternatives as strongly as possible on their own terms and not simply to utilize one as the "straw man" for the other. The assumption has been throughout the study that both Barth and Hartshorne have developed positions that warrant serious consideration as possible contemporary theological visions.

However, despite this effort to argue for these positions in their strongest forms, the visions postulated by Hartshorne and Barth were both revealed to be beset by significant and serious internal contradictions and dilemmas that this study could find no way to resolve according to the tenets each thinker proposed. Chapters 2, 3, 5, and 6 explored a variety of these difficulties, and it is not my intention to reiterate all these problems at this juncture. However, as a means of reaching an overall evaluation I do want to reconsider what I judge to be central or significant difficulties that arise within these thinkers' respective positions and which, thereby, stand as serious internal challenges to the views they seek to promulgate.

Barth

As this study has demonstrated, a central concern of Barth's theology is to articulate a conception of God, not as a static or impersonal absolute whose intentions are obscure, but as a dynamic, living, related being for whom relationship is the core of divine reality. Both Barth's understanding of the Trinity and of the God-world connection speak of his conviction that divine decision and the relationships which are its fruit are the center of what is meant by the Christian God. However, Barth also posits a conception of divine power, conceived in the double form of divine self-determination and divine world-determination, which is absolute and unqualified in character and which results in a version of determination which closely resembles the idea of omnipotence associated with the traditional deity Barth rejects. Barth, for his part, sees no tension between these two sets of claims nor does he understand his conception of all-determining power to be in conflict with his equally fundamental assertion that the creaturely realm, as God's partner in relation, has integrity and positive worth. Rather, Barth contends divine power, identified with God's gracious and purposive activity, in no way undermines that creaturely integrity and significance but, instead, is their ground and guarantee. Divine power is absolute and all-determining, but the identification of that power with God's loving purpose circumvents the difficulties traditionally associated with the idea of omnipotence and permits Barth to maintain all these claims simultaneously.

The analysis of Barth's position revealed, however, that these claims are indeed in serious tension. Time and time again it became evident that there is a difficulty of balancing the claim of completely determining power, understood not only as the ground for, but also the determining factor in all worldly occurrence, with the assertion of creaturely, especially human, integrity and responsibility. This was perhaps most clear concerning the relation of divine power to evil and sin and the recurring question of what meaning and content human freedom could have within this schema. And the conclusion reached through this analysis is that absolute power, even though gracious in character, cannot be reconciled with creaturely freedom and accountability except by sheer assertion. Barth's intention is clear: to maintain both the all-determining scope of divine power, and the freedom and responsibility of creatures with the notions of divine love and purpose acting as the bridge between the two. The conclusion of this study is also clear: Barth cannot carry out this intention without seriously calling into question or undermining one or both of his claims. The question that must be asked is why Barth fails, why Barth's central assertions concerning divine decision, relationship, and power cannot be reconciled with his claims for creaturely integrity and significance.

In reflecting upon why Barth finally fails to integrate and harmonize his various tenets in a satisfactory manner, I have come to some conclusions that bear not only on the issues presently before us but that will also be significant for my evaluation of the Barthian enterprise as a whole. My first thought was to interpret the tensions suggested by the analysis to be the result of an attempt by Barth to graft a traditional notion of omnipotence onto his own nontraditional conception of God. That is, it might be argued that while Barth's thought as a whole has taken great strides in revising, perhaps even revolutionizing, the concept of God along dynamic and relational lines, this aspect of his thought, for some unclear reason, remains tied to the presuppositions of an earlier and outmoded manner of conceiving of deity and the God-world relationship. According to this reasoning, Barth's conception of divine power could be understood to be in tension with the general direction of the rest of this theology and a revision of this idea of power along those more basic lines (a revision perhaps more attentive to his supposed christological norm) might result in the more adequate safeguarding of the integrity, freedom, and responsibility of creaturely reality. Barth's theology as it stands might then be understood to be a half-way stage on the road to the thoroughly relational understanding of God Barth seeks to develop.

While there is some plausibility in this way of thinking about the problem, I have finally concluded that it does not quite reach the heart of the matter. I think finally that the difficulty lies in that while Barth makes the notion of relationship central to his understanding of deity and while he further argues that power and with it love, freedom, and knowledge must all be interpreted in relational terms as well, he nonetheless never conceives of God's relationship with the world as truly social in nature. That is, while Barth makes the God-world realtion central, he does not conceive of it as entailing any of the social dimensions normally associated with relationship: reciprocity, mutual conditioning, and social interaction. While, I would argue, such elements characterize even the most bifurcated or hierarchically patterned relationships within the world to some extent, Barth suggests that they are dimensions essentially absent from the God-creature relation. For Barth, although God is different because of the relation, this difference is solely the result of God's unconditioned self-determination, not any determination of God by creaturely reality. Barth even, as the analysis uncovered, treats the cross primarily as an instance of God's initiative and self-determined activity rather than an example, even in part, of either divine receptivity or creaturely conditioning. Barth has, therefore, envisioned a relationship that is characterized by strict dichotomy; the terms or attributes applicable to one side of the relation are inapplicable to the other. Thus, God is always cause, creatures effect; God is always active while creatures are ever and only reactive. A further result of this dichotomized view of relation is that even when Barth does want to utilize the same notions, such as power, freedom, or love to characterize both God and the world, he must do so in such fundamentally different ways that such common usage is confusing and ultimately highly questionable. Hence, divine freedom entails creativity and choice among alternatives, while creaturely freedom is equated with obedience. Or again God's love is fully gratuitous, never responsive or receptive, while creaturely love is always reactive in nature.

Many of these difficulties arise, I would suggest, because these notions are all, in common usage, intrinsically social ideas receiving their meaning contextually and presupposing the reality of distinct social entities. However, in the Barthian schema these ideas, when applied to God, originally receive their meaning apart from God's relationship with realities that are ontologically distinct from Godself and bring it, so to speak, to the relationship. As Chapter 2 demonstrated, for Barth God is first, in Godself, omnipotent, loving, and free, and all of this apart from any relation with the world. It may be objected that while not socially defined in reference to the God-world relationship, these attributes are socially conceived in terms of God's intertrinitarian life. That is, while dichotomy and with it one-directional conditioning and activity characterize the God-world relationship, mutuality and social interaction characterize the internal life of God. Although it may be true (though Barth often sounds a dichotomous note in relation to the Trinity as well) that the Trinity does point to a more social interpretation of God's internal being, it functions, ironically, to undermine a genuinely social conception of the God-world relationship. For God's intertrinitarian relation is so perfect and complete that the end result is that Barth proclaims a socially self-sufficient and self-completed being for whom the significance and content of a relationship with the nondivine world is not clear. In the words of theologian Daniel Day Williams,

> Since he is complete love in himself, it is said that he needs nothing. The divine society becomes the alluring pattern of what the world would like to be but cannot, and God's communion with the world

really adds nothing to the completeness and blessedness of the circum-
cession of the Father, Son and Spirit. [1]

Thus, while Barth argues that a trinitarian interpretation of God lays the
foundation for understanding God's relationship with the world as natural
and grounded in God's intrinsically social nature, it can also be concluded
that this interpretation, insofar as it entails an understanding of God as self-
completed being, leads us to a conception of the God-world relation in
purely dichotomous terms which finally divest the notions of power, freedom, and love of their social content. Although Barth has argued for the
importance of the God-world relation, he has done so on a basis which
finally mitigates against a truly social interpretation of that relation and its
various components. The end result is that claims of creaturely integrity,
power, freedom, and responsibility always stand in danger of being rendered
meaningless in the face of the underlying and more primary assertion of
God's omnipotence and ontic and noetic independence.

Therefore, I would argue that the tensions that arise between Barth's
claims of divine all-determining power and human responsibility and
integrity are not the result of Barth's failure to carry through his general
intention nor can they be resolved by an appeal to his guiding presuppositions. Rather, they are conflicts that arise out of those very presuppositions,
and they serve to illustrate the difficulties that lie at the heart of Barth's
theological program. In the last analysis a conception of relationship which
is built on the premise that one of the participants is a self-completed,
totally self-sufficient being and the posssessor of all-determining power will
inevitably raise questions concerning the status of the other participants. It
will always prove difficult if not impossible, to move from a notion of self-
sufficient, self-completed, self-positing being to that of creative and fulfilling
relationship in which the integrity of all participants is safeguarded. However, to reinterpret the relation between God and the world in more
genuinely social terms would, in turn, undermine Barth's original and primary premise of divine independence and absolute power. Hence, the tensions remain within the Barthian schema and with them doubts concerning
the viability of his vision.

Hartshorne

Hartshorne, just as Barth, has as a central concern the development of a
conception of deity in primarily relational terms. However, unlike Barth, he
brings to his analysis a far more socially defined understanding of these
terms and categories. The result is that Hartshorne's vision avoids several of
the dilemmas that arise within the Barthian schema, but at the same time

---

[1] Williams, "New Theological Situation," 462.

the particular Hartshornian interpretation of these social presuppositions present significant problems of its own. If Barth's theology presents the dilemma of how to construe a social relation between a completely self-sufficient and all-determining God and an utterly dependent creaturely realm, Hartshorne's philosophy suggests almost the opposite difficulty: how to conceive of the relation between God and the world when God is understood to be related to the world in such a manner that the world is literally included within the divine life. That is, how is the God-world relation to be construed when God and the world are taken to be reality at different stages of development? While Barth's problem is how to introduce genuine social relation, Hartshorne's is how to keep that social relation from collapsing the distinction between divine and nondivine reality.

Hartshorne bases his position concerning the God-world relation on the premise, which he claims is metaphysically derived, that reality is intrinsically social and that such social relatedness entails the literal inclusion of ontologically distinct individuals within the life of other such individuals or momentary units of experience. From this premise that social relation means social inclusion, Hartshorne argues that God as the perfect social entity possesses the power or capacity to receive into Godself other realities on a universal and unlimited scale and that this receptive power results in the inclusion of all reality within the one unified and integrated divine reality and that, furthermore, this inclusive divine life can finally be interpreted as Reality itself or the Cosmic Whole. Thus, his understanding of social relation and, with it, power as the capacity for receptivity leads him to the equation of God and the world as a unified entity.

However, as the examination of Hartshorne's position demonstrated, while this vision is highly suggestive concerning the status and importance of receptive power and the meaning of social relatedness, the resulting identification of God and Reality as a whole is accompanied by numerous difficulties that apparently are not resolvable according to the tenets Hartshorne has set forth. A number of these internal conflicts were delved into in Chapters 5 and 6, but most siginificant among them are the following:

1) The equation of God and Reality, as unified and integrated, creates profound tensions between the assertion of the integrity (some would contend privacy) of individual experience and the claim that the divine inclusion leaves nothing outside God's experience but rather transforms or translates all experience into divine experience.

2) Hartshorne's assumption that God as all-inclusive is the measure of reality stands in contradiction to his alternate claim that God neither experiences nor includes contemporaries.

3) Even if these difficulties concerning receptive power are overcome or, more likely, ignored, the problem of how to conceive of power in its more agential forms remains. That is, how is this Cosmic Whole, Reality itself

to be understood, as Hartshorne wishes, in the individual, personal, moral terms historically associated with the idea of God? And further what can be meant by the claim that Reality itself acts upon the world in a definite, conscious, purposeful and even loving manner?

Hartshorne's difficulty with dealing with this latter issue has been clearly illustrated by his lack of clarity and apparent uncertainty concerning just how God can be said to operate in the world. Thus, while Hartshorne has argued eloquently, if finally problematically, for a vision of divine power and relationship that positively assesses receptivity, he has left his readers ultimately uneasy concerning his notion of social inclusion and finally unsatisfied with his treatment of the agential forms of power and how these can be coherently and meaningfully conceived in relation to a God who is understood as Reality itself.

Therefore, Hartshorne can be judged, on the one hand, to have avoided some of the pitfalls that characterize Barth's position. By grounding his position in thoroughly social premises he is able both to attribute to God, in a positive manner, the power of receptivity and reciprocity that escapes Barth and to attribute to nondivine individuals the power of initiative, determination, and creativity that equally is beyond the possibilities of the Barthian view. Thus, those social presuppositions with which he begins permit him to construct a vision of the God-world relationship which is not characterized by the Barthian dichotomies but rather can be conceived in terms of mutuality and genuinely social interaction. However, on the other hand, Hartshorne's interpretation of these social presuppositions along the lines of literal inclusion continually creates problems that, at every turn, threaten to render his position internally incoherent. Thus, while his position offers a number of correctives to Barthian tendencies, it does not of itself offer a definitive alternative. What it does do is suggest the importance and indeed promise of a thoroughly social interpretation of reality and the God-world relation, while raising fundamental doubts concerning the viability of his own particular interpretation of social relatedness.

In conclusion, it can be stated that while both Barth and Hartshorne set their theological programs in interesting and provocative ways and while they each further argue persuasively for the centrality of certain issues, their explicit formulations of their respective visions entail internal tensions, inconsistencies, and contradictions that seriously undermine either position's hope for contemporary appropriation. In a way they can be said to have set the theological questions but to have failed to provide wholly adequate answers to those questions.

If, however, they are beset by internal difficulties, the visions articulated by Barth and Hartshorne also stand challenged by certain presuppositions that have become commonplace for many thoughtful persons in the twentieth century. There are a myriad of external criticisms, arising from a variety of perspectives, that can be directed at Barth and Hartshorne.

Because of the limited scope of this study I have alluded to only a few of these external challenges. However, as a means of drawing some final conclusions I would like to turn now to one such external challenge, that of historical consciousness, which seriouly calls into question the Barthian and Hartshornian enterprises alike. I have chosen to focus on this particular critical perspective, on the one hand, because it is one with which I strongly align myself and, on the other, because it raises issues that neither Barth nor Hartshorne have taken account of adequately and thereby it strikes close to the heart of their proposals. And while, in this context, I cannot argue this critical perspective thoroughly or in detail, I do hope to indicate the direction and fundamental importance of its challenge.

The Challenge of Historical Consciousness

In the Introduction to this dissertation it was noted that the positions developed by Karl Barth and Charles Hartshorne both reflect and cohere well with many of the commonly held convictions of twentieth-century life and thought. A central way in which the contemporary sensibility was seen to find expression was in Barth and Hartshorne's shared concern to conceive of reality and with it God in dynamic and relationally determined categories. Both the promise and the problems of these thinkers' positions are grounded in their respective attempts to work out such socially and dynamically oriented visions of reality. And in this sense they have been deeply attuned to their age.

However, in another crucial way neither Barth's nor Hartshorne's work reflects or finally adequately takes account of another prevalent and significant presupposition of modern and especially twentieth-century western thought: the historical and socially circumscribed character of all thought and experience. Over the last several centuries the findings of a number of intellectual perspectives have pointed to the conclusion that all thinking, experiencing, and valuing is shaped and given content by the cultural and social context in which it occurs. [2] Representatives of such diverse perspectives as sociology of knowledge, cultural and social anthropology, historical studies, psychology, ethics, linguistic analysis, as well as proponents of certain theological perspectives, and even a growing number of the scientific community have agreed, if on little else, on this historicity and

---

[2] For classic statements concerning the nature and consequences of historical consciousness see the works of R. G. Collingwood and Ernst Troeltsch. For more contemporary analysis of the issue see Peter L. Berger and Thomas Luckmann, *The Social Construction of Reality* (Garden City, New York: Anchor Books, 1967); Clifford Geertz, *The Interpretation of Cultures* (New York: Basic Books, 1973); Gordon D. Kaufmann, *Relativism, Knowledge and Faith* (Chicago: University of Chicago Press, 1960); and idem, *An Essay on Theological Method* (Missoula: Scholars, 1975).

the social character of human existence and thought. And with this conviction there have emerged a number of related assumptions concerning the
processes and objects of knowledge and experience that can be seen to
conflict, in the most fundamental manner, with the claims set forth by both
Barth and Hartshorne. It is important to examine, if briefly, what some of
these assumptions are and how the Hartshornian and Barthian positions
relate to them.

Stated in overarching and general terms, it can be argued that the basic
conviction that has been the fruit of modern historical consciousness is that
all thought and experience is mediated through and given shape, content,
and value by the linguistic and symbolic forms available to a society and
that these linguistic and symbolic forms are themselves products of social
and cultural development; that is, knowledge and its medium and expressions are all thoroughly historical in nature. Humans do not know or
experience in vacuums nor from value-free or so-called objective perspectives. Rather, they do so in and through social contexts, and both the
experiences themselves and the ideas and symbols which give them public
expression reflect the historically and culturally defined possibilities and
limitations of those contexts.

One of the sources and most significant confirmations of this historical
and social sense has been the recognition of the plurality and diversity of
human experience and the growing recognition of the historically and
socially defined uniqueness of these multiple forms of knowledge and experience. With this assumption of historically grounded diversity has come as
well the conviction that all knowledge, truth, and value as well as the concepts and symbols that express them are relative to the context within which
they emerge. Furthermore, this historical consciousness and the relativism
which has been its product have given rise to the radical reassessment of
cognitive capacities and parameters and to the corresponding negative
evaluation of claims to universal truth or validity for cognitive assertions. In
the disciplines of theology and philosophy, this reassessment has entailed a
radical and ongoing reconsideration of the human capacity to know God, of
the possible status and meaning both of the object of religious experience
and theological reflection, and of the concepts and symbols that seek to
explain, describe, or embody it.

The revelation-based theology of Karl Barth and the metaphysically
grounded philosophy of Charles Hartshorne, distinct as they otherwise are,
both represent attempts to circumvent the consequences of this historical
relativism.[3] Each asserts a status for his truth and value claims and for the

---

[3] For criticisms of Barth and Hartshorne concerning this lack of historical and social sense
see Langdon Gilkey, *Naming the Whirlwind* (New York: Bobbs-Merrill, 1969) 100–103; Williams, "New Theological Situation," 450; Parsons, "Religious Naturalism and the Philosophy

cognitive process through which they were attained that exempts them from the limitations and historical conditioning that characterize all other forms of knowledge. And by doing so they set themselves and their positions in radical opposition to much of the spirit of the present day.

Barth, while generally acknowledging the relativity and the anthropologically circumscribed nature of knowledge, nonetheless contends that in faith this relativity is transcended through the presence of the divine Spirit who transforms human concepts and symbols into the instruments of God's purpose. Thus, while all other forms of knowledge are relativized and their character as human cultural and historical products is acknowledged, knowledge obtained in faith experience is elevated to the status of divinely communicated truth; faith knowledge, as knowledge given and guaranteed by God, thus evades the critical judgment of historical consciousness.

Hartshorne, in his turn, also seeks to place knowledge of God and the concepts that embody it outside the reach of historical relativism. He, too, acknowledges the relativity and historically conditioned nature of ordinary (for him, empirical) knowledge but also asserts that, in contrast, metaphysical knowledge of the universally (and eternally) true, is of a different logical type that transcends the limitations of that ordinary human knowing. Metaphysical concepts, while human, somehow transcend the cultural, social, and historical milieu from which they emerge and attain a level of universal validity and certainty that make them illuminating of and applicable to all historical circumstances no matter how diverse. He makes this claim on the presuppositions assumed but not proven: that the structure, if not the content, of experience is everywhere and in all times the same, that the human mind has the capacity to penetrate to this structure, and finally that human ideas and concepts are capable of corresponding to this universal reality. It is the reason in its metaphysical mode that can transcend the particularity of specific historical circumstances and attain to the universal structure of all reality. Insofar as the concept of God is a metaphysical idea, it, too, can be reached and can be securely defined by such metaphysical reason. Thus, as faith is the medium or vehicle of this circumvention in the Barthian schema, metaphysical reasoning plays a comparable role, from the perspective of historical consciousness, in the Hartshornian vision.

Thus, while Barth and Hartshorne acknowledge the claims growing out of the modern sense of the historical and social structuring of experience and ideas in relation to ordinary experience, they both argue for conceptions of knowledge of God and the ideas that express this knowledge which are not subject to the relativistic and limiting structures that circumscribe all other knowledge. Such argument for, or more accurately proclamation of, the transcendence of the historical and social character of knowledge runs

---

of Charles Hartshorne," 557–59; Keeling, "Feeling as a Metaphysical Category," 65; and Neville, *God the Creator,* 145.

counter to and is finally unacceptable in terms of the insights of historical consciousness. Both Barth and Hartshorne take the claims of historical relativism into account by applying those limitations to other forms of knowledge and exempting their own positions from such strictures, and they do so on premises that finally, so to speak, run around historical relativism instead of working through it. From the perspectives that take seriously the human and, hence, social and historical character of all thought and experience, both Barth's theological positivism and Hartshorne's metaphysical pretensions appear as arbitrary and ill-advised attempts at special pleading. As such they appear to be revisionistic rather than visionary; they are attempts to recapture a certitude and a status of universal truth that many thinkers, including myself, in the modern era no longer believe possible. Insofar as Barth's and Hartshorne's over-all approaches and methodologies reflect this historically uninformed tendency, their entire enterprises will appear suspicious and ultimately unacceptable to many of their twentieth-century intellectual compatriots.

This lack of a sense for the anthropological nature and ground for ideas and all the implications such a sense entails has repercussions for Barth and Hartshorne not only in relation to the form of their positions and the status they claim for them but also in terms of the content each develops. As I stated above, I am convinced that many of the tensions that arise from Barth's treatment of power are the result of the fact that he takes a notion that has arisen in and given meaning within human contexts involving social interaction and reciprocity and then attempts to define it in a manner that ignores those elements. If he had acknowledged and explored more fully the anthropological content of the notion, then perhaps when he had utilized it in reference to God it would have been more comprehensible. When ideas are taken out of their contexts and utilized in fashions that contradict their contextually defined meaning they inevitably encounter the danger of being rendered meaningless or illegitimate.

As I have argued above, Hartshorne's position, especially as it concerns the understanding of power as both receptive and outgoing, has less difficulties than does Barth's position. This is so, I would suggest, precisely because Hartshorne's procedure keeps his concepts closer to their anthropological sources. His method of generalization from human experience, although it is certainly problematic in other respects, nonetheless functions to keep his ideas meaningful in relation to the context from which they arose. As a result Hartshorne develops a conception of power and its related ideas that reflects a greater consciousness of the relational and social dimensions of these notions. From beginning to end these are relational terms, receiving their meaning from the human contexts in which they arose, in a way that they never are for Barth. The result is that Hartshorne's conceptions retain their meaningful applicability in relation to that human world in a way Barth's ideas finally do not. Further, I would suggest that where

Hartshorne's position is especially problematic this is, at least in part, the result of his straying, in his speculative flights of imagination, too far from those anthropological sources. This might indeed be the case in terms of the interpretation of social relation as inclusion, an interpretation that has difficulties being intelligible in light of human experience despite Hartshorne's claims that its model is human memory.

These remarks are not meant to be read as reductionistic, claiming that theological reflection consists merely in taking human ideas emerging from human experience and applying them to God in bigger and better ways. Although there is much truth in this claim, as Feuerbach and others have sought to demonstrate, theological construction is far more complex than mere projection. However, the insight of historical consciousness is that no matter what our sources may be, whether revelation or logical analysis, anthropology or mystical experience, they are all human experiences or activities. Theological ideas and visions, no less than the visions of any other perspective on reality, reflect and bear the marks of their origin, and their legitimate use must always take this factor into serious consideration. And it is my conviction that insofar as Barth and Hartshorne fail to do this in relation to their positions, those views are weakened and made less viable by the absence of such self-consciousness.

Hence, it can be argued that while Barth and Hartshorne often mirror the concerns and sensibilities that characterize this particular era, they also, in methods and presuppositions as well as sometimes in content, contradict several of the most fundamental tendencies and assumptions of our time. In this lack of historical and social consciousness (ironic in thinkers for whom the notions of history, process, and relation are so important), they both equally stand in opposition to much of the modern spirit and its challenge. And to the extent that they cannot reconcile their positions with the insights of this contemporary consciousness, both visions will appear very vulnerable and less than viable to those thinkers who take these insights seriously.

Final Thoughts

This dissertation has had as its task the explication and evaluation of the conceptions of God and divine power constructed by Karl Barth and Charles Hartshorne. Such an examination was undertaken on the assumption that both Barth and Hartshorne offer important and distinct alternatives whose validity must be carefully assessed by the contemporary theological world. However, this study has revealed, somewhat to its author's surprise, that the positions developed by these two thinkers each have profound internal difficulties and that, moreover, both face a serious and potentially devastating challenge from those perspectives that acknowledge and accept the presuppositions of historical consciousness. Thus on the levels of both internal coherency and external meaningfulness and viability the visions of Barth and Hartshorne, if not totally undermined, can be seen to be open to serious criticism. While they both are interesting and provocative, neither is ultimately compelling or sufficiently persuasive as it stands. Does this somewhat negative conclusion warrant total rejection of these positions, or, stated otherwise, what positive contribution can these views make to contemporary theological reflection?

It is my conviction, based on the outcome of this study, that indeed neither Barth nor Hartshorne can be appropriated on his own terms. I think both the methodological approaches they espouse and the material content they construct are open to such telling criticisms and questions on fundamental issues that their viability is greatly compromised. Having said that, however, I must state as well that I believe that the monumental efforts of both Hartshorne and Barth have made significant contributions to the direction and content of theological reflection. In the first place this is so since with great eloquence and subtly argued nuance they have carried their distinct perspectives to the outer limits. With intellectual precision and passionate conviction Barth and Hartshorne have pursued their positions to their farthest implications and conclusions. And by so doing they have shown us, perhaps in incomparable fashion, the consequences of thinking in certain ways. Thus, if their positions are unacceptable at certain points, they have nonetheless shown those who follow, to borrow Hartshorne's own phrase, "where the shipwrecks are buried."

There is a sense, I think, in which Barth and Hartshorne have set or at least contributed greatly to the determining of the contemporary theological agenda by being both problematic and compelling. If, indeed, both the revelational approach of Barth and the metaphysical approach of Hartshorne are open to question, this very status as problematic serves to emphasize, perhaps epitomize, the crisis of identity that continues to characterize present-day theological thought and it indicates once more the need to clarify anew the task of theological reflection and the status of theological language and claims to truth. If both revelational and metaphysical theology fail to satisfy contemporary requirements, the question must be asked again if such failure is finally one more manifestation of the demise of theology as a whole or a call once more to the creative task of revitalizing and reconceptualizing the role and status of theological thinking.

Although no definitive answer to this question has yet emerged, such reconceptualization is being carried out on a number of fronts, including within Hartshorne's own process perspective, and with greater attention to the insights and claims of historical consciousness than Barth or Hartshorne managed. It is with these efforts to redefine and reconceptualize the theological task that I identify my own efforts as a theologian. And while I think that such efforts, on my own part and that of others, may well find — indeed must find — the approaches as well as particular theological formulations articulated by Barth and Hartshorne untenable, I think that we ignore the questions posed and the agenda set by these thinkers at the risk of losing great wisdom and insight. This is particularly true, as this thesis has sought to demonstrate, in reference to Hartshorne and Barth's shared conviction concerning the centrality of the idea of relationship and its related notions of power, freedom, and love. These thinkers have clearly and forcefully argued for the central significance of these conceptions for any understanding of God, and they have further indicated their profound interconnection. They have argued, though to different ends, against any disassociation of these primary notions and warned of the dangers for human self-understanding and for the conception of any God-world relationship that would result from such a separation. By so arguing they are, I think, not only descriptively accurate but also prophetic and visionary.

Thus, I would contend that the Barthian and Hartshornian treatments of these issues offer ways of formulating the problems and posing the questions that are particularly relevant to our times. If their own ways of resolving these dilemmas are not totally satisfactory, nonetheless these thinkers have been convincing that these are indeed central concerns that any adequate vision must take into account. Both in terms of their failures and successes they have marked the places where theological reflection must be directed. If finally not definitive models, these visions are nonetheless suggestive points of departure for future theological convictions.

In closing this study, it can be stated that Barth and Hartshorne offer ways of doing theology that are approaches not open to many contemporary thinkers and that they have developed conceptions of God and particularly of power that are informative and suggestive but ultimately inadequate in the detailed forms in which Barth and Hartshorne have argued them. But in so constructing their visions, they have helped set the problems that present-day theologians and philosophers will have to resolve, and they have done so in a manner so compelling that future theological reflection will bear their imprint if only in opposition.